F. RODERICH-STOLTHEIM

THE RIDDLE OF
THE JEW'S SUCCESS

OMNIA VERITAS

F. RODERICH-STOLTHEIM

THEODOR FRITSCH (1852-1933)

THE RIDDLE OF THE JEW'S SUCCESS

1927

Translated from the German

by Capel Pownall

PUBLISHED BY

OMNIA VERITAS LTD

ⓞMNIA VERITAS

www.omnia-veritas.com

I

PREFACE

If there are riddles in the history of the nations, then the Jews most certainly present one of the chief instances; and, whoever has occupied himself with the problems of humanity, without advancing so far as the great problem of the Jews, has, so far as knowledge and experience of life are concerned, merely skimmed the surface of the subject. There is scarcely a field, from Art and Literature to Religion and Political Economy, from Politics to the most secret domains of sensuality and criminality, in which the influence of the Jewish spirit and of the Jewish entity cannot be clearly traced, and has not imparted a peculiar warp or trend to the affairs in question.

Indisputable as these facts are, it is nevertheless equally certain that Science, Literature and the Press, which concern themselves, not only in Germany, but all the world over, with all manner of valuable knowledge, display the utmost anxiety to avoid casting any light into the secret and mysterious sphere of Jewish influence. It is, as if a silent mandate had been issued, that the essential relations of life with Jewdom are on no account to be disturbed — that the Jews, in fact, are not to be discussed. And thus, one is entitled to maintain, that in no department of knowledge is the ignorance of our learned men so pronounced, as it is in everything, which is connected with the Jews.

If, however, the influences and activities, which the Hebrews exert upon the spiritual and political destinies of the nations, are of an extraordinary nature, one must finally supplement this recognised fact by the further recognition, that Hebrewdom avails itself of extraordinary powers and means to produce such results.

It is, in this respect, that the present book furnishes disclosures. To start with, one point must be made perfectly clear: religious views and religious motives are excluded from this work. The author is completely neutral to the religious parties, and cannot subscribe unconditionally to any one of the same. When Jews are spoken of in the course of this book, we are not thinking of a religious community, but rather of a particular people, a nation, a race. Consequently, whenever it would be advisable to avoid the use of the word "Jew", on account of the unpleasant flavour or taint which invariably accompanies that expression, use has been made, to a great extent, of the names "Hebrew", or "Semite".

That the Jews, however, in spite of their dispersion amongst the nations, still feel, at the present day, that they are a special people and a special race, and that they feel themselves united more by their common blood and race than by their religious creed, is testified to by one of the most illustrious amongst the people of Israel.

Disraeli, who later on became Prime Minister of England, and was created Lord Beaconsfield, makes, in his novel *"Endymion"*, which was published in London in 1844, an influential, elderly Jew speak to a young man as follows:

"No one must treat the racial principle, the racial question, with indifference. It is the key to the history of the world; and history is only so frequently confused because it is written by people, who are unacquainted with the racial question, and ignorant of everything which has a bearing upon it. Wherever you find the same in operation, whether amongst communities, or, in the case of individuals, it has to be reckoned with. But, on the other side, there is no other subject again, which demands such a fine power of discrimination, or, where the principle, if it is not completely understood, may show itself to be as misleading as an Ignis Fatuus.

I find in Europe three great races with pronounced characters — the Germans, the Slavs and the Celts, and their behaviour is determined precisely by these distinguishing characteristics. There is, however, yet another great race, which influences the world — the

Semitic. The Semites are, without question, a great race, for, amongst all the things in this world which appear to be true, nothing is more certain than the fact that they invented our alphabet.[1] But the Semites, at the present moment, exert through their smallest but most peculiar family, the Jews, an extraordinarily great influence upon all affairs. There is no other race, which has been endowed to such a degree with obstinacy and talent for organisation. These qualities have secured for them untold possessions and immeasurable credit. As you advance in life and acquire a more extensive knowledge of business and affairs in general, you will find that the Jews cross your path and frustrate your plans, wherever you go. Long ago they stole their way into our secret diplomacy, and have become almost complete masters of it; in another 25 years they will openly claim their share in the government of the country. Now here we are dealing with races: men and cliques of men who are guided in their behaviour by their peculiar organisation, and a statesman must reckon with this situation. On the other hand — what do you understand by the Latin race? Language and Religion do not make race — blood makes it".

At this juncture we shall only occupy ourselves with the signification and importance of the Jews in trade, that domain where they have laid the foundation of their power, and over which they are always extending their influence and authority in the endeavour to make a Jewish monopoly of it.

In his meritorious book: "Die Juden und das Wirtschaftsleben", (*The Jews and the Economic Life*) Professor Werner Sombart is at pains to prove nothing less than that the economic destinies of states and nations stand in immediate relation to the wanderings of the Jews. What further conclusions he then proceeds to attach to this theory, can best be summed up as follows: to whatever spot the Jews turn their footsteps, there trade and culture at once blossom forth; but, if they withdraw, commerce decays and prosperity disappears.

If this fact also, as a fact, is not to be disputed, it still seems to me that the reasons, adduced by Sombart, to account for this

---

[1] This has long been shown to be erroneous (The author.)

phenomenon, do not satisfy. And, as his conclusions also appear to me to be unsound, I consider it necessary to supplement the work of this scholar, who depends almost entirely upon literary and documentary evidence, by examples and experiences taken from practical, everyday life.

According to the impression, which is left upon one after reading Sombart's book, one might almost fancy that proof had been actually produced that the Hebrews were the real supporters of modern culture.

Sombart speaks of the "Culture of Capitalism", and endeavours to show how this culture rests preponderantly, or almost exclusively on the shoulders of the Jews. The perception, that humanity is extraordinarily indebted to the Jews with regard to Culture, has been vigorously and continuously propagated in more modern times, and may well have given rise to the opinion, which is widely held, that Culture and Religion have come to us mainly from the Hebrews, and consequently that the other nations owe an everlasting debt of gratitude to this Oriental people. In fact, in many quarters, it is actually maintained that all progress proceeds from the Jews, and that Culture without Jews is unthinkable. Such notions are, however, no longer tenable at the present day, by reason of our extended insight into the most remote periods of national history. One must remember that highly developed systems of culture have come into being in lands, in which a Jew has never set foot; that great systems of culture even existed at a time when no such thing as a Jewish nation had put in an appearance in the history of the world. The discoveries, made at the ancient seats of the Egyptian, Babylonian, and Assyrian nations, testify to this. The Aztecs, and the Incas in Peru as well, attained to a high degree of culture, and yet they knew nothing about the Hebrews. The culture of the Chinese and the Japanese gradually unfolded itself for thousands of years without the Hebrews contributing in the slightest degree thereto, for even at the present day, the Jew is only to be found as an isolated individual in China and Japan. The strongly developed racial feeling of these nations knows how to keep him at an arm's length. But, above all, what may perhaps be regarded as the highest and most exquisite blossom of culture, which humanity has ever brought to maturity — Grecian culture — developed at a time when Jewish influence was quite out of the question.

Thus, to hold up the Hebrew to universal admiration as the supporter of culture, is simply not admissible. On the other hand, it is conceded, that that, what is so commonly called "Culture", at once acquires an acceleration in pace, as soon as the Hebrews lay hands on it, and that, under the influence of this singular people, the external appearances of Culture develop in an astonishing manner. Only, at this stage, we ought to make a finer distinction, and not call "Culture", i. e. constructive work, what is really "Civilisation", i. e. a refinement or polishing-up of the mode of living. The increase and enhancement of the forms of life, which proceed under Jewish influence, affect preponderantly the externals of life. Trade and business increase, production receives a powerful stimulation, the circulation of money and the amassing of capital become more conspicuous than was formerly the case. Life seems to assume a richer and more luxurious aspect, and an impression of universal prosperity and augmentation of real property is created. All this, however, must be included in the conception of civilisation, whilst real culture, which is the cultivation and encouragement of the highest human capabilities, the improvement of organic and moral arrangement, and the deepening of religious feeling, is more or less disregarded. In fact, it appears that these deeper, cultural values actually suffer injury by the externalization of all existence. The dynamic conformity to law throughout Nature is not to be evaded even in human life; too much on one side always causes a deficiency on the other. It is not possible to develop extraordinary powers externally, without incurring a loss in internal values. We shall therefore be obliged, in order to treat this matter conscientiously, to throw light upon the highly- praised enhancement of culture by Hebrewdom from other points than Sombart has done, so that this obvious phenomenon can be viewed and comprehended as a whole.

II

JEWISH METHODS IN THE ECONOMIC LIFE

The question, why the economic life flourishes wherever the Jews direct their footsteps, has not been answered by Sombart in a way which satisfies us. He is under obligation to us for important disclosures. We shall, to the best of our ability, present these as follow. The facts and phenomena, upon which light must be thrown, can be separated into groups, according to the points of observation:

1.   The Hebrew enhances and accelerates the circulation of Money.
2.   He mobilises slumbering values: lets loose balanced and reposing forces.
3.   He practises "Raubbau", (Predatory culture)[2] at the expense of the stored-up forces of Nature and Mankind.
At this juncture must also be taken into consideration:
4.   The "Playing into one another's hands" (secret understanding) of the Hebrews.
5.   The strange Morality.

THE HEBREW ENHANCES THE CIRCULATION OF MONEY,

ENLIVENS BUSINESS

The sound merchant of the old school held the opinion that his duty was satisfactorily discharged, by satisfying the actual purchase-requirements of his customers. He allowed the latter to approach him of their own accord, and waited until they called upon

---

[2] Translator's note. It is very difficult to find in English a concise equivalent for the admirable German expression "Raubbau". "Predatory Culture" is, perhaps, the best.

him, believing that he had conformed in all respects to his business obligations, by procuring for the customer, at a suitable price, the goods which the latter required. He regarded it as beneath his dignity to run after customers, or to entice them, by all manner of tricks, to buy from him; in fact, in olden times, conduct of this kind was regarded as unbecoming and quite unworthy of an honourable trader. Far less did it ever occur to him to talk a customer into buying some article, which the latter would not have bought of his own accord. Thus trade remained a peaceful, and not unduly exciting occupation, and still the customer got what he wanted. The Hebrew introduced into these relations, a new tendency and a violent revolution. Wherever he invaded trade, he refused to adopt this quiet and peaceful method of satisfying requirements. He endeavoured to entice the customers by advantageous offers and promises of all kinds. Above all, he emphasised the cheapness of his goods, and knew well how to delude the purchaser, by suggestion, into imagining that, in this cheapness, the latter would find an enormous advantage. He recommended his goods, loudly and publicly, by methods, which were formerly known and forbidden as being those of a mountebank, and which are now called advertising, and very soon brought the practice almost to the verge of an art.

Yes, and when all these means of attracting customers proved of no avail, he went and looked for them, not only by sending out circulars and price-lists, but personally, by pedlars, agents and travellers. Thus, he did not wait until the requirement arose, and the demand set in of its own accord; he created an artificial demand ; he aroused requirement by persuasion, and by other means. In this manner, a new and alien trait was introduced into all business life. Commercial business activity now became a wild hunt for customers, for each tradesman sought to tear away the buyer from his rival. Certainly all this resulted in a violent application of the spur to business life, and the exchange of commodities was accelerated and increased thereby, but this kind of activity was of less service to political economy, in its higher sense, than it was to another purpose. If it was the aim of sound economy solely to satisfy a genuine want, and to direct goods wherever the same were really required, the new way of proceeding aimed mainly at gathering up or "assembling" actual money. Trade, according to the new perception, was no longer a useful link in the chain of calm, constant economic development, but was rather a means to direct the circulating money as quickly as possible again into the hands of the trader. It was not the transfer of goods, which was so important, but the fact that the transfer of goods gave the opportunity for getting hold of money.

Thus, extraction of money from the pockets of customers instead of satisfactorily meeting the need for commodities, now became the main purpose of trade. But trade forfeited thereby its proper and honourable character, and its former reputation as an important contributor to the well-being of the community. One can only learn to understand correctly this particular tendency of the Hebrews, by considering their peculiar relations to their environment. The old-fashioned merchant was not particularly envious of his trade-competitors; his motto was, "Live and let live"; and he knew that if he conducted his business, honestly and conscientiously, that if he served his customers honourably and fairly, a portion of the universal volume of trade would fall to his share, through which his individual existence would be assured. The merchants of olden times did not feel themselves competitors with one another, to the extent which the modern ones do. They were not so numerous; and, through the guild privilege, each was assured of his particular market or sphere of activity. The mania to supplant one another did not force its way to the front, and was kept within bounds by the respect felt for the vocation. A feeling of goodwill and of mutual tolerance — an attitude corresponding to the Christian view of life — prevailed amongst merchants and tradesmen, just as it did in other circles.

The attitude of the Hebrew towards this state of affairs was quite different. He came as a stranger into this kind of existence, which was a new world to him, as a supernumerary, whom nobody had summoned, and whom nobody desired to see. Moreover, he was not united to the native inhabitants of the land, either by the tie of blood, or by a common history, or by patriotism, or by religious and social views. He felt himself to be an alien, and regarded the others as strangers, who did not interest him; but he desired to force a place for himself amongst them by any and every means. He did not look upon other competitors, striving all around him, as being either entitled to live, or as compatriots. His view of life, derived from his religion, had taught him that his nation was something out of the ordinary, that it had been "chosen", and its holy books contained the promise that he should possess himself of all the riches in the world in order to rule over all other peoples. The "Nations of the World" were represented in the law of the Hebrew as strangers and as enemies. He had neither respect nor tolerance for them. All he cared about was to dispossess them, and to make them tributary to him. This is simply what stands written in the books of the Old Testament, which we also have accepted as "sacred books"; and it stands written still more distinctly in the laws, which Hebrewdom teaches within itself, but prudently conceals from the rest of humanity.

We shall return to these facts later on.

At all events, the Hebrew was not content to keep step with the other merchants, and to confine his attentions to those customers, who came to him of their own free will. He considered it as his right — yes, even as his duty towards himself and to his nation, to seize for himself as much as possible out of the total volume of trade, and to deprive his non- Jewish competitors of as many customers as he could. He also recognised what a great advantage it was, to attract to himself as much as possible of the money in circulation, in order to obtain, by this means, power and mastery over the economic life.

This assiduity grew out of his natural disposition, for the sense of gain and the impulse towards self-enrichment have always been very pronounced in the Hebrews. The greed for Gold is an ancient and hereditary evil in the tribe of Judah. But one only half understands the situation, if one forms the opinion, that the Jew is actuated in his business operations solely by the desire for gain, or by the love of money. Certainly the

Hebrew is fond of money; but the mere possession of the metal is not enough for him; he knows that behind the glittering gold lurks the secret also that the precious metal gives him power over others. In his case, the possession of money is not solely a means for leading an independent and luxurious existence, but is, at the same time, a means for exercising power; he will, by means of money, rule and oppress.

And, through his intense — one might almost say, artificially forced — business activity, by which he strives to bring back all the circulating money quickly into his hands again, he achieves something further. By gathering up money on all sides, by every means in his power, and by retaining it in his possession and allowing it to accumulate, the Hebrew knows how to cause a scarcity of money in the nation; and the scarcity of money brings him fresh custom — not indeed as a merchant, but as a money-lender.

If anybody understands how to bring back the money, which is circulating amongst the people, quickly into his own hands again, by enticing, for instance, in his capacity as merchant or tradesman, his customers to make purchases, for which there is no immediate necessity, he withdraws money from the "market", and money at once becomes scarce if unforeseen wants put in an appearance. Whoever then finds himself in monetary difficulties, is compelled to apply to those, who have known how to attract all the money into their own hands. And, in this way, commercial activity, which had been so violently stimulated, became simultaneously an auxiliary to the loan-monger and usurer. It was not chance, nor was it by any means the pressure of circumstances in former times, which made a money-lender of the Jew, but a carefully thought- out system. Money is a very peculiar commodity, and whoever trades in money has a tighter grip on the economic life than he who trades in ordinary goods. For this reason, all trade, as far as Jews are concerned, is, strictly speaking, merely a means for gathering together or "assembling" money, again and again. For the Hebrew follows the money, which has been lent on loan, also with ever-watchful eyes, and knows well what precautionary measures to take, to ensure that it will soon find its way back into Jewish safes.

It is not disputed that the Jewish method of doing business produces a showy splendour, both in trade and traffic, in which everybody appear s to be prospering. We often stand still, absolutely dazed by the precipitate development, which has overtaken all trade and traffic arrangements during the last few decades. But, — and we labour under no delusion in this respect — this blossom of external life, dazzling in all its splendour, is only produced by heavy sacrifice on the other side.

THE HEBREW MOBILISES SLUMBERING VALUES, LETS LOOSE BALANCED AND REPOSING FORCES

I once knew a man, who could not behold any stately tree, either in garden or park, without indulging in an outburst, somewhat on the following lines; "How crazy the people must be to allow a tree like that still to be standing! What an amount of capital is lying there locked up! What fine beams and planks could be sawn out of it!"

The man had Jewish blood in his veins, and gave vent to a feeling, which must be keenly alive in many Hebrews, although they do not venture to express it in such a barefaced manner. The Hebrew is incapable of allowing anything to rest in calm peace, which can be turned to some economic use. Instilled into his mind is the urgent impulse to make everything "liquid", to convert everything into money, to "mobilise" everything. And, on all sides, we see Hebrewdom, driven by this impulse, hard at work in order to scoop up with greedy hands the treasures of Nature and of Human Life. Certainly existence is enriched and broadened thereby, and civilisation is enlivened. From the common economic point of view it has the appearance of being highly meritorious, when a forest, which has been standing for a hundred years in peace, slowly and laboriously growing up by virtue of the creative power in Nature, and has become a great potential source of value, that somebody should set to work with axes and circular saws to liquidate the reposing capital. Hundreds of men are employed to lay the trees low, and to cut up and transport the timber, and thus life springs up in the district; wages are paid, and sales are effected. Regarded from this point of view, the man, who "mobilises" these sleeping values, may well appear to be a benefactor to the neighbourhood where he provides useful work for so many hands. But, not only will the lover of nature be saddened by what has taken place; the serious economist will also be of a very different opinion. Certainly the forest is there, reduced at last to a form, in which it can be utilised by the community as building-timber and fire-wood. The wise forester, however, goes to work with care and restraint, and does not fell any timber without making provision for afforesting an area equivalent to that, which has been cleared. Or, at any rate, he only allows the mature trunks to be felled, and spares all the younger timber. The Hebrew obeys an entirely different principle — his true commercial principle: he clears the ground to the last sapling; the afforestation he leaves to others.

The above is an example of reality rather than of symbolism. The Hebrews have actually laid low enormous stretches of primeval forest, not only in our Fatherland, but also in Russia and in Poland; by doing so, they have certainly given a stimulus to business and commercial intercourse, and have caused money to circulate, but the reverse side of this activity will perhaps only be appreciated to its full and disastrous extent by future generations. The cut-down forest certainly brings profit for the moment, but, for the more or less distant future, it means nothing less than impoverishment of the district — in many cases, actual devastation. The springs dry up all over the now bare surface; permanent drought sets in, and when heavy rains do come, they simply sweep away the valuable upper layers of soil. The extirpation of great forests means, accordingly, nothing less than the exhaustion of fertility, and the conversion into desert land of vast tracts of country. Italy and the Balkan States furnish a grave enough warning. As in the case of the forest, so does the Hebrew comport himself in other spheres of activity. He is for ever intent upon mobilising or stirring up sleeping values, and bringing them into circulation, in order to derive an ostentatious and momentary benefit therefrom; but organic breadth of vision is completely wanting in this individual. He does not trouble to consider what the further consequence of this reckless and predatory method of proceeding on his part will be. This is quite in accordance with his nomadic nature. He does not feel himself in any manner linked to the soil; he forsakes the devastated territories, and seeks fresh profit elsewhere in the world. The conception of the

Fatherland is altogether foreign to him, and, in this respect, he is true to his nature as a member of a desert and nomadic race.

THE HEBREW PILES HIS PREDATORY CULTURE AT THE EXPENSE OF NATURAL AND HUMAN RESOURCES

Once more, as in the case of the forest, the same fate befalls the treasures contained in the bosom of the earth. What has here been slowly formed in Nature's laboratory by processes, which have taken hundreds of thousands, or even millions of years, are dragged to the light of day with insatiable greed; it must take its part in enriching and adorning life. At first this sounds very plausible — but how long can it last? Careful economists are already asking uneasily how much longer the world's supply of coal will suffice to shield the human race against the ever-menacing forces of the cosmic cold. Certain geologists have spoken reassuring words: the world's coal supply is plentiful, and will suffice, at any rate, for many centuries, perhaps, even for three or four thousand years. The foresight of humanity ought to enable it to project its conscience across this span of time, for it will be our descendants, who will — even if it is after the lapse of thousands of years — raise bitter reproaches against us because we have squandered the irreplaceable treasures of the earth, greedily and blindly. And there are other treasures of the earth as well, which are not so plentiful as coal. The world's supplies of iron ore, which are nearly all known, as they can be discovered and marked down by means of the magnetic needle, have been subjected to close calculation with regard to their extent and richness; and the result is, that if we continue to use up iron in the same way, as we have been doing for the last few decades, all the iron-ore fields of the world will be exhausted in from 50 — 60 years. And then what?

Whether such calculations prove true or not, they provide us with a glance into the future, which must arouse apprehension, and cause us to regard the lordly culture, of which we boast so readily today, in a very questionable light.

The Hebrews are certainly not the only ones who practise Predatory Culture at the expense of the treasures of the earth, but it can be maintained with justice, that it was that class of men, who introduced the principle of ruthless mobilisation of values and of pitiless money-making into our economic life. And it is precisely that which Sombart wishes to demonstrate, or actually does demonstrate, whether he does so intentionally or not; the Hebrew has made the principle of pitilessly carried- out capitalisation supreme in the economic life, and it is not to be wondered at if others try to copy him — or rather, are compelled to do the same, in order to withstand the Jewish competition.

Not only do we squander these natural treasures, but we are dissipating another treasure as well, which finally is the most important of all, as far as culture is concerned. The mobilisation of the treasures of the earth, and the tremendous activity of economic life, which has risen to an almost morbid degree, impose a terrible strain upon man and his creative powers. He may, perhaps, feel a pride in the results of his work, in the thousands of roaring and clattering machines, in the boldly executed constructions, with which he spans rivers, estuaries and mountain ravines, and in the ingenious technical appliances, which convey him with the speed of the wind across the face of the earth. But what does he run down and secure as booty or prize at the end of this wild pursuit? Generally only the loss of his best powers, and an early end to his days.

Who can now refuse to recognise the fact that the harassing hunt after business, which characterises modern economic life, is rapidly leading to an exhaustion of mankind, and that the race itself, in spite of all the technical perfections of the external world, is slowly sinking, as far as its personal constitution and powers of accomplishment are concerned, i. e. is decaying steadily both physically and spiritually?

In this respect also, the modern economy is carrying on ruthlessly another method of Predatory Culture. Industrialism entices men from the country into the town, and consumes them. It is a well-known fact that the families, born in the towns, very soon fade away, and that they seldom extend to more than three generations, and that the large towns and the industrial areas can only maintain themselves by a constant influx of human beings from the rural districts. But even the reserve of human strength in the country, taken as a whole, is not inexhaustible. It already shows an alarming retrogression. Sixty years ago, two thirds of the inhabitants of Germany lived in the country, and derived their livelihood from agriculture and from forestry, and only a third of the population lived in the towns. Today, the proportion is almost reversed. The rural population has now shrunk to 37 per cent of the total, and will no longer be able to make up the deficiency in the births amongst the 63 per cent of the population, who now dwell in the large towns, and in the industrial districts.

We see accordingly how the magnificence of modern culture can only be produced by the expenditure of powers, which cannot be revived. It requires but a few more decades of this mode of existence, and the German Nation will have used itself up; foreign national and racial elements will stream in from all sides, and make themselves comfortable in the bed, which we, in our excessive and suicidal diligence, have so carefully prepared for them.

A typical example of the fanatical pressure, which impels the Hebrew to mobilise all values, is furnished by his attack upon the "Fidei-Kommisse", namely the indivisible family estates. The land-owning nobility, in particular, has frequently made the arrangement that the family estate shall descend undivided to the heir, in order to guard against the breaking-up and dispersion of the estate. It is of incalculable value, both for state and community, if, in this manner, strong, independent existences can be maintained; moreover, the community cannot suffer any detriment thereby. Notwithstanding this, the Jewish Press has, for years past, fiercely attacked this arrangement, as if it were an offence and an injury against the majority, and Parliament is overwhelmed, from the Jewish side, with motions to do away with the "Fidei-Kommisse", as if the eternal happiness of the whole nation depended upon this. The innate hatred felt by the Jew towards the nobility plays, in this respect, no small part. The Jew wishes to see this nobility destroyed, which presumes, both by breeding and tradition, to be something out of the ordinary, while the "chosen people", according to his opinion, alone possess a claim to pretensions of this kind. Do not the Jews, with predilection, refer to themselves as the "natural aristocracy of mankind"?

Moreover, this aversion to the "Fidei-Kommisse", (the indivisible family estates) is only the old Hebrew urgency to mobilise values expressing itself afresh: there must not be anything durable or constant: everything must be cut up and handed over to speculation.

The new revolutionary government, directed by Jews, has no more urgent policy than that of breaking up all the "Fidei-Kommisse", and of prohibiting the formation of any new family estates. Who can compute today the harm which will be caused by such a policy? The undermining of the economic foundations must also make itself felt in the social and intellectual structure of society. Genuine men of nobility will become scarcer and scarcer: the nobility has already, in many respects, degenerated, and become degraded by the intrusion of the Jewish money- and business-spirit. The Jewish principle of life drags mankind back from the heights, which it has scaled. The final result is: universal vulgarisation.

We hear the ready answer: but wealth has increased enormously! Have we not collected huge quantities of capital, which are a sufficient guarantee for the future? In this respect also the modern idea of economy arrives at a fateful and most erroneous conclusion. Even Sombart represents the situation as if the Hebrews brought riches with them wherever they went, and were continually producing new wealth. Even if we understand under the expression "wealth", merely the gold and silver treasure of the earth, it certainly cannot be maintained that these are increased by the Hebrew and his economic activity. We have already seen that his art consists in collecting and re-collecting these treasures into his own hands, as quickly as he can. But the Gold and the Silver in their totality form only an insignificant portion of the riches of the nation. What we call capital does not generally consist of coined metal. Today we reckon also as capital, landed property, such as cultivated fields, forests, buildings etc. But the Hebrews certainly do not increase this kind of property either.

There is, however, another kind of capital, which plays the most important role of all in modern political economy: this is the Loan Capital those sums, which are lent out in return for the payment of fixed rates of interest. And it cannot be denied that the Hebrew possesses an extraordinary talent for increasing this particular kind of capital.

Let us, first of all, make it quite clear to ourselves of what such capital really consists. Whoever owns a million marks, which brings him in interest, does not possess this million marks in the form of gold and silver coins, lying in his safe, but has lent the million marks out on loan. But even the borrower— the debtor to the man who owns the money — no longer holds the actual money; he has passed it on further in the course of his business. All that is left to him of it is the obligation to pay interest. He has taken over for himself — and generally also for his descendants for illimitable time — the duty of paying to the creditor, certain sums of money as interest, at certain stated intervals. Out of all this the fact next emerges, that an equally great debt, on the other side, faces this sum of Loan Capital. Whoever is in a position to call his own a million marks of Loan Capital, and draws interest from the same, must hold other people as his debtors to the extent of a million marks. And thus arises the peculiar equation: the more Loan Capita l there is here, the more Debts there are there. An increase of capital of this nature means, in reality, nothing else than an increase of debt.

Loan Capital thus consists of acknowledgment of debt, and of obligation to pay. It takes visible shape in the form of mortgage-deeds, bonds, shares, original or founder-shares, rent- charges and similar devices. And, if we boast today that the number of rich people has increased enormously, that millions and thousands of millions are accumulated in the hands of single individuals, we must not forget that the debts and obligations of other people have increased in equal measure. It is accordingly a bold assumption to maintain, that the general welfare of the nations is promoted by the increase of capital of this kind, i. e. Loan Capital. Whoever speaks of modern Wealth ought, if he is conscientious, to speak at the same time of the monstrous nature of the modern system of creating indebtedness. In whatever direction we look, we see an enormous development of this creation of debt; in the kingdom, in the province, in the parish, in the business, in the family — all are carried on by means of debts. The registered mortgages on land throughout the German Empire are computed at 60—70 thousand million marks[3] (three thousand to three thousand five hundred million pounds sterling).

It is a very remarkable and significant fact that we have no statistic s whatever concerning this so important question of political economy, while we are overwhelmed with statistics on all other matters.

If the above-mentioned sum of debt is approximately correct, it simply means that the nation has to find something like 3000 million marks (one hundred and fifty million pounds sterling) every year in order to pay the burden of interest, placed upon the ground, composing the Fatherland. Who, in the last analysis, provides this sum of money? It is simply the working and productive class of the citizens: the peasant, the craftsman and the workman. These are the powers, which create productive values, and who must, by the excess of their labour, produce the burdens of interest in order to satisfy the owners of Loan Capital.

If we reckon that there are 15 million working-men in the German Empire capable of production, a yearly impost of 200 marks (ten pounds sterling) is laid upon each of them in order to satisfy the owners of Loan Capital. That this crushing impost is not consciously perceived, is simply due to the fact that it is split up and distributed in such a way, that it is almost impossible to check or trace it, and that all kinds of roundabout ways and tricks are utilised, which make it quite impossible for the ordinary man to discover the source of his misery. The Loan Capital, which burdens our land, sucks in its interest by raising the rents of tenements, workshops and business premises, by increasing the price of food-stuffs and other necessary commodities, and by other similar indirect methods.

---

[3] According to Jewish computation (v. Gwinner in the Prussian Upper House) the capital value of the land in the German Empire amounts to close upon 300 thousand million marks (Fifteen thousand million pounds sterling) and, according to other authorities, 220—250 thousand million marks (eleven thousand to twelve thousand five hundred million pounds sterling). Certainly, in most districts, the debts on the land are higher than 25 p. c.

Thus, the productive worker is not directly conscious of this impost, but feels only an inexplicable pressure on all his business activity. He sees that, in spite of all his effort and industry, the fruits of his toil disappear out of his hands, without his being able, at the same time, to discover any satisfactory explanation of this. In spite of all his toil, he cannot make any advance and prosper, becomes discontented with his lot, and vents his resentment in all directions, mostly against those, who are quite innocent of his hard fate. He complains about the high taxes and rates, which form only an insignificant particle when compared with that impost — the interest on Loan Capital. He grumbles about the increasing cost of living, of rent, of food, of clothing, and of other things, including "bread-usurers" and bad government, and does not seem to have even the faintest idea, that it is just this invisible impost of the interest on Loan Capital, which is oppressing him by making everything dear.

Thus, this modern system of creating capital, by casting an intolerable burden on the entire national life, produces universal oppression and consequently discontent, which is causing an ever-growing resentment between the various classes, which compose the community, without the oppressed people being at all clear as to where the source of the oppression really is.

* * * * *

It is not very probable that the Hebrews invented that work of art —the loaning-out of capital against interest; it is quite likely that it was known and practised before their time. It is quite certain, however, that they first introduced this branch of business to us in Germany, and, supported by the prohibition against practising usury, enforced by the Christian Church against its members, promoted and developed it to an extraordinary extent. Owing to their peculiar dexterity in always attracting to themselves again the money, which is in circulation, they know how to produce a constant shortage of money amongst the people. In this manner they compel the productive classes to borrow, and to continue borrowing.

The money, which has been gradually collected by commerce and other means, leaves the hands of the Hebrew, for the most part, only as Loan Capital, and continuously creates for him fresh circles of people, pledged to pay him tribute.

Is it then really such a great blessing for a nation if it can be shown, that the Hebrews, living in their midst, possess thousands of millions of marks in the shape of Loan Capital, for which the productive class have to find the interest? What does the saying now mean: wherever the Jews turn, there appear new riches, new capital? Should one not, before all other things, state emphatically: there arise, to a terrifying extent, fresh debts? It is not the real wealth of the nations, which is increased by the Jews, but their debts and obligations, which, under the deceitful name of "mobile capital", accumulate until they amount to sums of incredible magnitude, but which are in reality, only a phantom possession — an imaginary value.

We read, with aversion, the descriptions of the persecutions of the Jews, which are said to have taken place in the Middle Ages: if these were, in all cases, as many people imagine, can be left an open question; at any rate, one ought to explain conscientiously, what led up to these persecutions, and what was the real cause of the same. We can read, in every record, that it was by no means a religious hatred, which incensed the citizens against the Jews, because at all times and in all countries, a remarkable tolerance has been displayed towards the religious rites of the Jews, some of which rites are of a very peculiar nature. No one has prohibited their noisy method of praying; no one has disturbed their Sabbath and Passover festivals. Nobody has prohibited even their Purim, their festival of revenge, which they still celebrate annually, with unquenchable thirst for revenge, in recollection of the massacre of 75,000 Persian enemies of the Jews, by the direction of the minister Mordeca i more than 2000 years ago. What really incensed the people against the Jews were the insatiable hunger for interest, and the unchristianlike usury of the latter; by reason of this diabolical greed for money, which stopped at nothing, this slinking, alien race became so repugnant to the ordinary German man, that he considered the Jews capable of anything.

As has been already stated, during the time when the influence of the Church was predominant (from the 11th till the 18th century) Christians were forbidden to practise usury; only the Hebrew was allowed to do this. Thus it naturally came about that everyone, who wanted to borrow money, was obliged to go to the Jews. According to the law, the Hebrews were aliens and on sufferance, and their sojourn, in either town or district, was only permitted when a tax ("Jew-tribute") had been paid to the ruling prince or potentate; but it was precisely this arrangement, whereby the mild or stern treatment of the Jews depended essentially on the attitude of the ruling house, which relieved the situation to an extraordinary degree for the Jews living in the Empire, which was, at that time, split up politically to an endless extent. Generally speaking, the legislation was very considerate, and allowed the Hebrew to devote himself wholeheartedly to his favourite occupation, viz traffic in Money, and to claim unheard-of rates of interest for his loans. A rate of interest of 30 — yes, even of 50 and 60 per cent per annum, was already known from the 12th to the 15th century, and was so well-established during the 16th and 17th centuries, that it was regarded as nothing out-of-the-way. Under these circumstances, and owing to the scarcity as well as to the extraordinary fluctuations in the value of money throughout that period, it was an easy matter for the Hebrew always to collect all the money again into their hands, and to force the remaining citizens to raise fresh loans.[4]

A particular trick facilitated the obtaining of an exorbitant rate of interest. Even when the rate of interest was moderate, the debtor

---

[4] "At the end of the 14th century, the social position of the Jews deteriorated, chiefly on account of their arrogance and usuriousness. Up till then, they had been respected, were qualified to own landed property, and were appreciated as being necessary for the development of the towns. They had, in some instances, even found an entry into the municipal bodies, for instance at Cologne and Worms. In many towns, the highest admissible rate of interest reached 86-2/3 per cent for the year! Ludwig of Bavaria (1314-1347) decided, as a particular favour for the citizens of Frankfort, that the Jewish rate of interest was to be restricted to 3 2 ½ per cent. Since the canonical prohibition against the lending of money for interest was enforced sternly and universally against Christians, and the cloisters no longer loaned out money, the money-business remained almost exclusively in the hands of the Jews for a long period." (Dürr and Klett) *History of the World II*, page 139) — "Thus a regular monopoly of usury by the Jews established itself, which was only broken into in the 18th century, to the extent that, towards the close of that century, it was permitted to charge generally a 5% rate of interest." (Rich. Schröder: "Deutsche Rechtsgeschichte" II, 15, [German History of Law II, 15].

had, for the most part, to pledge himself to pay back his debt on a fixed date by weekly or monthly payments of interest. In case he was unable to keep to the appointed date, he was bound by the terms of his bond, to pay double the rate of interest from that time onward; often indeed, the whole debt was doubled. The well-meaning debtor, who had the best intention of paying off his debt at the appointed time, entered into such contracts with a light heart, in the certainty that, at the appointed date, money, from other quarters, would be at his disposal. The Hebrew, however, who had a complete understanding with his fellow-tribesmen, and knew accurately what call there was for money, and how much there was in circulation, took good care that his debtor did not get the expected money at the appointed time, and thus he compelled the latter to accept the new and still more onerous conditions. The Hebrew only granted an extension of the term on the condition that his claims, both with regard to interest and capital, should be increased, and as, thanks to the cooperation of Jewish friends, of which we have already spoken, delay in the repayment of the debt was frequently repeated, the Jew was more successful then, than now, in entangling, by means of a comparatively small loan, a whole family in the bondage of debt throughout their lives, or even in expelling them from their house and land.

Thus there is nothing strange in the fact that, already from the time of Charlemagne, unceasing complaints about the Jewish usurer were directed both to the civil and clerical authorities. The earlier peasant-insurrections also, were not due to the "Priests" and to the Nobility, but to money-lending Jewry; for example, the Peasants' Rising at Gotha in 1391, and the Peasants' Rising at Worms in 1431. Later — when the Jews had drained the extravagant and quarrelsome nobility of their riches, and the latter had made an alliance with the clergy to oppress poor "Hans Karst"[5], with tithes and compulsory labour, the peasants turned against all three tormentors. In 1450 the cup-bearer, Erasmus von Erbach, an ancestor of the present Princes von Erbach (in the Odenwald), who personally was quite prosperous, raised his voice thus against the Jews: "The poor man is robbed and flayed by the Jews to such an extent that it has become intolerable, and may God have mercy on

---

[5] The German Peasant.

him. The Jewish usurers settle down, even in the smallest villages, and when they lend five gulden, they take six-fold security and take interest upon interest, and yet again interest, so that the poor man loses all that he possesses."

How well founded this complaint was, is proved by the testimony of all contemporaries.

Elsewhere it is stated that, "Jewdom sits on the necks of the citizen and of the poor man, and is the cause of the rapidly increasing poverty". The Jews are referred to as "vultures", who "do not desist until they have consumed the marrow in the bones, and reduced the citizen to beggary". (Petition of the Frankfort citizens June 10th 1612). Sombart also mentions in his conscientiously collected material a number of similar expressions of opinion, taken from the same period, which confirm what has been said above.

Thus, it was not religious hatred, which incensed the people against the Jews, but the actual plundering of the masses by a system of charging an immoderate rate of interest. The wealth which the Jews "brought into a land", was thus of very doubtful value. It was a kind of wealth, which had a dazzling appearance in certain places, whilst everywhere else it produced only poverty and misery.

Thus: the Hebrews did not create new values in the shape of goods, and consequently, actual new wealth; they merely understood, in a masterly fashion, how to obtain possession of the prosperity of other people; they did not produce any new possession, but only brought about a change of possession. What they produced was merely an appearance of wealth, which in reality consisted only of the debts of those people, who were not Jews.

III

PARTICULAR BUSINESS TACTICS OF THE JEW

The commercial practices of the Hebrew require that more light should be directed upon them. It is conceded that the Jew, in matters of business, displays great dexterity, and has at his disposal a particular method of operation, which procures for him the admiration of extensive circles of people. Many are inclined to ascribe an extremely high degree of cleverness to the Hebrew, because he knows very often how to give a particular turn to his business machinations, which surprises and confounds all concerned. As soon as we look more closely into the matter, and ascertain upon what principles these business measures are founded, we learn to think less highly of the renowned cleverness of the Hebrew. It becomes a matter of a number of tricks, carefully guarded and transmitted by tradition amongst the Hebrews, and with which this dexterous race of traders overreach every man, who thinks in a natural manner. A short story out of actual life will give us an idea of what goes on in this sphere of activity.

A well-to-do elderly married couple had decided to dispense with their footman, and consequently with the latter's livery as well. The lady of the house offered the garments for sale. A Jew appeared punctually at the appointed time, in order to inspect the livery. After carefully examining the same, he made an offer of 50 marks. The lady was astonished that the dealer was able to offer such a high price, as the suit could not have cost much more, and was, moreover, a kind of clothing — being a uniform with particular badges — for which there would naturally be very little demand. She thought at once that she could do a good business with him, and hurried away to fetch an armful of discarded clothing, which she offered to him as well. The Hebrew examined everything, and offered quite respectable prices. Apparently he could make use of it all. The lady of the house, delighted with the prospect of unloading her wardrobe in this way of unnecessary ballast, continued to fetch more clothing. The Hebrew chose out most of this as well, and laid it in a great heap together. The only article, which did not find approval in the eyes of the Hebrew, was a fashionably- cut, light summer-suit, which the master of the house had only worn once, and had then laid aside, as it did not take his fancy. The Jew threw this on one side with the remark: "this is out of fashion, and nobody will buy it". When he had laid all the remaining articles of clothing together, and had offered quite a reasonable price for the same, the old lady asked him again to take the summer-suit; she wanted to see the last of it as the sight of it annoyed her husband. Finally the Hebrew agreed to take the suit for 5 marks. The lady accepted this offer, because of all the other clothing, she had been able to dispose of. The entire sale amounted to about 200 marks. "I have not got so much money with me", said the Jew, politely, "because I was not prepared to buy so many things. I will, however, have the clothing fetched away shortly, and will send the money at the same time. I will leave a deposit of 5 marks, and may as well take the summer-suit with me so that I do not make the journey empty-handed". With this the Hebrew took his departure, and, up to the present moment, has not returned.

The worthy lady related the episode to me herself, and was quite at a loss for an explanation. The Jew must have been taken ill, or something unforeseen must have happened, as otherwise he would have returned, "for he made such a favourable impression". I am afraid that I hurt the lady's feelings, for I had to laugh in her face, before I proceeded to explain the incident to her as follows: "the summer-suit was the only object of any value to the Jew, and consequently the only thing, which he was willing to buy. The other articles of clothing he had never intended to buy; only, in order to gain your confidence, he offered such good prices. Your confidence once gained, you did not observe how he was overreaching you with regard to the good summer-suit. He accomplished his object, and will take very good care not to let himself be seen again".

It took a considerable time before I was able to convince the good lady of all this; she then exclaimed with astonishment and almost with admiration: "Gracious me, what a clever fellow he is!" — "No, madam", I replied, "that is not real cleverness; it is a mode of operation, partly inherited, partly the result of instruction. It is an ancient receipt, according to which the Jews have conducted their operations for centuries — even for thousands of years. It is the "art" in business of deceiving one's opponent as to the value of the goods, and as to one's real intentions. I will relate to you a short story of a similar kind, which will make quite plain to you how this mode of operating proceeds, according to a certain pattern and custom."

A Jewish lad, who could not have been more than 10 or 11 years old, was accustomed to go from village to village, buying up hare- and rabbit-skins. He was instructed what he should pay for the wares, and soon acquired such knowledge of the business by constant practice, that he was able to carry it on to the satisfaction of his father. A peasant, from whom he had bought several rabbit-skins, produced also the fur of a marten. The young Jew held it to his nose, and said contemptuously: "This is only the skin of a stinking marten, and is not worth anything". The peasant, who understood little about such matters, urged the young Jew to take the fur of the marten as well, and finally the little business-man purchased it out of pure compassion for five half-pence! As soon as the young rascal had reached home, he called out: "Father, look what a stroke of business I have done! I have bought a valuable marten-fur for five half-pence!" — and he related what had happened. A neighbour, who, unobserved, had witnessed the episode from the window of a stable, made it known. Even this diminutive man of business already possessed the "cleverness" to speak disparagingly of the most valuable goods in order to deceive the seller with regard to the real value, and thus to enable himself to buy them up at a very cheap rate.

Anybody who has once thoroughly grasped the mode of operation, which has been systematically made use of in these cases, need not express any great astonishment as to the measure of "cleverness" required. It is always the same trick. The Hebrew, who has lived for thousands of years by dealing, and by overreaching other men, has developed, in this direction, a cunning and superior tactic. He knows that the desire — the demand, causes the price to rise. Whoever allows it to be seen that he would like to buy certain wares, or, that he is urgently in need of the same, will soon tempt the seller to demand a higher price. And, on the contrary, whoever offers his wares in a pressing manner, and allows it to be seen that he must get rid of the same at all costs, probably because he is in urgent need of money, has to put as cheerful a face on the matter as he can, when advantage is taken of his situation to reduce the price to the utmost.

The old saying: "Supply and Demand fix the price", has a certain justification — so long as upright and honest merchants are concerned. Today, we know that Supply and Demand can be artificially produced, simply to influence the price. And the Jew "runs", or carries on the most insignificant business in accordance with these sagacious measures, just as if he were operating, on a large scale, on the Stock Exchange. He knows how to deceive the other side as to his real intentions: he pretends that there is Demand, when he knows that, in reality, the Supply is more than sufficient, and also the reverse. The Hebrew, who goes to the Produce Exchange, under the necessity of buying several waggon-loads of wheat, because he has contracted to deliver this amount to a mill, takes very good care to conceal his real intention. He assumes an attitude of complete indifference; and, if anyone offers him wheat, he replies, shrugging his shoulders: "Wheat? I have enough wheat. Do you want to buy any?" And, as all the other Jewish business people present, who, perhaps, also want to buy wheat, assume the same attitude, as if by some secret understanding, and behave as if they had no need whatever of wheat, but wanted, on the contrary, to sell it, they create the impression that there is a superfluity of wheat; thus, they force the price down, and succeed in buying the wheat cheaply.

A simple or open-natured farmer, on the contrary, who has gone to the Produce Exchange, in order to get rid of his produce, because he needs the money urgently to pay the interest for the impending quarter, will at once offer his wheat eagerly. But, strange to say, he encounters cold refusal on all sides. And the same thing happens to all the other sellers; Supply preponderates, and the prices fall. Our farmer now returns to the first Hebrew, to whom he had offered his wheat, and who, in reality, urgently needs wheat, and the latter appears at last to relent, and says with apparent generosity: "Now, as you are an old business friend of mine, I will relieve you of your wheat, but only at a price, which is 2 marks (2 shillings) under the current price" — that is 2 marks cheaper than the official price, quoted for that day on the Exchange. In the end the farmer is glad to have found a purchaser at any price, and is secretly grateful to the Hebrew for having purchased his wheat out of sheer good nature. Several days later, when the supplies have been, for the greater part, bought up by the Hebrews, one notices a marked rise in the prices.

Business has been carried on in this manner, at the markets and on the exchanges, for decades and for centuries, without that simple section of humanity — the producers — perceiving what is going on; they — the producers — have always all the toil and disadvantage, the Hebrew dealer all the benefit. And this benefit or gain, on occasions, mounts up to millions. One example of this will suffice, compared with which, the so-called "Bread-Usury" of the Agrarians, about which the Jews and their hangers-on, especially the Social Democrats, are always crying out, is mere child's play.

In the year 1892, the corn-merchants Cohn and Rosenberg, supported by God only knows how many of their friends behind the scenes — the Chawrusse — by buying up on a gigantic scale, and then withholding from the market all available supplies of rye, produced such a shortage of this indispensable food-stuff, that the price of rye rose, in a few months, from 140 to 290 marks. They then "unloaded', and "earned" by this business, in a very short time, about 18 million Marks (£900,000). Most of our newspapers and of our so-called "Liberals" — the friends of the people — had not a single word of abhorrence or even of disapprobation for this "Bread Usury" according to the Old Testament pattern.

The game is made much easier if the Hebrews have a secret understanding, that is to say, if they have consulted beforehand, amongst themselves, about the condition of the Market, and have decided what the attitude of the other side is likely to be. Still any such understanding is scarcely necessary, for all Jewish business-people respond to one and the same instinct, are schooled in one and the same tactic, and act as one without any previous arrangement.

The "Killing" or "Slaughtering" Principle

There is another mode of operation, by which the Hebrews secure an advantage in business, and to which they are indebted for their present dominating position. Again, an instance of this mode of operation will make the same clear to everyone. Take, for example, a town in which there have existed for a long time ten separate businesses of the same kind or trade, and all of about the same size. The owners of these businesses have confined themselves, each to his or her circle of more or less regular customers, in accordance with the principle, "Live and let live", and have all been able to make a tolerable, and even comfortable living. Suddenly this old harmony is disturbed. One of these businesses changes hands, and the new owner, a man with a large amount of capital, or with extensive credit, brings a new business principle along with him. He calculates thus: What has been formerly sold by ten businesses, can be just as well sold by one business. I will make it my task to attract al l the customers in the town for this kind of business into my shop. This will not be difficult. I have sufficient money at my disposal to live comfortably, even if I make no profit whatever for several years. I will therefore offer all my goods at prices which show no profit whatever, i. e. at cost price. The result of this will be that all the customers in the town for this class of business will be attracted to my shop.

This business-man with the "New Principle" orders a new price-list to be printed, and sends it to every customer in the neighbourhood. He has reduced the prices so much below what used to be customary in the trade, that all purchasers are attracted without fail to the new shop.

The remaining nine businesses or shops now either lose their customers, or are compelled to reduce their prices correspondingly. As in either case no profit is made, those, who have no means to fall back upon, must sooner or later give up the contest. Others, who may possess enough capital to support them for the remainder of their lives, remark that it is useless and stupid to continue to carry on a business, in which there is no profit. These simply discontinue business. Others again, try to keep pace with the new competitor, but only see what means they possess, gradually disappear, and they also, sooner or later, are compelled to retire from the ruinous struggle. Thus, after a few years, the man with the "New Principle" remains the master of the situation, and now that he is without competitors, and is practically a monopolist on his own territory, endeavours to make up for the loss, which he has undergone, by gradually raising the prices, until finally the customers are at a greater disadvantage than they had ever been before.

This is no principle of life; but is, on the contrary, a principle of destruction or death; it carries on business for the mere sake of business, that is to make money; it does not ask what becomes of the other people. Here we are, face to face, with a tendency, which places acquisition before life itself; for business and political economy are, in the last analysis, only of importance when regarded as a means for preserving life. The supreme law of political economy should always culminate in the question: how can we arrange matters economically so that the people shall secure the maximum benefit in body and mind? A political economy, which certainly enables riches to be accumulated, but which, at the same time, causes the people to degenerate both physically and morally, cannot be regarded as ideal.

Seen from a purely business point of view, it may appear to be an improvement when material advantages are secured by concentrating all the trade into a single business. Certainly many purely economic advantages may be attained by the uniting of the scattered individual branches of any trade or business into one large central establishment; at any rate, the concentration of the management effects a saving in space, time and energy. Any person, however, who does not recognise business advantage as the supreme aim of life, but asks, on the contrary: what becomes of the people concerned? — such a person must have the gravest doubts as to the beneficial influence of such a business development as that described above; he would feel himself compelled to ask: what has become of the nine families, who have been thrown out of action by the "New Principle?" And he will then have to confess, that this "New Principle", however profitable it may seem at the first glance, leads finally to the expropriation and impoverishment of extensive classes of people, and thus, by its ultimate results, becomes a curse to the national life.

The man with the "New Principle", of whom we have just spoken, is not necessarily a Hebrew; others can also adopt this business method as their guiding principle. But, as a matter of fact — at any rate in our European affairs — it is almost invariably the Hebrew, who has introduced this principle. By so doing he has certainly created a great deal, which corrupts the eyes of many by its dazzling appearance, as, for instance, the great retail shops; but what kind of fruit this sort of development will produce in the more distant future of our nation is a question, which is well-warranted, and also very serious.

Another example, taken out of everyday life, occurs to me at this moment; it illustrates, in an allegorical manner, the action or operation of the Hebrew on the community.

For a great many generations there had been a number of small mills on a little river in Posen. There was not always sufficient water in the river at all seasons of the year to keep the mills working regularly; but one of the mills, on the upper part of the river, possessed a reservoir of considerable size, in which water could be stored up to provide for times of drought, when the sluices could be opened according to requirements. When the upper miller had water enough to work the mill for a day, or even for half a day, he started his mill, and thus the motive water flowed down regularly to all the mills situated below. There was no written law to regulate the use of this water; the practical requirements and common sense of the owners sufficed to maintain this arrangement to the complete satisfaction of all concerned.

One day, however, a disturbing element crept into the harmony, which had so long prevailed amongst the milling industry along this particular stream. The upper mill, together with the reservoir, passed into new hands. Whether it was that the new owner did not understand much about his business, or did not make himself agreeable to his customers, in short, the old customers gradually deserted the upper mill, and went to the other mills, lower down the stream. This annoyed the new owner, and he did his utmost to disturb the business of his neighbours. One means of offence he had always at his disposal, and that was his reservoir. He no longer allowed the water to run off, at regular intervals, but stored it up for days, and even for weeks, to the utmost capacity of the reservoir. Then, he would suddenly release the water by opening all the sluices, generally at night or on a Sunday, so that the accumulated water rushed down the stream with great force. The mills, on the lower part of the river, could make little or no use of this sudden head of water, and were obliged, as they did not possess any reservoirs for storing the water, to open their floodgates, and to allow this superfluous water to flow uselessly away. Any methodical management of the lower mills was thus rendered impossible. The injured parties complained in vain to the local and other authorities; they could obtain no redress because there was no law, which compelled the miller, on the upper part of the stream, to let the water run off at regular intervals.

The mills, on the lower reaches of the stream, would most certainly have been ruined by these spiteful tricks, if chance had not put a sudden stop to them. On one occasion, after a heavy rain-fall, the upper miller stored up the water to such an extent, and then let it rush through the sluices so suddenly, that a regular inundation ensued, which caused considerable damage to the embankments, dams and machinery of the lower mills. Now, at last, there was cause to take legal action against this disturber of the peace to force him to desist, and to make him pay compensation for the damage, which he had brought about.

Also, in this case, it does not necessarily follow that the disturber of the peace was bound to be a Hebrew; but as a matter of fact, he was; and, one is entitled to say, that the example given is typical of the onslaught made by the Hebrew race upon our economic life. The organic connection of economic examples, which results from the love of order, innate in the Aryan element, and from a voluntary adjustment to the harmony of life, which instills common-sense, and is supported besides by a moral feeling of duty and a respect for the respect of other men, collapses immediately when the Hebrew puts in an appearance.

The hitherto quiet and regular development of business relations suffers a considerable disturbance in all directions, as soon as this Oriental stranger, with his strange principles, and in whom the sense for social harmony is completely wanting, interferes with the economic life. He displays an utter disregard for others, and pursues, only and always, his private advantage. By the ruthless manipulation of this principle, he has become everywhere the destroyer of the economic life. He checks the even flow of development, creates "corners", produces artificial shortage and superfluity, and knows how to make profit out of both. Thus, in the economic life, he is nothing less than a disturber of the peace, a revolutionary and an anarchist.

IV

THE INTERNATIONAL CONNECTION AND

SECRET LEAGUE OF THE HEBREWS

Amongst the various causes of the tremendous advance of the Jews, special emphasis must be laid upon one of the most important — the way in which they play into one another's hands internationally. The Jewish success can be attributed, in a large measure, to the cooperation of many in conformity with a principle of unity.

The House of Rothschild stands, before the eyes of all, as the most striking example of this, and is testimony at the same time to the avalanche-like growth of the property, which is strictly confined in Jewish ownership, and which plays the chief part in sucking dry the national prosperity, not only of entire Europe, but also of most other countries.

1. THE ROTHSCHILDS

The role of the great millionaires, who control the economic life of America, has been played in Europe, until quite recently, almost exclusively by the House of Rothschild with its five branches in Paris, London, Frankfort on the Main, Vienna and Naples.[6] The Rothschilds, however, can only be compared with the former, i.e.

---

[6] The founder of this house, with its world-wide connections, was Mayer Anselm (Amschel) Rothschild at Frankfort on the Main (1743-1812). He had five sons, of whom Anselm (1773—1855) took over the management of the Frankfort House, Salomon Mayer 1774 — 1855) that of the Vienna House, Nathan Mayer (1777 — 1836) that of the London House. Karl (1788-1855) that of the House at Naples, and Jacob (James) Rothschild (1792 — 1868) that of the Paris House.

the American millionaires so far as their actual riches are concerned, and not with regard to their economic position. The money-princes of America are always striving to utilise their gigantic fortunes for the further economic development of their country; the Rothschilds, on the contrary, compose a cosmopolitan company, without any country of its own, devoted to the mere acquisition of money, and which lives solely from the "financing" of the productive power of others. And, in order to ply this business on as great and as safe a scale as possible, the House of Rothschild has devoted particular attention to that chronic want of money, which is displayed by the Governments of the various countries. For the last 50 years, scarcely a single national loan of any importance has been negotiated and concluded without the Rothschilds; they have their fingers on the pulse of every exchange, and no one knows better than they how to skim the cream off all important economic operations. If one was desirous of writing an appropriate description of the various influences, which the Rothschilds exercise on our economic life, and upon our politics, the material would fill volumes. In this case a mere indication must suffice, and reference must be made to other books. Even in Sombart's work there is something on the subject. The so-called "Ger- manicus-Broschüren" (pamphlets) published during the years 1880-1888 by G. Richter at Frankfort on the Main, contain most instructive matter. Also F. v. Scherb: "Geschichte des Hauses Rothschild" (*History of the House of Rothschild*) Berlin 1892. "Germanicus" is evidently a well-informed judge of all matters relating to the Exchanges, and particularly so of the Jewish fraternity of Frankfort, and he lays bare relentlessly the fraudulent machinations of the great Jewish firms. But although some of these pamphlets passed through several large editions the voice, which spoke, therein died away, completely unheard in authoritative circles, and has not led to the slightest proceeding against the systematic plundering of the people, which takes place on the Stock Exchanges — a proof of the terrible ban, which Jewry has already cast over our public life. Nothing which runs counter to Jewish interests can any longer obtain publicity.

If Social Democracy were a genuine movement of the people, it would find, in this respect alone, its most urgent call to come to grips with the real robbers of the nation; but the genuine friend of the people learns to his astonishment, that the apparent representatives of the Proletariat extend their hands protectingly over the machinations of the Stock Exchange, and march, arm in arm, with the very men, who arrange how the people are to be deceived. With what notorious assiduity the leaders of the Proletariat have earned their title, "The Truncheon-Guard of the Jews", can be learnt from the fact, which has never been challenged, that during all the incendiary destruction, which took place at the time of the Paris Commune in 1870, the only property, which remained completely unharmed, was that of Mr. Rothschild.

Further material for the chapter on the Rothschilds and their companions is to be found in the writings of Otto Glagau: "Der Börsen- und Gründungsschwindel in Berlin" (*The Stock Exchange and Establishment swindle in Berlin*) and also "*in Germany*" (1877).

Old Meyer Anselm (Amschel) Rothschild laid the foundation of his fortune in Frankfort on the Main, as is known, with the capital of the former Landgraf and later Kurfürst, William I of Hesse who, during the time of the Napoleonic wars (1806—1813), handed over the whole of his fortune, amounting to 12, or, according to other authorities, to 21 million thalers, and the whole of which had been acquired by the sale of soldiers to other powers, partly by his father, and partly by himself, to the Frankfort money-man at 2 per cent (some say, free of interest) for many years, in order to guard it from the hands of the enemy. As money is very scarce, and is in very great demand during times of war, the clever banker earned, not only 5 and 10 per cent interest, but even higher rates, by means of the royal treasure. And those, who held the purse-strings for the German Federation, were guilty of the criminal folly of entrusting the huge sums of money, paid by France, as war reparation, and which had been marked for the erection of fortresses for the protection of the Federation, to the Frankfort Jews, and in particular, to the House of Rothschild, at the rate of only 2 per cent for 20 years!

Thus, the House of Rothschild has utilised the millions, belonging to princes and states, to make a foundation for its own world-wide power, and to still further extend its usury amongst princes and peoples. It became the money-lender and the money-broker for the Governments of all the European states, and from then onwards exercised a fateful influence upon all political proceedings.[7] It is significant that Amschel Meyer Rothschild, the eldest son of the founder of the business, was present at the Vienna Conference in 1815, spoke on that occasion, and was altogether a personality of considerable importance. In 1845, Prince Metternich wrote to the French Ambassador in Paris: "The House of Rothschild plays a far greater rôle at Frankfort than any foreign government, with the exception, perhaps, of the English. There are natural reasons for this, which one certainly cannot regard as good, and which, from a moral point of view, are still less satisfactory. Money is the great and final tribunal in France" etc.

The fine art of the Hebrew has always consisted in ascertaining, by means of espionage, the approaching shortage in goods and provisions, in buying up the same, and then, when they are urgently needed, only parting with them at a profiteer's price. In times of war it is scarcely possible to satisfy the requirements of the army without the aid of the Jews, as they have already laid their hands on all available stores, and secured the same by deeds of purchase and payments on account. That the House of Rothschild is quite at home in this underhand business, is proved by the following passage out of a letter from Nathan Rothschild, the third son of Meyer Amschel, to his friend, the politician Thomas Buxton:

When I had established myself in London, the East India Company[8] sold gold to the amount of 800,000 pounds sterling. I

---

[7] This is best shown by the drastic speech of the old tribal mother Rothschild, when she said to her sons: "Don't give the Princes any money, so that they will not be able to make war."

[8] According to an article in the *Quarterly Review*, June to September 1848, page 127, reviewing a book called, "*Memoirs of Sir Thomas Fowell Buxton, Bart.*," the amount is given as 800,000 lbs. of Gold! As twenty Troy pounds of Standard Gold, i. e. 22 carat Gold, are coined into 934 sovereigns and one half-sovereign, the above-mentioned amount of 800,000 lbs. would represent in minted gold the enormous sum of £37,380,000, that is to say if Troy Pound s and Standar d Gol d are meant in Buxton's memoirs; if Avoirdupoi s Pound s and Fine Gol d are intended, the minted value would be still larger — far over £40,000,000! It is incredible that Nathan Rothschild, or even the East India Company, had such an enormous amount of Gold at their disposal. The great probability is, that the actual amount of Gold, whether "standard" or "fine", was represented, as Fritsch has stated, by a minted value of £800,000. (Translator's note)

bought it all, because I knew that the Duke of Wellington must have it; I had bought up a large number of his bills at a cheap rate.[9] The Government sent for me, and declared that they must have the money. As soon as they had it, they did not know how to send it to Portugal. I undertook this as well, and sent the money across France. This was the best piece of business, which I have ever done.

And the members of this firm, which has become rich through countless, unclean, financial operations, have been ennobled (Amschel Meyer by the Emperor of Austria already in 1815), have been loaded with orders and decorations, and have been entrusted by princes and persons of rank with the management of their fortunes, and princes and persons of rank did not regard it as degrading to maintain relations with these wholesale usurers — yes, they sank almost to subserviency in their eagerness to help this descendant of a Frankfort Jew, who dealt in old clothes, and who had no other name than that of the house in which he lived, to play a more important part even than that assigned to kings and princes of the royal blood. And sprigs of the oldest and most illustrious nobility, who desired that everyone should know that their honour was a rare and costly possession, bent the knee before men, whose ancestor had adopted as his watchword; "My money is my honour".[10]) The increase in the wealth of the House of Rothschild is calculated as follows by the writer on political economy - Dr. Rud. Herm. Meyer — in the eighties:

The Parisian Rothschild (II) died in 1875, and left 1000 million francs. One is entitled, therefore, to estimate the combined fortunes of the members of the House of Rothschild at 5000 million francs. The Rothschilds make more than 5 per cent interest. Let us reckon in the meantime, that this "Plus" is utilised for their maintenance, and that their capital only doubles itself every fifteen years. One is entitled to assume this, because it has actually

---

[9] Wellington, who was a spendthrift in private life, was first Lord of the Treasury from 1826-1830.

[10] Mayer Amschel Rothschild writes as follows in a dunning letter to the agent of the Kurfürst Wilhelm II of Hesse: "He, who has my money, holds my honour, and my honour is my life; he, who does not pay me my money, takes my honour away from me." The original letter was sold by auction by Rud. Lepke in Berlin.

increased more quickly since the founding of the House. If it had only doubled itself every 15 years, it would have amounted to

1875	5000 million Francs
1860	2500 „ „
1845	1250 „ „
1830	625 „ „
1815	312 „ „
1800	156 „ „

It may be pointed out, however, that old Rothschild had no fortune whatever to speak of in the year 1800. One is therefore entitled to assume, that if a remedy is not to be found by means of anti-capitalistic, truly economic legislation, the fortune of the Rothschilds will continue to double itself every 15 years.

With this fact in view, one is quite in order in asking what relation does the income of the remainder of humanity bear towards it. The kingdom of Saxony is one of the richest and most prosperous of the German states. In the year 1876 the income, which had been assessed for income-tax, of 2-3/4 million inhabitants, amounted to 459 francs a head, and in 1877 to only 430 francs a head. The fifteen per cent income derived from the present fortune of the Rothschilds is therefore as large as the combined incomes of 581,400 Saxon citizens in the year 1877. If one assumes, that the average income throughout Europe always remained the same as that of the Saxons in the year 1877, and, bearing in mind the fact that the income of the Rothschilds doubles itself every fifteen years, one arrives at the following result:

The fortune of the Rothschilds amounted, in the year 1875, to 5000 million francs; the income out of this was as great as the combined income of 589,000 ordinary individuals; in 1890 the fortune of the Rothschilds amounted to 10,000 million francs; the income out of this was equal to the combined incomes of 1,150,000 ordinary individuals; in 1905 the fortune would amount to 20,000 million francs providing an income, from which 2,320,000 human beings — half the population of the kingdom of Saxony in the year 1905 — would have to live. In the year 1920, the fortune will have swollen to 40,000 million francs; in the year 1965 the fortune will amount to no less than 320,000 million francs, providing an income equal to the sum of the incomes, upon which 37,120,000 human beings must exist.

Thus writes Rud. Meyer. This survey, even if it can lay no claim to absolute accuracy, shows nevertheless, in a very instructive manner, how a great mass of capital, which is constantly increasing by means of compound interest, grows after the manner of an avalanche, and, like a sponge, sucks up the whole economic life. For these huge accumulations of property do not, of course, consist of real money, but simply of the debts and obligations of others; their growth, therefore, indicates a progressive indebtedness of the productive and owning classes, and also of the countries themselves.

The success of the House of Rothschild is entirely attributable to the fact that the firm possessed simultaneously an establishment in each of the five most important countries in Europe, and maintained, by means of their representatives at these establishments, a constant service of news, relating to all political and economic circumstances, which was utilised to exercise active influence in every direction. The five great banking houses, which all worked on exactly the same lines, and played into one another's hands, formed, whenever a crisis arrived, a united power, opposed to which the governments of countries were but little better than powerless.

2. THE "PLAYING INTO ONE ANOTHER'S HANDS", AND SECRET UNDERSTANDING OF THE HEBREWS

This particular instance is not necessary to demonstrate how valuable organised collaboration is to business interests. The superiority of the Jewish organisation over individual activity is apparent in countless cases of everyday life — from the buying of rags, and the operations of the auction-room hyenas, to cattle-dealing and traffic in stock-exchange shares. The Hebrew, however, is already quite capable, as an individual alone, of out-stripping all sound and honest competitors in the business arena; not only does his innate and trained sense of business give him the advantage, but, before everything else, he is enabled to do this by particular tactics and by the unscrupulousness of his procedure. And, granted that the Hebrew possesses an eminent talent for commerce, and all kinds of remarkable characteristics, which enable him to force the average German business-man out of the saddle, these powers increase until they become absolutely irresistible when several cooperate to exert them in the same direction.

The German business-man, as a rule, stands as a single individual, opposed to all the rest; he endeavours to advance his business by his own power and ability, and nowadays it is quite the exception for him to receive any special help or advancement from relatives or friends. With the Hebrews it is quite different. The strong "holding-together" of this foreign national element is a world-wide historical fact. One hears them extolled in all quarters, because they stand by one another and support themselves. That is certainly a praiseworthy characteristic, and, as such, may appear worthy of imitation. In the case of the Jews, this "holding-together" does not arise from unalloyed mutual goodwill; it is rather a duty of life, created by tradition, and indispensable for this people. The Hebrew recognises the fact that, owin g to his peculiar behaviour, and to his peculiar designs, which are hostile to the rest of humanity, he would be powerless in the world as a separate individual. The co-operation of kindred powers, in the same direction, appears to him as necessary law of life. It is solely due to the fact that many of his kind — either by agreement or impelled by the common instinct — incessantly oppose the established regulations of the honest and productive nations, that that kind of dissoluteness, and that kind of confusion are produced in the social structure, which are essential to the prosperity of the Hebrews.

For this reason no one finds "holding together" so necessary as the Jews. In all their business, whether it be as agent or middleman in the country, or as wholesale merchant or stockbroker in the towns, the Hebrews are organised everywhere in bands or gangs. Even in the domain of theft where, until a few decades ago, they were considerably more active than at the present moment, they had developed theft by gangs, until it could almost be regarded as an art.[11] Each one had a separate part to play. For instance, there were the "scout", who had to "provide" the opportunity, the "Schmiere-Steher" (Grease Stander) whose business it was to keep a look-out, while the theft was being committed, fellow-conspirators who received the stolen goods, and all kinds of other people, who helped to make "gang-robbery" so successful. One has only to read the writings of the criminal actuary Thiele, which were published in the forties of the last century under the title: *"The Jewish Swindlers in Germany"*, to learn on what a magnificent scale the people of Judah showed their skill on every occasion, both in organisation, and in the assignation of the part, which each should play.

In one particular case — Rosenthal versus Löwenthal — there were no less than 700 thieves and accomplices prosecuted, who were, almost without exception, Hebrews, and whose communications extended, from certain towns in Poland, as far as the Rhine, with branches all over Germany. This powerful "Chawrusse" carried on burglary, embezzlement, artificial bankruptcy, and the traffic in stolen goods, on a truly grand scale. Anyone, who reads the account of the trial at the time, cannot help being struck by the fact that quite a number of characteristic names of various [members of this band of thieves are to be found today amongst the magnates of finance and the matadors of the Stock Exchange in Berlin, until the impression gains ground that the present-day Jewish corporation of the Stock Exchange is a direct continuation of the old swindling "Chawrusse" of Bentschen and Neutomischel. One must not, by any means, believe that the connection between thieves and bankers belongs to the past. When four Jewish burglars were captured recently in the act of robbing a warehouse in the vicinity of Paris, a large number of letters were found in their possession, connecting them with some of the leading

[11] The "Thieves' Jargon" or "Rotwelsch" is, on this account, full of "Yiddish", which is a corrupt form of German spoken by Hebrews: compare also Avé-Lallemant: "Das deutsche Gaunertum* *(German Swindledom)* 4 Volumes 1854.

Jewish firms in London and Antwerp. The public press unfortunately remained silent concerning what other discoveries were made in the course of the investigation.

3. NOMADISM OF THE HEBREW

Internationality presumes, of necessity, a departure from the stationary habit — from the attachment to the soil, to the home, to the Fatherland. Since the Jew knows no Fatherland in our sense of the word, Internationality is an essential part of his peculiar disposition, and impels him, on principle, to assume a hostile attitude towards all national effort. For this reason the German disposition is especially hateful to the Jew.

Sombart very appositely represents the Jews as a nation of wanderers —of "nomads", compared with the stationary nations.[12] Out of this fundamental opposition arises a wide divergence in the views taken with regard to life and to economic principles. The stationary individual must, of necessity, favour well- regulated conditions and stability, in order that he may have full scope for his productive and constructive activity. The nomad, animated by the impulse to convey all his possessions along with him, and to make them as portable as possible, must always foster the wish to make things and values moveable; in fact, to "mobilise" them. Consequently he is not in love with fixity and constancy of relations and regulations; he desires, on the contrary, to see everything in a state of flux and revolution. The ground with its surface-soil, which is the preliminary condition, and forms the foundation for all productive and stationary nations, has little meaning for the nomad — if he is not able to convert it into moveable, liquid values. He accomplishes this by the production of "paper values", for which the immoveable goods of stationary citizens are pledged. Therefore he holds sides with mortgages, pledge-papers, stocks and shares,

---

[12] He was certainly not the first to remark this, for we have possessed, since 1887, the masterly work of Professor Adolf Wahrmund († 1913): "Das Gesetz des Nomadentums und die heutige Judenherrschaft": (*The Law of Nomadism and the present-day domination by the Jews*).

bills of exchange, and all other paper values, which can be stuck comfortably in the pocket, and carried away.

Just as little interest is shown by the Hebrew in the production of the native soil; his instinct for "dealing", drives him to desire that all articles, on their journey from producer to consumer, should travel as far as possible, and consequently be made to pass, as frequently as possible, the turnpikes of his middleman monopoly. The more that goods wander about the world, and the more that nations become dependent upon what they import from foreign countries, so much the better for the Hebrew. It is on this account that he endeavours, by all means, to check and to complicate the simple and straightforward course, which the exchange of goods would naturally take. He thrusts himself everywhere between producers and consumers, and strives, wherever it is possible, so to arrange matters, that not even the smallest business shall be completed without his interference. In countries where the Jews sit close to one another, this system has been perfected to a marvellous extent. J. C. Kohl, for instance, relates in his *"Journeys in the interior of Russia and Poland"*, that in Poland it is not possible to conclude either an important or unimportant piece of business without the mediation of a Jew. "The nobleman sells his wheat to the shipper through the Jew, the master of the house engages his servants, his steward, his cooks, yes, even the instructors and tutors for his son through the Jew. Estates are let, money is collected, stores are bought etc. through the agency of the Jew; in short, one feeds, travels, rides, lodges and clothes one's self through the mediation of the Jew. Formerly the Jews were also the sole tenants of the Customs, Mines and Salt-works in Poland.[13] T. von Langenfeldt in his book "Russland im 19. Jahrhundert" (*Russia in the 19th Cen*tury[14] gives a picture of the interaction of Jewish business activities, and of the far-flung net of their helpers and helpers' helpers:

At the annual markets where the Jews are permitted to do business, the dealing takes on a certain feverish aspect. They appear

---

[13] Leipzig 1841. — This work is still regarded by those acquainted with the conditions as correct and reliable. — See also Richard Andree: "Zur Volkskunde der Juden" (*National information concerning the Jews*) page 213.
[14] Berlin 1875. — See "Handbuch der Judenfrage" (*Handbook to the Jewish Question*) 27 Edition pages 100—111.

in enormous numbers, and sell their goods, both wholesale and retail, from booths and stalls, or hawk them from house to house. Around each Jewish wholesale dealer swarm hundreds of poor Jews, who obtain goods from him on credit, and sell the same retail. One Jew supports another; they have their own bankers, brokers, agents — yes, even their own carmen. Over the whole of western and southern Russia there is spread an innumerable host of commission agents and factors, employed by rich Jewish wholesale merchants. These form the connecting link between the merchants and the producers, between the more distant markets and the commercial centres. The duties of these agents consist in purchasing goods, and in writing periodical reports, with which they have to furnish their masters, concerning every economic novelty, concerning the prices of every possible product, imparting at the same time their views as to the advantage of this or that commercial operation".

And further: "Besides the commission agents, the brokers are absolutely indispensable for Jewish trade. The business of the broker consists in knowing everything, hunting up everything, bringing the interested parties together, watching the actions of those people who have any kind of relations to the merchant — in one word: to represent all the interests of his principal. The broker is a living price-list, in whom the prices, the quantity, the quality, and the location of the goods for sale — in fact everything which can interest the purchaser, is recorded. Almost every Jew is a broker; yes, one is entitled to maintain that he is born to the part".

"The brokers on any particular market do not allow any stranger to enter the same, and do not themselves attempt to enter any strange market, but recommend their clients to go to a broker known to them, at the place in question. There are special brokers for the grain, tallow, salt, and timber trades. Where Jews exclusively live, the whole country is covered with a net of brokers, who penetrate into the most remote economic corners of each district. The broker understands how to make himself indispensable everywhere, and to everybody. The estate- owner, and especially the Polish estate-owner, is the born friend of the Jew, who flatters him, abases himself before him, knows always where and how money can be procured, and where he — the estate-owner — can dispose of his produce to the best advantage".

From the above characteristic motives springs the mania of the Hebrew to give the preference to all foreign goods. He is always the first to bring novelties from foreign countries, and is an indefatigable praiser of everything foreign. He is always ready with an assurance that the foreign article is better than the native; he even goes so far as to maintain that foreign corn is more nourishing than that grown by German peasants. He knows full well that the native product very easily discovers the direct road from producer to consumer without requiring his services as middleman; and this sticks in his gizzard.

He would like to make production just like consumption — dependent upon himself, and to get it completely into his power; he therefore tries to separate the two processes, and to thrust himself between them. The business of the middleman has become to such an extent the second nature of the Jew, that he regards it with favour also, when practised by others, so long as he does not lose any advantage thereby. Manufacturers, who deliver exclusively to their representatives, the latter themselves, as well as the great army of agents, brokers, and commission men, who do not stand in direct competition with Jews, are wont to praise the Jews on account of the punctilious respect, which the latter pay to every kind of middle-man business. The Jew's ideal would be to convert Germany into a one-sided industrial country, importing all raw material and food-stuffs from abroad, and compelled to export again the greater part of its industrial products. In this case both the raw material and the finished article must pass through the hands of the middle-man, and his control of the market would be complete. But this would be accompanied also by the political control of the state. The nearer this ideal brings the Hebrew to the social-democrat of Marxian[15] tendencies, the further it separates him from all representatives of national work.

[15] Karl Marx (1818-1883) was of Jewish origin, like Ferd. Lassalle (1825—1864) and many other notorious social-democratic magnates.

Therefore the Jew is a sworn enemy of agriculture in the home country. He persecutes with fanatical hatred the "agrarian", who by his diligent production, interferes with the commercial monopoly of the Jew. For this reason the latter is never tired of singing the praises of international free-trade, of abusing protective duties, of inciting the inhabitants of towns against the country-folk, and of endeavouring, as far as possible, to sow discord between the two.

The Hebrew fraternity is favoured by yet another circumstance in its control of the economic life, and that is: — the peculiar morality.

V

THE PECULIAR MORALITY OF JEWDOM

That the Hebrew is not very particular with regard to his moral obligations towards other people, is fairly well known. One is wont to excuse him much in this respect, and to overlook his lack of conscientiousness with the remark that he had been frequently unjustly persecuted in "olden times", and thus had been driven, by dire necessity, to the adoption of a lax moral code. In this respect also, many "worthy souls" are inclined, out of ill-considered amiability, to speak disparagingly of their own nation by imputing the responsibility for the moral deficiencies of the Hebrew to their own Christian ancestors. These fine folk could easily ascertain from the Bible, that the bad ethics of the Hebrew are as old as that nation, and already existed before there were any Christians. The Hebrews were already decried, far and wide, in ancient Egypt, Babylon, and Syria on account of their questionable morality and business tactics; consequently, the Christians cannot be blamed for the moral shortcomings of the Jewish people.

Already we can learn out of the Old Testament that their law allows the Hebrews to treat the "non-Jew" — "the stranger" — very differently to those of their own faith and blood. In this respect already, the "Chosen People" place themselves in the strongest contrast to all other nations, who are designated as "strangers". It is continually reiterated that it is permissible to do all kinds of things towards a "stranger", which it is forbidden to do towards the fellow-Jews. Thus, for example: "You may practise usury against the "stranger", but not against your brother." (5. Moses 23, 20).

A sharp distinction is always drawn between the Jews, and the rest of the nations. All the moral commandments of the Hebrews extend only to members of their race; all other races are excepted. What is forbidden to be done to Jews, is permitted towards those, who are not Jews. 5. Moses, 15. 3: "You may put pressure on the stranger, but you must be lenient to him, who is your brother." The contempt shown for all those, who are not Jews, goes so far as to regard unclean food and garbage as good enough for the "stranger". 5. Moses, 14, 21: "You shall not eat offal; you may give it to the 'stranger' in your gate so that he may eat it, or sell it to another 'stranger'".

All the commands, made with reference to one's neighbour, are not comprehended by the Jew as by the Christian, who regards them as referring to all men; he — the Jew — accepts them quite literally, and as referring only to the actual neighbour, the member of the same race, the fellow-Jew. When we read in 3 Moses: 19, 13: "Thou shalt neither overreach nor rob thy neighbour", the Jew considers that he is released from any like duty towards those, who are not Jews. The writings of the Rabbis express this particular comprehension of the text quite unmistakably.

* * * * *

This peculiar comprehension on the part of the Jews of their particular rights as human beings goes, however, still further back; it rests, in the last analysis, on the fact that the Jews not only separate themselves as a "chosen people" from all other men, but have their own particular god. It is a fatal mistake of our theologians to regard the Jewish God as identical with the Christian. On a closer examination, Jehovah (whom the more modern science calls Jahwe) is found to be the exclusive God of Jewdom, and not, at the same time, that of other men. One can convince one's self from 1. Moses, Chapter 17, that this Jahwe-Jehovah concluded his formal agreement expressly only with Abraham and his seed (descendants), and that this covenant bears a hostile meaning for all non- Jewish peoples. As a sign of the covenant, circumcision is introduced, and Jahwe declares: all who are not circumcised, will incur his vengeance, and will be completely destroyed.

It is at once clear that this covenant between Jahwe and Abraham's seed is a warlike covenant, the point of which is directed relentlessly against all non-Jewish nations — the unbelievers, the heathens (Goyim). In the eyes of the Jews, however, heathens are all those, who are not of Abraham's seed, all who are not circumcised, all who have not entered into the blood-pact with Jahwe. Dominion over all other nations is promised to the Jews, and the possessions of the former will be given to them as a reward if they — the Jews — are true to their pact with Jahwe:

"Ask of me, and I shall give thee the heathen for thine inheritance, and the uttermost parts of the earth for thy possession. Thou shalt break them with a rod of iron; thou shalt dash them in pieces like a potter's vessel." (Psalms 2. 8. 9)

Yes, open hostility is declared against all non-Jewish nations, and their extirpation and annihilation are to be the life task of the Jews:

5. Moses 7, 16: "Thou wilt devour all nations, which the Lord thy God will give thee. Thou shalt have no mercy on them, and shalt not serve their gods, for to do so will be thy condemnation.[16]

The oriental scholar, Adolf Wahrmund, is therefore justified in referring to the journey of the Jews across the earth as an expedition for the capture of the world — certainly not by open force of arms, but by other means, a plentiful store of which, is placed at their disposal by the Talmudic teaching of the Rabbis.

The most important weapon of the Jews against non-Jewish nations is Money; they therefore endeavour to obtain possession of this in every form. For this reason Jews are allowed to practise usury against non-Jews, and the lending of money, and the receiving of interest are recommended as an important means or instrument for dominating other nations.

---

[16] Consequently it was a fatal blunder of Luther, always to translate the word Jahwe as "Lord God", and thus to help to obliterate the fundamental difference between the particular god of the Jews, and the "Heavenly Father" of Christ.

5. Moses 15, 6: "For Jahwe, thy God, has conferred blessings on thee, as he has promised thee, so that thou shalt lend to many nations but shalt not need to borrow thyself, and that thou shalt rule over many nations but that no one shall rule over thee!" —

Truly a wonderful compact with God, which is payable in cash, and which promises domination over other nations by money-power — whilst Christ teaches: "Ye cannot serve God and Mammon."

The peculiar Jewish perception of life which results from such doctrines, is made the utmost of in the Talmud. It would take too much time and space to quote even extracts here from the mystical books of the Rabbis; therefore reference is made to the work by Th. Fritsch: "Mein Beweismaterial gegen Jahwe" (*"My evidence against Jahwe"*)[17] in which a strong light is cast upon domains, which we can scarcely glance at.

Thus, the segregation of the Hebrews from all other nations is conscious and deliberate, and is in nowise due to possible dislike on the part of those nations. The devotional books of the Jews furnish us with plenty of proof on that point. Warning is incessant never to make common cause with the foreign nations:

"Give heed that thou makest no treaty with the inhabitants of the land, into which thou comest, so that they may not become a vexation to thee." 2. Moses 34. 12 and 13.

The boundary-line between the Hebrew and the rest of humanity is everywhere most sharply defined, and the peculiar morals of Jewdom rest on this separation of interests. They were first set out, however, in characteristic form, by the Rabbis, who "laid down" the Jewish system of morals in the "Talmud" (= Doctrine), from the 2 n d to the 5 t h Century after the birth of Christ.

"The Talmud — a comprehensive work, divided into many parts — is the real code of laws for Jewdom since the time of Christ,

---

[17] Hammer-Verlag, Leipzig C 1

and is the foundation of its religious and civic arrangements". (Brockhaus Conv. Lexicon). And it is precisely in this book, where the perception impresses itself most forcibly upon the reader, that it is only the Hebrew, who is a man in the real sense of the word, and that all the remaining nations stand far beneath him, and are, in fact, comparable to animals.

"The nations of the world are like the baskets, in which one puts straw and dung. They have a soul, which is only equal to that of the animals."

is an example of what is to be found in the "Midrasch schir haschirim", and a further specimen in the treatise "Baba mezia" is as follows:

"You Israelites are called men, but the nations of the world are called not men, but cattle."

Jalkut Rubeni expresses himself still more distinctly:

"The Israelites are called men (human beings) because their souls are derived from God, but the souls of those, who are not Jews, are derived from the unclean spirit, and therefore they are named swine."

But, in case a believing Jew might be of the opinion that those, who are not Jews, are just as good men as the Hebrews, because they possess the same form, Schene-tuchoth-habberith is prepared to give instruction upon this point, for it is stated there:

"A human form is only given to those, who are not Jews, in order that the Jews may not be waited upon by beasts."

With such a perception it is comprehensible how all intercourse with those, who are not Jews, is most strictly forbidden to all true Hebrews. It is a matter of common knowledge that the Old Testament warns the true Jew, in the most emphatic manner, not to enter into marriage with those, who are not Jews, and the

Rabbis of the Talmud repeat and accentuate this commandment on many occasions.

Consequently, when the suggestion is made that a mutual contempt exists between Jews and non-Jews, it is well to remember, first of all, which side started this; it is in consequence of the racial conceit of the real Hebrew that he regards his nation as quite out of the ordinary, and especially chosen, and permitted to look down upon other men with contempt. It is certainly nothing to wonder at, if the other nations, in their turn, pay back this aversion in the same coin, and they are more entitled to do so, as, in their case, it is a counter- stroke to a brutal challenge.

But, whoever regards those, who do not belong to his race, as no better than beasts, cannot possibly recognise that he has any moral obligations towards such inferior creatures. Upon this fundamental perception rests the entire system of morality of the Rabbis; it teaches, with constant repetition, that one has duties only towards one's neighbour, one's race, and towards nobody else. The Law states: "Thou shalt do no wrong to thy neighbour", and the discerning Rabbi adds, to make it clearer: "the other people are excepted". Again, one reads in the treatise Sanhedrin: "An Israelite is permitted to do a wrong to a "Goi" i.e. non-Jew, because it is written: Thou shalt not do wrong to thy neighbour, without however, paying any heed to the Goi.'" It cannot be wondered at then, when the Talmud draws the following conclusion for instance: "Lost property, which belongs to a Goi, need not be returned."

But the writings of the Talmud do not confine themselves to such general instructions. Just as business forms, as it were, the soul of the entire Jewish existence, so great importance is given in the Talmud also to all business relations, and all manner of good advice is imparted therein as to how one is to comport one's self during business developments. For this belongs also to the Jewish religion. When one recollects how little the doctrine of Christ concerns itself with money-matters and business, and how it, to a certain extent, rejects any such thing as Money, relying on the Word: "Ye cannot serve God and Mammon", one must feel what a contrast exists between the Christian and Jewish perceptions of life, and one, across which no bridge can ever be built. How important, however on the contrary, are all business matters to the Hebrew! Thus, we find in the writings of the Talmud directions, of which the following are examples:

"If a Goi holds the pledge of an Israelite, and the Goi loses it, and an Israelite finds it, the latter shall return it to the Israelite, but not to the Goi; if, however, the finder desires to return it to the Goi for the sake of the sacred reputation[18] then, the other (Israelite) shall say to him: 'If you wish to keep the reputation sacred, do so with what belongs to you.'" (R. Jerucham Seph. mesch. f. 51. 4)

It is also taught:

"It is permissible to take advantage of the mistake of a Goi, when he makes a mistake (to his disadvantage). Thus, if the Goi sends in his bill, and makes a mistake, the Israelite shall say to him: 'See, I rely upon your bill; I do not know if it really is as you state, nevertheless I give you what you demand.'"

Not only in purely business matters is the Hebrew allowed to treat those, who are not Jews, in a different manner to his own race, but Rabbinism inexorably extends the sharp division between Jew and non-Jew into all remaining domains of life. The Jew is commanded, when acting as Judge in law-suits, to influence the course of the proceedings in favour of his racial companions. In the book *Baba Kamma* (= the first door) we find Fol. 113a, paragraph 2:

"When an Israelite and a non-Jew come before you in the Court, you shall, if you can, administer justice to him — the former — according to Jewish law, and say to him: 'it is so according to our law'. When the law of the worldly nations is favourable to the Jew, you shall administer Justice to him accordingly, and say to him: it is thus according to our law'. But when this is not the case, use cunning."

---

[18] A mode of speaking, which frequently occurs, much to this effect: "In order that our Religion and our God do not incur a bad reputation."

The following passage, for instance, bears eloquent testimony to the assertion that the despicable doctrines of the Talmud towards the Canaanites, Edomites and Amalakites, refer, not only to the peoples of antiquity, but also to the present:

"The inhabitants of Germany" says Kinchi (Obadja 1,20) "are Canaanites, for when the Canaanites fled before Jehoschua, they went into the land Alemannia, which is called Germany, and even to the present day the German s are called Canaanites. "

In more recent times, the Hebrews eagerly assume the appearance of possessing a warlike spirit, boast of their participation in the various campaigns, and endeavour, through their patrons and press, to bring it about that they will even be admitted to the rank of officer. That they, however, prize safety rather than valour is shown by referring to the passage out of the Talmud Pesachim 112b:

"If you go to war, go not first but last, in order that you can return home first".

Also, the extensively held idea, that the Jew was compelled by foreign influence to confine himself to trade, because other vocations were forbidden to him — a matter, which, later on, we will go more deeply into — is shown to be fallacious by the actual writings of the Rabbis. The same prove that the Hebrew has, from the remotest periods, always displayed a preference for trade, because other activities, and especially agriculture, appeared too tedious to him, and brought in too little profit. Thus we read in the Talmud:

"Rab Eleazar has said: "No handicraft is so unprofitable as agriculture for it is said Czech 27. 29 'You will come down' (grow poor)!" R. Eleazar beheld a field, across which cabbages were planted in beds. He then said: "Even if cabbages were planted for the whole length of the field, trading would still be the best." On one occasion when the Rab was walking through a wheatfield, and observed how the wheat swayed to and fro, he said: "continue to sway, trade is to be preferred to you". — Rab has further said: "He who expends a hundred Sus in trade, can enjoy meat and wine every day, but he, who expends a hundred Sus on agriculture, has to be content with cabbage and salt, must sleep on the earth, and is exposed to every kind of misery."

Thus, the preference for Trade, and the contempt for Handicraft and Agriculture are a very ancient legacy of the Jewish race, and no one has ever found it necessary to compel them to turn to trade.

* * * * *

It would be a fatal mistake to imagine that these ancient views and laws in the Talmud do not possess any validity today. On the contrary: the doctrines of the Talmud form, uninterruptedly, an important item in the Jewish religious education, and every young Jew receives instruction according to the views expressed in the Talmud — however much he may assure one, later on in life, that such matters are entirely unknown to him. Moreover, the law, set out in the Talmud, has been modernised by a recent revision — the so-called Schulchan aruch — and the validity of this law is so undisputed, that the Imperial German legal authorities, in law-suits, in which both parties were Jews, have relied upon the precepts of the Schulchan aruch.

In this more recent law-book of Jewdom is to be found that remarkable prayer, which is said every year on the Day of Atonement, in all synagogues, accompanied by great solemnity, the so-called Kol-Nidre-Prayer. It is as follows:

"All vows (Kol-Nidre) and obligations and conjurations and oaths, which we shall vow, enter into, and swear, from this day of Atonement until the next, we repent of, and the same shall be dissolved, remitted, abolished, destroyed, and shall be of no force and invalid: our vows shall not be vows, and our oaths shall not be oaths".

The contents of this peculiar prayer have often been used as a reproach to the Jews, who usually argue their way out of it, by maintaining that the vows, declarations and oaths, which are spoken of in this prayer, refer only to religious matters, more especially to vows and oaths, which the Jew makes or takes to himself, or to his God. It is difficult, however, to see why anyone, who regards his oaths to God so lightly, should take a more serious view of his affirmations or vows to his fellow-men. In any case, the praying Hebrew has the right, when reciting the "Kol", to connect this prayer secretly with his own particular vows and oaths.

* * * * *

There is nothing to wonder at then, if a nation, with such a remarkable system of ethics, obtains a tremendous advantage over men, who possess a more sensitive conscience, and a finer sense of justice, and who not only abide by their oaths and vows, but adhere punctiliously to their ordinary promises and assurances. That ethical perception of the Talmud, which forces the Hebrew to observe his duties towards his racial and religious brethren with almost painful exactitude, but absolves him of his duties towards other men, must introduce a curious kind of discord into our life. The Hebrews are thus united in a strong union, which not only possesses a strong common-interest, but directs itself, at the same time, in silent hostility against all other men. And, since the Hebrews are forbidden in addition in the sternest manner according to their laws, to disclose anything of their secret legislation to those, who are not Jews, Jewdom acquires, with such a basis, the nature of a conspiracy which is aimed at all men, who do not happen to be Jews.

The situation is aggravated by the following circumstances: the doctrines and laws of the Rabbis are — with few exceptions — only to be found in the Hebraic language and characters, and are, for that reason, practically unapproachable for the rest of mankind. Besides, the written language of the Hebrews resembles a cryptograph, the reading and explanation of which are taught by tradition in the schools of the Rabbis. The Jews are consequently in the position to maintain to the uninitiated that the rendering of the latter is incorrect. For, as a matter of fact, those scholars, who are not Jews, but who, having learnt the Hebrew language and examined the writings of the Rabbis, have then proceeded to translate some of the awkward passages, have become the objects of the most violent hostility on the part of the Jews. Only with the help of converted Jews has it been possible, in certain cases, to ascertain the correct reading or version. But for centuries reliable Christian scholars have made translations of the immoral passages, which all agree, so that it is scarcely permissible to entertain any doubt as to the correctness of the version. One need only mention the Heidelberg Professor of Oriental Languages, Johann Eisenmenger, who produced a translation of extracts from the Talmud in the year 1700; the Canonical Professor, August Rohling, of Prague, who published his "Talmudjude" (*Jew of the Talmud*) in 1878, and since then has been made the object of most odious enmity from the side of the Jews. Further, the Orientalists, Professor Johann Gildemeister of Bonn († 1890), Dr. Jakob Ecker of Münster, and Professor Georg Behr of Heidelberg, as arbiters in court, have confirmed the correctness of these same translations of the rabbinical writings, when the opportunity presented itself in law-suits, relating to such matters. Since, however, the Jews always renew their denials, there is really a most urgent necessity, in the interests of both sides, that the disputed passages in the Talmud should be examined by impartial experts; all conflict about the matter would then be removed from the world in the simplest manner possible.

It is, however, a most remarkable fact that the Hebrews oppose any such procedure most emphatically and, strange to say, the state officials have also declined to move in the matter when application has been made to them. When, in the year 1890, a petition was sent from the anti-Jewish camp to a number of Imperial and local authorities, containing the request that a commission of independent savants should be appointed, whose duty would be to examine carefully the passages in dispute, in not a single instance was the request granted. The Prussian Ministry of Culture dismissed any such step as being "impracticable." If one compares the thoroughness with which the morality of the Jesuits has been and is still discussed in public, one is forced to accept the view, that the zealous friends of truth and opponents of those, who work in an obscure and devious manner, know how to restrain their zeal for enlightenment in a truly remarkable way so far as the Jews are concerned.

The position is thus a very peculiar one. This much is established: The German national representative bodies and governments have given the Jews equal civic rights, and have recognised them as a separate religious community, without making any inquiry whether the moral instruction of the Jews is compatible with the welfare of the state. There is, therefore, no cause for wonder if attacks are constantly being delivered by the National German Party against this untenable position, and if the demand is made upon those, in positions of authority, to undertake, even at this late stage, a thorough examination of the Jewish doctrines. There will be no end to this dispute until the matter has been made clear beyond any possible doubt. Joh. Ludwig Klüber, the diplomatist and authority on International Law (decd. 1837) calls the Jews plainly, "a political-religious sect, under the strict, theocratic despotism of the Rabbis", and "a completely separated society of hereditary conspirators, with certain political principles and commandments for the general life and for commercial intercourse." (Thus, not merely with religious aims). And this is, in concise, sober language, the essence of the matter. For the Jews do not compose, like the Christians for instance, simply a religious community, which depends upon certain moral doctrines, and worships its God according to certain established forms; their — the Jews' — law extends to all manner of practical affairs in life, and, under the influence of a peculiar morality, concerns itself particularly with the cultivation of trade and usury. They form, in spite of their dispersion amongst other peoples, an absolutely distinct nation, even, as Fichte expresses it, a separate state. And, as they are at the same time intent upon preserving the purity of their blood, and intermarry, as far as it is possible, they form also a self-contained race. Of all the rulers in Germany, no one has recognised this fact more clearly than the greatest of all practical politicians amongst them, Frederick the Great, who considered it necessary, even in his political will of 1752, to impress most strongly upon his successors: "Moreover, the ruler must keep his eye on the Jews, prevent their interference with wholesale trade; check the growth of their population, and deprive them of their right of sanctuary whenever they commit an act of dishonesty. For nothing is more injurious to the trade of the merchants than the illicit profit which the Jews make."

The racial peculiarity; however, is visible to the eye, so that the Jew can be recognised immediately and picked out from all the other peoples of the world. And, further, there can be no doubt whatever upon this point: by means of their Talmud and their system of Rabbis, the Hebrews are held together in a rigid caste, which carries on a cooperative war against the remaining nations, chiefly by means of material expropriation and the undermining of morality.

Our Moltke, who had the opportunity of studying Jewdom thoroughly, during his residence in Poland from 1830 to 1832, sums up his observations in the following words ("Darstellung der inneren Verhältnisse in Polen") (*Description of the internal conditions in Poland*, Berlin 1832):

"In spite of their dispersion the Jews still remain closely united. They are guided consistently by unknown authorities for mutual purposes. As they reject all the attempts of governments to incorporate them in the nations, the Jews form a state within a state, and have become a deep wound in Poland, which has not healed even at the present day. Even now each town has its own Judge, each province its Rabbi, and all are subordinate to an unknown chief, who lives in Asia, and who is bound by their law to travel round continually, from place to place, and whom they call the "Prince of Slavery". — Thus, retaining their religion, their government, their morality, and their language, and obeying their own laws, they know how to evade those of the land they live in, or, at any rate, to nullify the same for all practical purposes: and, closely united amongst themselves, they resist all attempts to fuse them into the rest of the nation, just as much on account of their religious belief as on account of their self-interest."

* * * * *

It simply does not do then, to complacently ignore, with Christian tolerance and sentimental charity, this singular and firmly organised hostile state of Jewry. This hostile state has declared war on us — war to the knife — for it is attempting to appropriate our

F. RODERICH-STOLTHEIM

material as well as our spiritual values.[19] It is an error to represent the Jews to one's self as a harmless "Concession", which lives peacefully besides us, and is only desirous of serving its God in its own particular way. The most excellent Adolf Wahrmund sees the ancient principle of the nomadic desert robbers, who sweep across the cultivated spots in order to leave the pastures grassless and barren behind them, surviving in our Jews. He says:[20] "According to the view taken from the Talmud, and expressed by the Rabbis, the path of the Jews across the world is a warlike expedition for the conquest of the same — nothing else. They regard themselves as soldiers on the march, hiding themselves in secret camps, or concealing themselves under a false flag — in the midst of the enemy, always waiting for the signal to attack and surprise."

None of these facts are altered in the least, because, now and again, this or that Jew appears to us to be quite a harmless and perhaps even an amiable individual. Without doubt the Jew possesses many human and social virtues, but who will guarantee that this external aspect of his disposition can be regarded as genuine, mixed as the latter quite comprehensibly is with bitterness on account of imagined slights, or imbued with feelings of revenge? The peculiar situation of the Jew, in the midst of a community, which is inwardly foreign to him, compels him to adopt a cautious and discrete attitude. It would be foolish on his part if he openly displayed his pride and his aversion to all men, who are not Jews. How could he thus accomplish his aims? Slyness commands him to adapt himself by mildness and pliancy to his environment, and to present the appearance of entertaining good will and a kindly disposition towards his fellow-citizens, in order to captivate the latter in their artlessness, and to win their confidence. Only thus is he enabled to promote his own business interests, and those other secret aims of Hebrewdom, to the best advantage. One must not then accept the plea that there are also some extremely nice and honest Jews as a proof that they are not dangerous. Exceptions prove the rule, and amiability and apparent harmlessness are

---

[19] Dr. Moritz Goldstein stated in the "Kunstwart" 1912, that it could no longer be disputed that the Jews ruled over, not only the material, but even the spiritual values of the German Nation, however much the Germans might deny their capacity to do so.

[20] Page 41 in the writing under his name.

70

amongst the most deadly weapons, which the Hebrews employ against those who surround them. If, occasionally, a kind heart may prompt a Jew to act unselfishly, and even to display self-sacrifice where others are concerned, (an occurrence which, on account of its rarity, is wont to be trumpeted forth a hundred times as loudly as it would be in the case of anybody, who is not a Jew) the best and most moral Jew still remains a member of a most secret society, which directs its front against us. And, at the moment, when the decision must be made whether to defend Jewish interests against other interests, the noblest and most high-minded Jew will also take the side of his racial comrades, and will treat everyone, who is not a Jew, as an enemy. Luther already summed up the situation correctly when he spoke as follows, concerning the Jews:

"But if they do anything good, know that it is not done out of love, nor does it happen for your good; but because they must have room to live amongst us, they must of necessity do something. But the heart is, and remains, as I have said."

Therefore, do not forget: we are in a state of war with the Jews. But, if a nation has declared war upon us, and advances with hostile intent into our country, it no longer behoves us to ask: is that particular individual a good or a bad man? — but, from that moment, each of them must be regarded as our enemy, and against whom we must defend ourselves.

VI

AN EXPLANATION WITH SOMBART

After we have sketched in outline our own attitude to the question, which lies before us, the task still remains to follow up Sombart's work,[21] in order to supplement the same, partly by confirming it, and partly by making another comprehension valid. Sombart, himself, allows that his book is one-sided, and is meant to be. He has, in fact, supplied a written history of the economic method of the Jews, which — although the author obviously has taken pains to keep to the point, and to abstain from all appreciations — has nevertheless been written preponderatingly from the sunny side. Anyone, who did not know anything about the history of the world, would, on reading this book, easily acquire the impression that the Hebrews were the sole moving principle — not only in political economy but chiefly in Culture, that we were indebted to them alone for all great undertakings, and for all progress. It can scarcely have been the intention of the author to create this impression, and he would simply disclaim any such explanation. But it can be easily understood, that at a time when so many disparaging remarks are made about Hebrews, the wish might arise, for once, at any rate, to muster everything, which could be said in their favour. Sombart still says — although he wishes to refrain from appreciation:

"Israel traverses Europe like the sun; new life bursts forth where it arrives; on its departure what has hitherto prospered, wastes away." It would be scarcely possible to utter a more pretentious appreciation of a people than the above, and it is certainly opportune, for once in a way, to examine in detail how far such a pronouncement is justified or not. Sombart has collected, out

---

[21] "Die Juden und das Wirtschaftsleben" (*The Jew and the Economic Life*).

of literature, with extraordinary diligence, everything, which could possibly throw a favourable light upon the activity of the Jews. He acknowledges that other factors have contributed to the building-up of the modern capitalism — which seems to him to be equivalent to modern Culture — but does not wish to mention the same in his book. He is of opinion that one will search in vain throughout his work, "to discover in any single passage anything approaching an appreciation of the Jews, their affairs, their performances," and yet, a few lines further on, he says concerning the Jews; "They, above all other nations, are an eternal nation". That is a frequently-expressed opinion, and yet the ancestors of Jewdom can scarcely date further back than the ancestors of other races, for it is not recognised that the incarnation of the remaining nations only happened within historical time; just as little is the national existence of the Hebrews any older than that of the other nations. It is quite the contrary — for it must not be forgotten that ancient cultures were already known in the history of the world before the Jewish people put in an appearance. And when Sombart goes on to reckon up, amongst the accomplishments of the Jews, the following:

"They have presented us with the one and only God, with Jesus Christ, and consequently with Christianity", this is not only an appreciation, but an extravagant eulogy, which, in the face of our modern knowledge of these matters, may even be called frivolity.

The contention that the Hebrews invented monotheism — the one God doctrine — belongs to the domain of thoughtless phrases, all the more as the most ancient Jewish documents recognise a whole line of gods, such as Elohim, El-Schaddai, El-Elyon, Adonai, Zebaoth, Jahwe etc. It was first of all Luther's translation — which was frequently extremely free — of these names by the universal designation "God the Lord", which is responsible for this semblance of Jewish monotheism.

Moreover, it has been sufficiently established for many decades that the Jewish God has nothing in common with the Christian Father-in-Heaven, or the universal Father of the Germanic nations. Jahwe, as we have already discussed, is the exclusive tribal God of the Hebrews: he has absolutely no desire to be the God of other peoples, for he persecutes the latter with unappeasable hatred, and assigns to his favourite the task of annihilating the remaining nations, or, as Luther translates: "to devour them." It is quite clear in this case that we have not to deal with the one and only God of all nations, but with a tribal or separate and national God. Therefore Jewdom can, by no means, lay claim to have presented "the" only God to the rest of the world. The discoveries of the Egyptologists and Assyriologists have furnished sufficient proof that these ancient, civilised nations already worshipped an only God before the Jewish nation was known of.[22]

Our Germanic ancestors also worshipped an only God and universal Father, in the form of their Ziu (Dius), and the Egyptians did likewise with their Ptah, the Indians with their Dyaus Pitar (from which the Roman Jupiter originated), the Greeks with their Zeus, and the Persians with their Ahuramazda (Ormuzd) etc.

The way, in which Sombart misleads his readers with regard to Christ, is still more flagrant. Upon this point also we are at the present day sufficiently well-informed to know that Christ was not of Jewish extraction, but was a heathen Galilean. The enmity of the Jews towards him shows itself in every chapter of the Gospels; the Jews persecute him incessantly so that he must always seek refuge from them "in the land of the Heathen." Their hatred against him is so fanatical, because, out of his teaching a spiritual world, which is strange to them, is speaking. It is the spirit of the other race, which here opposes the Jewish nature, for the teaching of Christ signifies, in all respects, a complete reversal of the Jewish system of morality. Christ had, accordingly, nothing in common with the Jews, neither outwardly nor inwardly. His teaching is the most pronounced contrast, yes, the most emphatic protest against Jewish morality and the view, which Jews chose to take of the world, and the whole life

---

[22] Compare Wahrmund: "Babyloniertum, Judentum, Christentum" (*Babylondom, Jewdom, Christendom.*) Lagarde: "Deutsche Schriften" (*German Writings*); Fritsch: "Beweismaterial gegen Jahwe" (*Evidence against Jahwe*); Further *"Hammer"* No. 257: "Zur Entstehungsgeschichte des Alten Testaments" (*The History of the origin of the Old Testament*); particularly W. Schmidt: "Ursprung der Gottesidee" 1. (*Origin of the idea of God*); 1912. A. Lang: *"Making of the Religion"* (1909). Fritsch endeavours to prove that Jahwe is identical with El-Schaddai, whom he indicates as the "Geist der Finsternis", (*Sprit of Darkness*) and as the personification of the Principle of Evil. The philological comparisons upon this point are striking. (Compare "Beweis-Material gegen Jahwe", 9. Edition, pages 77-86.)

of Christ was a continual fight against Jewdom. The excellent Lagarde (celebrated both as an orientalist and an authority on the Bible, died 1891) said: "No nation crucifies its ideal, and whoever is crucified by a nation certainly does not correspond to the ideal of that particular nation." One must read the Gospel of St. John in order to convince one's self how, on every occasion, the racial contrast between the Galileans and the Jews bursts forth. But, when the Jews boast of being the children of God, Christ calls them the children of the devil (Gospel of St. John 8. 44—45). It would scarcely be possible to make a more trivial and thoughtless remark than that the Jews bestowed Christianity upon us, and therefore have a claim to our gratitude. But when this phrase is heard from the mouths of the Jews themselves, the very summit of senselessness is reached, and a piece of bluff is produced calculated only to deceive those, who are utterly incapable of judgement. It is only necessary to ask in return: If the Jews assign merit to themselves on account of Christianity — why are they content to pass on ungrudgingly to others, what can be proved to be a great advance in moral perception and in the ennoblement of mankind, instead of also enriching themselves therewith? And finally, above all, if the Jews of today, who still harbour the utmost contempt and enmity towards Christ and his teaching, claim merit for themselves by reason of the Christian doctrine, will they not also take over part of the responsibility for the torturing and martyring of Christ?

VII

Jewish Successes In modern times

S ombart points out that when the migration of the Jews took place in the 16th century, a remarkable displacement of the economic centre of Europe became perceptible. The Hebrews, who had been turned out of Spain, migrated, for the most part, (some authorities say 90,000) to European and Asiatic Turkey, where they are known to the present day as "Spanioles." Another large multitude (25,000) migrated to Holland, Hamburg, and England. The remainder, about 50,000, dispersed themselves amongst the various countries of Europe and America. It is not disputed that, from that time, the economic life of Spain suffered from a severe set-back, whilst, in those places, to which the Jews had directed their foot-steps, there was a sudden access of trade. There is, however, nothing extraordinary in this, and the same thing could have happened if people of another nationality and race had been concerned in these migrations instead of the Hebrews. The immigrations of the Huguenots, for instance, are a distinct proof of this. Every extensive emigration is bound to produce a set-back in the economic life of a country, whilst, on the other hand, every considerable influx of population, irrespective of whatever elements it may be composed, will always enliven the economic life. We experience this, on a small scale, almost every day — the removal of a factory, of a garrison etc —. In our case it must be taken into consideration that the Hebrews, for the most part, brought capital with them and brought it to countries, which were developing, and thus it would be doubly beneficial from an economic point of view. We have already recognised, earlier in this work, the kind of enlivenment, which the Jew introduces into the economic life. It is the mobilisation of all values and forces, by which he imparts a tremendous stimulus to political economy. But we have also seen how this inflated economic life, which is, at the same time, highly artificial, acts, in its final phases, devastatingly and destructively upon the nations.

Still, for the time being, the glory of enlivening trade and international intercourse may be conceded to the Jews. But, at the same time, one must not forget that they do not stimulate trade out of love for their fellow-men, but in order to make profit for themselves. They produce, in all directions, traffic and exchange, in order to derive the utmost benefits for themselves thereby.

It is enough to take away one's breath when Sombart endeavours to convince us that modern colonial affairs owe their development chiefly to the Hebrews. Certainly the Jews went out also to the newly opened-up colonies, just as they go anywhere where business prosperity entices them. And, for this reason also, they were certainly amongst the first in the newly opened-up America. Sombart serves up, for our edification, the unproved legend that a number of Jews were present in the ship of Columbus (but scarcely on the original voyage of discovery), and that the first European, to step upon American soil, was the Jew Luis de Torres. Yes, he even maintains that the expeditions of Columbus were fitted out exclusively with Jewish money, and that we have, accordingly, to thank the Jews especially for the discovery of America. Still more audacious is the conjecture that Columbus himself may have been a Jew, simply because some Columbus-investigator claims to have discovered a family "Colon," into which a Jewess married. This half-Jewish family Colon is therefore asserted to be identical with the family Colombo. A genealogical feat, which is not made any the more probable by the fact that the Christian name Christobal occurs in both families.

One can thus see how ready many people are, to assign everything remarkable in the world to the Jews: and Sombart surpasses himself, whilst calling attention to the fact that already in the period 1820—1830 there were numerous Jewish firms in America, by the audacious utterance: "America is, in all respects, a Jewish country." He mentions with satisfaction that, at the present moment, New York contains nearly a million Jews, of whom the majority certainly have not yet begun their capitalistic careers; and since all Hebrews, according to his opinion, carry a passport for the territory of the millionaires in their pockets, his exaggerated fancy sees in the America of the future a land where there will only be Slavs and Negroes to act as servants, and Hebrews to lord it as rulers. With the fantastic imagination of an oriental, he calls the Jews, "the golden thread, which runs through the texture of American political economy."

He utters the following remarkable words with respect to the colonies in general:

"Their economic body must have bled to death, if it had not been fed from outside with a constant blood-stream in the form of precious metal. Jewish commerce, however, directed this blood-stream into the colonies."[23]

Here also we meet again the extraordinary idea, either that all the Gold treasure in the world had always belonged to the Jews, or that the Jews had, in some way, produced the Gold themselves. In this respect one must always keep the fact clearly before one's mind, that the Jew, in general, produces nothing at all — neither goods nor money, but that he possesses an extraordinary knack of attracting the goods and money of others into his hands, in order to pass the same on further, after making a considerable profit for himself. And the simple fact arises of its own accord out of all this: if the Jews had not got the money, other people would have it; and other people would look after what commerce was necessary if the Hebrews were not always at hand to push them aside. Therefore again it is a curious kind of exaggeration when the learned man, who pretends to regard matters objectively, states: "The United States must thank the Jews that they — The United States — exist at all". Is it not most peculiar that these Jews, who are supposed to convey riches and life with them in all directions, are never able to exist alone by themselves? That they have never been able to create a self-

---

[23] It is a remarkable fact that no trace of the above is to be found in our colonies. Out of the 35 milliards of German capital, which Jewish trade has, for the most part, directed abroad, little enough has fallen to our colonies, although it was precisely there, where problems of incalculable importance for the development of the lands themselves and for the mother-country, awaited solution. These problems, however, were certainly not those of the money-bag alone.

supporting state, and always required other men on whom to live, and of whom to take advantage? If the Jews were really the great cultural nation, which they are represented to be, they would, for once and all, separate themselves from all other nations, and, established in their own colonial kingdom, would give proof of their power and productivity.

Very probably a Jew was always on the spot wherever there was prospect of business; but certainly not to benefit the commonweal, but rather to utilise the opportunity and to lay claim to the best for himself. Sombart himself has portrayed the process of the colonisation of North America as follows:

"A body of absolutely reliable men and women — say twenty families — advanced into the wilderness, in order to begin life anew there. Amongst these 20 families, 19 would be equipped with plough and scythe, ready to cut down the woods, and to clear the steppe by fire, and, by the work of their hands, to support themselves by cultivating the land. But the twentieth family would open a shop in order to provide their comrades quickly, by means of trade, with the requisite utensils. This twentieth family would then, very soon, busy themselves with the sale of the products, which the 19 other families would have won from the soil. This family would be the one which would first have ready cash at its disposal, and thus would be in the position, in cases of need, to provide the others with loans. In many such cases a "rural loan-bank" would attach itself to the shop etc etc."

He thus actually portrays, in sleek words, a picture of the part, which the Hebrew plays amongst the working and productive nations; it appears to us, however, that the real cultural work is done by the people with the pick-axe and the spade, with the plough and the scythe, and not by the shopman; and, there is no doubt that if no Hebrew is present to act as shop-keeper, amongst the 20 other families there will certainly be one, ready to act in this capacity as soon as the necessity arises. For, after all, nothing is so easily learnt as this elementary dealing in produce, and the lending of money; and we experience every day and in every direction how people of mean origin and very mediocre ability can take up this kind of business with complete success. That the Hebrew, with his peculiar talent for this branch of business, and, we may well add, with his ruthless exploitation of the situation, generally has more success than other and more ingenuous men, we are quite willing to admit.

Further, Sombart tries to prove to us nothing less than that the Hebrew has played an important part in the formation of the modern state. He acknowledges that the Jews are, by their very nature, a "non-national" or "unnational" people. Actually with the exception of the former Jewish kingdom in Palestine, they have never been able to found a state anywhere in the world.[24] Nevertheless Sombart wishes to assign to leading Jewish politicians an important share in the modern state. It sounds almost like biting irony when he says:

"But even if we do not find any Jews amongst the rulers of the modern state, we can scarcely imagine these rulers, we can scarcely conceive of the modern prince, being without Jews".

Who, on reading the above, does not recall Talleyrand's venomous words: "The Financier supports the state in the same way as the rope supports the man who is hanged!" And even Sombart, on referring to the conjunction of Prince and Jew, cannot refrain from the ironical observation that if you have a Faust you must also have a Mephistopheles. He continues then:

"I consider that it was they (the Hebrews), before all others, who placed the material means at the disposal of the state, as it came into being, by which it could maintain itself and develop further."

He certainly does not disclose to us where the Jews are accustomed to procure these means, namely: if not out of the state treasury, then out of the pockets of the people, who have been fleeced. Also, he does not disclose to us how the Hebrews, before all others, have practised the art of plunging all countries deep into

---

[24] Even in this case they did not form, strictly speaking, a separate country, but lived in the midst of the native Edomites, Canaanites, Hittites, Amorites, Philistines, Galileans, Samaritans, and formed, apparently, only the monied bourgeoisie, while the real cultural work fell to the lot of the others.

debt, and again, how these state loans are nearly all negotiated and created by Jews, in which process there lies a rich profit for the broker or agent, as the state becomes, so to speak, a cow to be milked for the benefit of the Hebrews. One is entitled to ask the question: Do the Hebrews provide this money out of love for the Prince and the State? — or, do not they rather provide it in order, by this means, to make State and Prince dependent upon them, and to create an economic system, by which they can, as it were, continuously suck the marrow out of the bones of the nation?

One must again and again recall to one's mind that all the so highly-praised services of the Jews do not arise from the promptings of a humane heart but simply from the mania for profit.

It is equally a matter for amazement when Sombart, with extreme conscientiousness, gathers together all the facts of how the Jews have always acted as army-contractors in times of war, and appears inclined to assign great praise to them for having undertaken a most meritorious service on behalf of the state. The Jews certainly had a strong predilection for army contracts, and it is equally certain that they always enriched themselves immoderately by this means.

In the disclosures about Poland (Page 42) it was shown that the Jews, by means of their widely-extended organisation, held the whole of the grain- and cattle-trade in their hands, and thus there is nothing remarkable, if, in times of war, they are the first on the spot — and are the best able — to undertake army contracts. Nobody should believe that they do this out of self-sacrifice for the state, and that they actually give something away, but it is a specific Jewish tactic to represent sly profiteering as kindly acts undertaken for the good of the community.

The following fact is immediately conceded; the non-Jewish nations, and especially the Germanic people, are somewhat simple and awkward as far as economic matters are concerned. There are excellent, highly spiritual natures, in whom all matters of money and accounting arouse an inward repugnance. And it is just this weakness — which one is equally justified in regarding as strength, and which certainly has its foundation in a lofty and spiritual constitution — which the Hebrew has always known so well how to exploit. He was always ready to encourage this dislike to all money and commercial transactions, which existed, as one would naturally expect, in aristocratic circles, and offered his services as obsequious assistant and agent. Sombart says of a Court Jew, Moses Elkhan, who lived in Frankfurt a. M. about 1700:

"The industrious man, who procured jewelry for the Princess, cloth for the livery of the head-chamberlain, delicacies for the head-cook, was also quite ready to negotiate loans."

This would constitute in itself a meritorious beginning, and would allow the Hebrew to appear as a useful member of society, if he had confined himself to taking a moderate remuneration for the performance of the above duties, and had not mixed himself up in other affairs. But the Hebrew has no time and no inclination for the simple discharge, for a moderate remuneration, of such duties as have been mentioned: for him they are rather the opportunity to make other people dependent upon him, and to acquire a determining influence over affairs. Everywhere he plays the rôle of Joseph in Egypt, whom Potiphar placed in authority over all his property, and who soon lulled his lord and master into such a state of comfortable indolence that it is said of the latter: "He made everything over into Joseph's hands, and no longer took interest in anything except eating and drinking." This was the first step for Joseph towards the all-powerful position of the Finance-man of Egypt, in which capacity he fleeced country and people to their very shirts. (See I Moses 17, 13—20.)

For the Hebrew does not aim merely at profit; he desires to exploit, to rule and to subjugate. He soon finds out how to place the yoke of compulsion on to his confiding clients, and to keep a tight hand over them. He is not acquainted with the maxim: "Live and let live;" he releases nothing until he has seized all for himself.

But it does not matter what the Hebrews do; Sombart always knows how to direct a ray of sunshine upon their deeds so as to beautify the same. Speaking of our time, he mentions boastfully, that, at the present day, the Court Jew has been done away with, and that the loaning of money (we could also say usury) to princes and states is no longer the business of one individual, but that all opulent Jewdom takes part cooperatively in the business. And Sombart regards this also as a virtue on their part. He says:

"And now again it is the Jews, who have helped to perfect this modern system of loans. It is they, who have made themselves superfluous as monopolizers of money-lending and, by so doing, have contributed so much the more to the founding of the great states."

What nobility of soul! — might one exclaim. But one really does not know if it is supposed to be praise or blame, when Sombart ascribes the "Commercialisation of the Economic Life" to the Hebrews, understanding thereby, the resolving of all economic occurrences into sheer commercial transactions. He discerns, as the final accomplishment of capitalism, the "transmutation of political economy into a series of Stock Exchange operations."[25] He says:

"First of all a process is completed, which one might call the manufacture of credit, and the materialisation of the same in the shape of paper securities. Closely connected with this is the occurrence, known under the name of "Mobilisation", or, if one prefers a German word, the marketing of these claims." (Page 60).

We have accustomed ourselves, in modern times, to understand by the word "Credit" something full of value, and precious in the highest degree; sober-minded people call it in plain English: "Begging for a loan economy", and one might just as well call the "making objective of claims", the "conversion of all values into paper form", that is to say: the transformation of all objects of value into easily transportable Promissory Notes. The creative part, which the Jews play in this transformation of the economic life, we will allow to pass unchallenged; it is quite another question whether this proceeding finally is wholesome for mankind. It is not denied that objects of value, when transformed into paper (shares,

---

[25] Translator' s note. To convey the exact sense of the word "Verbörsianisierung" one must coin an English equivalent viz "Stock Exchangisation".

mortgage-bonds, bills etc) are a commercial convenience, and facilitate the flow of business on the various markets. But, in this mobilisation of all values lies also a great economic danger. Let one imagine, for instance, that a millionaire finally acquires the power of buying an unheard-of quantity of such paper securities, including the title-deeds to a considerable portion of our Father-land, which he then sticks into his pocket in order to take up his residence in some foreign country. In every case, everything, including even the land itself, is thus easily made an object for speculation. And in all this, the Hebrew pursues — if not a conscious calculation — then solely his racial instincts. The nomad, in whom the sense of constancy and of a desire for a permanent habitation is wanting, wishes to make everything transportable, so that it may easily be carried with him wherever he goes, just like the silver and golden vessels and utensils were taken out of Egypt.

The fore-runner of the paper security, namely the saleable or negotiable promissory note, is already to be found in the Bible, and in the Talmud, as Sombart points out. The loaning of money and commercial business are actually the twin suns, around which the whole essence and being of Jewish life revolve, and so there is nothing to wonder at if these two conceptions find an important place in the religious writings of the Jews. One can learn from a certain passage taken from the Rabbi Schabbatai Cohen, and which Sombart quotes, that the activity of the Rabbis extended also into the business organisation. The passage mentioned speaks of regulations introduced by the Rabbis for the extension of commerce.

The Rabbi in question regrets that the trade in promissory notes cannot be very large on account of the amount of detail involved in a transaction of this kind, boasts, on the other hand, that in his time (in the 17th century) the turnover in note-of-hand or paper acknowledgments was considerably greater than in actual property, and states therefore that the decrees of the Rabbis for the extension of trade deserve the closest consideration.

One can see from this that the rôle of the Rabbi in Jewdom is something quite different from that of a Christian pastor or clergyman. The Rabbi is not only priest and guardian of the soul, but he is also adviser on business matters,[26] and — as we shall learn later on — political organiser and leader of his congregation.

The conversion of all economic values into paper arises, in the case of the Hebrew, still more from the mania for creating continuously fresh material for trade; for trade appears to him to be a purpose in itself —as the real object of life, and all his thoughts are concentrated on the extension of trade. To us, trade is only a necessary kind of evil, a servant, as it were, to production and consumption; the Hebrew, however, regards the world as having been created for the sole purpose of being turned into a huge shop full of goods. Whilst we regard each promissory note, each paper security, simply as representing a receipt for a loan or value received, the Hebrew makes "trade-material" out of the same. Sombart says:

"The effect (Paper Security) is intended by its very nature for traffic, and it has failed to perform its function if it is not traded with."

This is a specific Jewish perception, which is not clear to us without further explanation, but we hear at once that it is grounded upon the nomadic view of the world:

"Any peculiarity, which our economic life experiences from the perfectionment of the paper security, is derived exclusively from the mobility of the same, which makes it extraordinarily well adapted for quick transfer."

We ask: is then quick change of possession a necessity for a healthy condition of political economy? Is it indispensable for a settled and productive nation? Is anything of a positive nature accomplished by the continual "shoving-about" of values in all directions? Sound, economically-productive circles have no interest in such a constant change of proprietors; steadiness and certainty of duration must appeal to them as far more desirable objects. But the

---

[26] This is made manifest by the fact that the Stock-Exchange prices from Berlin are announced by telephone to the Rabbis in the provinces at the same time as they are announced to the banking businesses in the same places.

Hebrew combines with this easy saleableness of values yet another purpose; the traffic in paper securities, owing to the perpetual shifting in values on the Stock Exchange, means to him constant opportunity for profit-making; and we shall learn later on, how this profiteering is carried on at the expense of the honest and productive section of the community.

* * * * *

During the perception of such matters the contrast between two views of the world unconsciously reveals itself. The settled man desires continuance and steadiness, the nomad sudden change and mobilisation. Sombart admits that this strange principle of easy change of proprietorship, and of constant alteration of values, was foreign to the German, and also to the Roman Law, and that it, in all probability, had its origin in Jewish mentality.[27] Quite comprehensible, for the law of mobilisation is the law of sudden change and revolution. Sombart calls the Jewish Law "traffic-friendly": that is only a circumlocution for the idea of mobilisation and the shifting of values. While we should like to see trade confined to what is necessary, the Jew strives to extend it beyond all limits, and into every conceivable domain. The constant endeavour of the Hebrews is to procure for trade the utmost freedom from restriction. Under the expression "Protection for the market", they demand an unconditional recognition of, and sanction for all trade customs. They go so far as to demand that stolen articles, which are found in the hands of Jewish "receivers", shall not be reclaimed by the lawful owner. This principle has already been enunciated in the Talmud, and it has been repeatedly corroborated, especially in the Middle Ages, by the privileges given to the Jews. According to Jewish perception, the right to buy ranks higher than the right to own, and the relative legislation aims almost at giving privileges to receivers of stolen goods!

---

[27] Compare Richard Schröder: "Deutsche Rechtsgeschichte" (*History of German Law.*)

VIII

THE STOCK-EXCHANGE

The Jewish World of Trade and Mobilisation achieves its greatest triumph on the Stock-Exchange. The Stock-Exchange might well be — although Sombart does not put forward this claim on behalf of the Jews — in its present day form an invention of the Hebrews in every respect. Originally it was merely the meeting-place for merchants, where they bought and sold their goods according to sample. All trade on the Exchange related originally to "effective" goods, that is to say, to goods, which actually existed, and of which, samples had to be produced. Even today business of this kind is still transacted on the Exchange, but the extent of the trade there has increased considerably. Not only are goods bought and sold there, which are really warehoused somewhere, but also goods, which time alone can produce — yes, goods even, which do not exist and which never will exist. It is justifiable, under certain circumstances, to secure in advance, delivery of goods for a future date, and therefore purchase-contracts on the Exchange, which refer to a future delivery of the goods, are comprehensible. The manufacturer, who has pledged himself for months in advance to supply certain of his customers with certain wares at regular intervals, is naturally interested in also securing the necessary raw material in advance. He accordingly buys "on term", that is to say: he enters into contracts today at fixed prices, which contracts shall only become "effective" at a future date or "term." Trade of this kind has nothing actually objectionable in itself, although it was simply forbidden on the sound mercantile exchanges of the olden times. But, at any rate, this method of doing business opened the path to unlimited speculation. By this means large quantities of goods can be bought and sold, which are never delivered, and which are never intended to be delivered. Buyer and seller make a bet, so to speak, as to whether a commodity at some future date will cost more or less than at the present moment. Settlement is effected on the following lines, that one party has to pay out, on the appointed date, the difference between the arranged price, and the price quoted, for the day in question, on the Stock Exchange list.

Thus this "term-trading" becomes simply a business of differences, and does not rank any higher than gambling and betting. This game of "differences" might appear harmless if it were a private affair, and did not exert its influence upon the genuine fluctuation in the prices of goods. For, when business in "differences" is undertaken to a far greater extent than the real business purchases, the basic price, at which the business in "differences" has been concluded, must, of necessity, influence the price of the actual goods. The fixing of the daily price results from the general average of the prices, at which the purchases have been concluded, and, generally speaking, one is not able to say whether the latter represent genuine sales of goods, or merely a gamble in "differences." It can also be the case that someone buys himself free from his contract to deliver the actual goods, by paying the price-difference. Accordingly there is no hard and fast line between genuine purchases and mere speculations in prices.

The essence of the so-called "speculation" consists in making sham purchases on the Stock Exchange so as to create an artificial influence on the movement of prices; and, apart from the fact that this gambling in "differences" ruins many a person, it is thoroughly repugnant to the sense of sound political economy. Strictly speaking, every purchase, which does not aim at satisfying the requirement of the moment, but has rather the object of utilising the occasion to lay up cheap goods for a future date, is of a speculative nature. It is more usual, however, to understand by speculation on the Stock Exchange, sham purchases and the trade with imaginary values, as opposed to trade in real values.

The machinations, connected with unsound business on the Exchange, and which first appear on the Produce Markets, assume a more pronounced character on the Stock and Share Market. Here, along with the national loans, it is particularly the railway-stocks and the shares in industrial undertakings, which form an important object of trade. The computation of the value of the share depends, generally speaking, upon the rate of interest paid during recent years, which is not by any means an infallible guide as to what the returns will be in the future. The art of the guiding factors, on the Stock Exchange consists in creating, above all things, a favourable atmosphere. Reports are inserted in the newspapers in order to cast a more or less favourable light upon an undertaking, and to anticipate a higher or lower dividend as the case may be. The public is thus seduced into buying or selling the paper securities in question. Certainly a preliminary condition to the successful carrying-out of this manoeuvre is that the public press puts itself at the disposal of the powers in question. This is easily managed. Some of the matadors of the Stock Exchange are themselves owners of newspapers, or are connected with the same as secret partners, others again, through the agency of influential banking-firms, procure favourable notices from the press by making considerable payments to the latter in the shape of orders for costly advertisements. By far the largest portion of the public press, in all countries, is actually under the influence of the magnates of the Stock Exchange, and to this extent Sombart is correct when he states that the Jews took a substantial part in the development of the modern Stock Exchange.

But business on the Stock Exchange only yields a sure result when it is transacted by secret collusion, that is to say by gangs or bands. If individual always opposed individual on the Stock Exchange, the formation and quotation of prices would pursue an even and reliable path, and profit and loss would be more or less dependent upon chance. It might then well happen that what was lost one day might be regained on another. Matters take a very different course when a secret organisation of certain brokers exists, and when all the partners in the same, who have a mutual understanding, operate simultaneously according to a pre-arranged plan. In a case of this kind, the price is like a ball, which can be tossed about at the pleasure of this organised clique.

Let anyone represent to himself the following position: the number of shares actually on the market are limited. One knows, for instance, the exact number of shares in any undertaking. If now, several of the larger banking firms and stockbrokers are working in conjunction with one another, they can very easily ascertain what number of the shares of any undertaking are held by the public, and what number are in the hands of the operating banks and brokers. The aim and object of the secret confederates — we will make use of a Jewish expression and call them the "Chawrusse" — consist, as one can easily understand, in buying up paper securities at a low price, and in selling the same at a high price. And this business is effected in the simplest way possible. As soon as any particular paper security is held to a very large extent by the public, all that is necessary to do is to arouse suspicion about the same. The view is spread abroad by means of suitable and cleverly-worded press-notices, that the security in question has no prospects, and that only a poor dividend can be expected. At once a number of the holders endeavour to get rid of the shares in question, and the price steadily falls as the shares are offered for sale. The large stock-brokers help in the process by instructing their agents on other stock-exchanges to offer, whatever they hold of the security in question, at declining prices. They do not run any risk by doing this, for nobody wants to buy the discredited shares. Thus, by reason of these carefully planned and continued influences, the price of the paper security in question falls, day by day; and then, and then only, when a heavy fall in the price has set in, does the "Chawrusse" begin, in all secrecy, to carry out their purchases. They buy up the shares, at the greatly depreciated price, and know how to maintain it at this low level until they hold the greater number of the shares in their own hands. Then the page is at last turned over. All at once, the "well-informed" financial press announces that the former suspicions, with regard to the prosperity of the undertaking, were without any foundation, and that it promises, on the contrary, to pay an excellent dividend very shortly. Immediately the price of the shares begins to "recover", to use a stock-exchange expression, and here also assistance is given by the instigation of a zealous but absolutely artificial enquiry for the shares. But, for the time being, the "Chawrusse" withholds all the "material" i. e the shares. The tension, due to the growing demand and the scanty supply, contributes to a further rise in the price, and it is only when the "Chawrusse" consider that their profit is large enough that they begin to unload their stored-up shares at the enhanced price. If, after the course of several weeks or months, as the case may be, they have relieved themselves of enough of their treasure, they turn the point of the spear in the opposite direction. They suddenly make a forced sale of the remainder of their shares, and arrange that the financial press shall publish articles to correspond; the price gives way, and the old game begins once more. It is instructive to note that, in these transactions, it is invariably the "Chawrusse", who gain, and the dear Public who are duped.

Some simple-natured people look up with respectful awe to the ingenious heads, who direct our stock-exchange affairs, and who, in spite of all fluctuations on the Bourse, always contrive, with "miraculous certainty," to secure the advantage. The former imagine that an almost superhuman capability is requisite to survey the situation on the money-market aright, and to grapple with the circumstances as they alter. Good, trusting folk! If they only knew how it was done they might well say, to paraphrase an old saying: "One cannot believe what a little understanding is required to rule over the stock exchanges of the world."

The indispensable condition for success, however, is combined action: the Chawrusse. He, who ventures into the combat on the Stock-Exchange as a free-lance, must not be surprised if he emerges from the struggle stripped of all his feathers. Success is assured only to organised bands. It is a well-known fact that, in every game, if two or more of the players have a secret understanding with one another, they always gain the advantage, and "let the others in." They know how to communicate by secret signs, and play into one another's hands. On this account also, one of the conspirators can attach himself to the losing side, without the least apprehension, for he knows that he will receive his share of the profits eventually from his fellow-conspirators. This is the secret of the Stock Exchange. And it is only the elect of the people of Israel, who form the conspirators of the "Chawrusse." The transactions of the Stock-Exchanges, at the present day, are nothing less than swindling; the artificial quotations are made by the "Chawrusse," supply and demand are artificially created, and all this takes place with the sole object of fleecing the unsuspecting, productive nations by the continual rise and fall of the Stock Exchange quotations, and of adding incessantly to the wealth of Israel.

And this important secret, of which Sombart unfortunately has betrayed nothing to us,[28] is the secret combined action of the Hebrews, of which we spoke on page 39 and the following pages, and which extends over many other domains as well. This secret hand-in-hand working has always been the chief strength of the Jews, and which has naturally always given them an advantage over all sound, straightforward traders. We are not at all astonished when we read in Sombart: "Already in the year 1685 the Christian merchants of Frankfort were complaining that the Jews had gained possession of the entire broker- and bill-discounting business;" and that in the year 1733 the Hamburg merchants lamented that: "The Jews were entirely masters of the bill-discounting business, and had out-stripped our people."

Let us then grant to the Hebrews the glory which Sombart claims for them; i. e. of being inventors of trading in "Futures" and of being the fathers of speculation ("Jobbing") on the Stock Exchange. And this questionable practice is introduced by the Hebrews wherever they settle. During the 13th and 14th centuries, when they were present preponderatingly in Northern Italy[29], Sombart informs us that stock-jobbing was, at that time, in full swing in Genoa, and that speculation, in the form of "futures" and "differences", was carried on to a considerable extent at Venice — so much in fact, that in the year 1421, a prohibition had to be issued against trading in bankers' bills.

The mania for speculation accompanied the Hebrews to Holland as well, where, in the course of the 17th century, the shares of the East India Company furnished the material for an arrant piece of stock-jobbing. It is there where Sombart seeks the source of the modern Stock Exchange speculation. Here also was issued a proclamation of the States General in the year 1610, forbidding,

---

[28] Anyone, who requires further information on this subject, can find enlightenment in Kolk's "Das Geheimnis der Börsenkurse" ("*The secret of Stock Exchange quotations*"), Leipzig. Herm. Beyer 1893, and also in the Germanicus Pamphlets. See page 34.
[29] The business of loaning paper securities (Lombardising?) which takes its name from the Lombards, dates from this period.

"the sale of more shares than one actually possessed." This prohibition was followed by many others, whereby Sombart remarks: "naturally without having the slightest result." Our author (Sombart) boasts that the Jews invented dealing in shares. A questionable glory indeed, for, in a report from the French ambassador at the Hague to his government in the year 1698, the former expresses himself in an extremely outspoken manner: "the Jews have control of the entire business in paper securities on the Stock Exchange, and regulate it as they see fit"; and, according to the same report, "the prices of shares fluctuate so incessantly that they give rise to transactions several times in the course of the day, a kind of business, which rather deserves the name of gambling or betting, all the more, as the Jews, who are at the bottom of all this activity, carry out masterstrokes of artifice, by which the people are again and again 'let in' and made fools of."

Sombart informs us, with reference to the activity of the Hebrews in England, during the reign of William III. (1689— 1702), that the chief negotiators of the first loan were Jews; they were ready at hand with their advice when the Orangeman began his reign. The rich Hebrew, Medina, was banker to the English Commander-in-chief, Marlborough (1650—1722), and paid the latter a fixed yearly salary of £6,000 (120,000 Marks), for which he acquired the right to receive all the war intelligence direct from head-quarters.

"The victories of the English army brought as much profit to him as they reflected glory on the soldiers of England." (Sombart page 106) — All the tricks of raising and depressing prices, false news from the theatre of war, the pretended arrival of couriers, the secret coteries on the Stock Exchange, the entire hidden machinery of Mammon, were well- known to the first fathers of the Bourse, and were utilised by them to the utmost extent."

We learn concerning Mannasseh Lopez, the body-physician of Queen Elisabeth of England, that he made a large fortune by circulating a false report that the Queen was dead, and by buying up the public funds which consequently fell in value.[30] Nathan Meyer

---

[30] He ended on the gallows, a fate which he incurred for betraying the English interests to Philip II of Spain. (Drumont: *"La France juive."*)

Rothschild of London had reports sent to him in Brussels, by Jewish spies, concerning the issue of the battle of Belle-Alliance, so that he could travel back with the news to London by express post and special ship. On his arrival he circulated a false rumour concerning the result of the battle, which was the immediate cause of a tremendous drop in the prices of English and German paper securities. He bought up the depreciated securities secretly in enormous quantities, and, when 24 hours later, the London Stock Exchange learnt the true issue of the battle, and, at the same time, that Rothschild had made fools of them, he — Rothschild — was many millions richer.

Sombart allows that John Law (1671 — 1721) the author of the notorious fraud in the shares of trading companies, may have been a Hebrew, and that his real name was probably Levi.

Of kindred spirit to these Jewish "statesmen" was the notorious "Demon of Württemberg": Süss-Oppenheimer (hanged 1734). The Hebrews also introduced the traffic in shares into Hamburg, in the 18th century, and carried it on to such an outrageous extent, that the Hamburg Council issued a proclamation, in 1720 prohibiting the practice. Today, it is represented as being the narrow view of reactionary circles to speak of business on the Stock Exchange with anything but the most profound respect; but, as Sombart himself confesses, this view of those, who are called today "Provincials" and "Agrarians", was, in the 18th century, the settled opinion of the sound merchant. During the debate upon John Bernhardt Act in the English Parliament in 1733, the "infamous practice of stockjobbing" was condemned unanimously by all the speakers. What have not our Hebrews accustomed us to in the meantime!

Sombart has already said (P. 112) of the time in question:

"Public debts were regarded as the shameful side — "Partie honteuse" — of national life. The best men saw, in the rapidly advancing indebtedness, one of the worst evils, which could be inflicted upon the community."

The extension of the market in shares from 1800—1850 is regarded by Sombart as being of equal significance as the expansion of the House of Rothschild.

"The name of Rothschild means more than the firm; it means all Jewdom as far as the Stock Exchange is concerned; for, only with the help of their compatriots could the Rothschilds reach their position of power, which dominates all others, and obtain the entire mastery of the Stock Exchange."

This is a complete confirmation of the "playing into one another's hands", which characterises the Jews, and which we have always insisted upon; this is our "Chawrusse" and its secret; this is organised Jewdom, which has turned the Stock Exchange into a cupping-glass to bleed the nations (compare chapter IV).

Sombart says further:

"If, in this way, the sphere of the money-lender was considerably extended, the Rothschilds also took good care to adopt further measures for squeezing the last farthing out of the community. This was brought about by skilfully utilising the Stock Exchange for the purpose of emission or issuing into circulation."

This step on the part of the Rothschilds soon brought into this kind of activity other, and questionable followers and imitators, in the shape of "Banks of issue or emission." These deflect German "spare" capital abroad to an incredible extent (but not to our colonies!)[31] — thereby depriving the home- country of the money, which is required for economic purposes, and depressing the value[32]

---

[31] "The amount of German "working" capital, invested abroad, was estimated in 1912 at 35 Milliards of marks (France 30, England — colonies excepted — 33 Milliards of marks).

[32] On the occasion of the celebration of the 25th anniversary of the accession of the Emperor William II., when there was a great deal of grandiloquent talk concerning the "unexampled development" of the German economic life during the past 25 years, the T-gliche Rundschau" published, side by side, for the purpose of comparison, several Stock Exchange quotations from 1888 and 1913. According to this, the following prices were current:

		1888	1913
4% German Imperial	Loan	107.00	98.10
3½% " " "		102.00	84.90

of our national paper securities, upon which countless citizens depend for the proper and regular payment of their interest. These "banks of issue," at the same time, secure enormous profits for themselves by their activity, which is absolutely destructive to all national economy, and which is either inadequately taxed, or escapes taxation altogether. Only a severe legal restriction and even, from time to time, an absolute prohibition of the issue of foreign securities, by means of the Stock Exchange, could remedy this nuisance.

Sombart then continues:

"'Create a favourable atmosphere', was the watchword, which, from this moment, dominated all traffic on the Stock Exchange. 'Creating a favourable atmosphere', was the aim and object of the unceasing fluctuations in the market-prices, caused by the systematic sale and purchase of shares, just as the Rothschilds manoeuvred when they were about to 'launch an issue'. In order to obtain command of the Stock Exchange and the Money Market, all possible means, which stood at their disposal, were utilised; all paths, which might lead to the attainment of the desired object, were traversed; every conceivable trick of the Stock Exchange, and of anywhere else, was practised; all levers were put into motion; money was sacrificed both in large and small sums. The Rothschilds practised 'Agiotage' (Stock-jobbing) in the narrower sense which the French attach to the word. Up till then, the great banking- houses had never done this, at any rate, openly. The Rothschilds employed the expedient of artificially influencing the market by creating a favourable atmosphere, which practice had been introduced by the Amsterdam Jews for a new object viz the launching of shares."

4% Prussian Consols	106.90	98.10
3½% " "	103.50	84.90

Here is proof, in cold, hard figures, of crushing weight, with which to confront those who speak of the "unexampled development of the last 25 years", and of the blessings conferred on the nation by the "Emission-activity," or the "Activity in issuing", of certain "great banks", which "opens the doors of foreign countries", but which, however, only causes the empire, our states and cities, and finally our citizens, enormous losses.

This is a literal quotation from Sombart; and it is the same thing, which the wicked Anti-Semites have been saying for 30 years. This activity of a great banking-house had in view, the placing of golden fetters upon Governments, in order to compel the latter to create more public debts. The Rothschilds have made it their business to burden the different countries with the necessary public debts; with this object in view they understood how to create artificially the occasion for making a public or national debt. According to the latest reports (1913) they have reached Ecuador with their "opening-up activity." Soon we shall hear the Press tune up, preparatory to bursting into hymns of praise concerning this "land of promise".

In addition to the fabrication of public bonds and obligations by the gentlemen, who manufacture stocks and shares, the Flotation and Mortgage business soon made an appearance. The industrial undertakings were "financed" and "discounted", on a miniature scale, in just the same way as the various states were on a large scale. In order to provide new trading values for the Stock Market, it became necessary to buy up the sound businesses of private people, and to convert the same into shareholder companies; that is to say, to float them. Otto Glogau has bequeathed to us a valuable book about the Flotation Swindle in Berlin in the years 1870—1873.[33] It shows that, in this case also, the Hebrews were always the active spirits, and that it was only for the better concealment of this fact, as far as the public was concerned, that a number of more or less innocent Germans — aristocrats whenever it was possible to procure them — were pushed to the front as dummies. What Jews, and the companions of Jews, brought to pass on this occasion, belongs to the most impudent of political comedies. When, according to their opinion, they had sufficiently plundered the masses at the time of the Flotations, and saw their erections of swindles on the verge of collapsing, they put up their tribal companion, Lasker, the then leader and particular star of the National Liberal Party, in the Reichstag, to play the part of the suppressor of "Flotations". He then unearthed, with great tumult, several members of the Conservative Party whom, he asserted, were

---

[33] "Der Börsen- und Gründungsschwindel in Berlin" (*The Stock Exchange and Flotation-Swindle in Berlin*) Leipzig 1877.

implicated in "Flotations", but let the chief culprits, who were his tribal brethren and Liberal Party friends, escape scot-free. Thereby he secured the double advantage of diverting the resentment of the public, who had lost enormous sums, from the real culprits to the opposing political parties, and of posing, at the same time, as the guardian of public morality. The Jew-controlled press also helped, for all it was worth, to fan the universal indignation against the unfortunate scape-goats in the Conservative camp.[34]

* * * * *

Our professional political economists of the High Schools unfortunately do not report any of these ugly facts, any more than they mention the baneful effect, which the game on the Stock Exchange has on the National Wealth, and on the entire economic and public life: they even lift up their voices in praise of the beneficial development of the Stock Exchange, and all connected with it. Glogau, in his book, which we have already mentioned, calls the learned political economists the chief allies of the "Flotation" gang, because they so disgracefully neglect their duty as instructors and guardians of the people, and he regards it as being beyond doubt that many of these political economists are directly paid for their opinion and instruction by the Stock Exchange.

Sombart then proceeds to speak of the "commercialisation of Industry": it would be better to use plain English, and to call it "converting Industry into material to job and huckster with". Industry thus becomes a mere object of speculation for the Stock Exchange; Production is a matter of secondary importance. "In the Speculation Banks", says Sombart, "capitalistic development reaches its highest point. With their help, the commercialisation of the economic life is carried to the extreme, and Stock Exchange organisation becomes complete." He then says concerning these Speculation Banks:

"They take part, to a very considerable extent, in speculation, either directly or else by way of the "Report" business, which, it is

---

[34] The Jewish statistician, Ernst Engels, estimated the losses on the Berlin Stock Exchange alone, during the "Flotation Years", at 700 million Thalers, and Glogau estimated double.

notorious, has become, at the present moment, the mightiest and most important lever of speculation. By means of loaning speculative securities, the banks are thereby placed in a position, by acquiring other securities at a cheap price, to create the impression that money is plentiful and is accompanied also by a desire to buy. Thus, on the one hand, a power of creating an upward movement in prices is easily acquired, and this power can be reversed just as easily to depress prices, by depreciating the store of available securities. The great banks accordingly, hold the handle, which controls the machine called the Stock Exchange, literally in their hand." (Page 129) And further: "The heads of the banks, who control the Stock Exchange, tend more and more to become entire masters of the economic life."

Sombart refers to the notorious "Crédit mobilier" in Paris as nothing better than a speculation bank. This "bank" was founded by the Portuguese Jews, Isaac and Emil Pereira; other large share-holders in this undertaking are Torlonia of Rome, Salomon Heine of Hamburg, and Oppenheim of Cologne. Sombart also includes in the species of speculation-banks, the Berlin Diskonto-Gesellschaft, founded by David Justus Ludwig Hansemann, and the Berlin Handels-Gesellschaft, in close connection with which, stand the Darmstadt Bank, and the Berlin banking firms of Mendelsohn, Bleichröder, Warschauer, and the brothers Schickler. The above-mentioned also adds: "The Jewish elements also preponderate amongst the founders of the Deutsche Bank." (Page 129)

Thus, the international character of the "Speculation-Banks" is proved, and accordingly the part which they play in the trade and intercourse of the world.

IX

HOW SOUND BUSINESS METHODS ARE FORCED OUT OF THE FIELD BY THE JEWS

Sombart also recognises the Jewish influence upon the mental attitude adopted by the capitalist towards political economy. He acknowledges that, owing to the peculiar Jewish spirit, something of an alien nature is introduced into our life, and he is in a position to understand how it is that, merchants, who are not Jews, and their spokesmen resent these conditions, and display a deep sense of injury, which is quite comprehensible. He perceives in all this a "quite natural reaction against the Jewish disposition, which is of a fundamentally different order." He refers constantly to the pages of history in order to establish how the sound commercial spirit has protested for centuries, in a similar manner, against the disorder caused by the Jews in trade. Everywhere and always the same complaint. Thus, the various trades and professions in the Mark of Brandenburg, in the year 1672, complain "that the Jews take away the food from the mouths of the other inhabitants of the land." The mercantile community of Danzig, in the year 1717, expressed themselves in almost identical terms. In 1740 a petition to the Prince Bishop of Mainz complains "that it is a matter of common knowledge that the Jews are the cause of ruin and destruction to the rest of the community." And it is the same story in every country to which the Jews come. In England also, the sound mercantile community resists the intrusion of the Jewish spirit with similar expressions of opinion. The business people of Toulouse in France complained in the year 1745: "We implore you urgently to check the progress of this nation, as there is no doubt whatever that it will wreck the entire trade of Languedoc." In Sweden, in Poland, everywhere the same picture. A moralist of that period reports with reference to the Jewry of Berlin: "They support themselves by means of robbery and deceit, which, according to their ideas, are not regarded as crimes." The behaviour of the Jews was felt universally to be an offence against the good customs of the commercial community. Sombart concedes that, in all this, a battle between two antagonistic views or perceptions of the world is evident. In the settled organisation of society as it used to be, in what are called "the olden times," man was the centre of interest, and the object of all regulations and laws was to render the existence of the honest worker as secure as it could be made. The production of goods was proportioned to the actual need, and, in the sound development of all businesses, each honest worker and trader received his fair share. Struggling to obtain unlimited profit was regarded as improper and un-Christian; nobody deliberately endeavoured to enrich himself by damaging, or at the expense of, another. A spirit of social harmony pervaded all, each found his own path, and could exist honestly.

Into this state of social harmony the Jew now stepped, with his entirely different mind and irreconcilable disposition. He had nothing to give — neither productive talents nor capacity for honest, straightforward work; consequently he had to secure an existence by cunning. To him, trade was not only — as it was according to the Christian perception — the willing companion of, or the necessary complement to Production and Consumption, but a way and means also for the enrichment of the individual, and for the obtainment of mastery over others. A moderate profit meant nothing to him; he desired great surpluses, which would enable him to heap up capital and thereby become a despot with the power to oppress.

This new tendency naturally brought a very disturbing element into the organic nature of society as it was then constituted. Up till that time all business life and all social cooperation had been based on good-will and trust; now a hostile element stepped between, an element which did not lay claim to be trusted, and did not repose trust in anyone. The Hebrew considered that he was quite within his rights in abusing the confidence of others; he even despised them on that account, and designated trustfulness as sheer stupidity. This is the bottomless chasm, which separates the Hebrews' view of life from ours, and across which no bridge will ever be constructed. The contest has always been an unequal one for the two antagonists. The Hebrew arrived as conscious opponent, with no quarter for those who were not Jews; the artless Christian Aryan, however, took pains, in accordance with the teachings of his religious instructors, to see, in the Hebrew, a fellow-man who was to be met, before all others, with trust and love, because he belonged to the nation from which our Saviour was said to be sprung. Thus, heart and home were opened alike, in all directions, to the foreign intruder. The latter knew well how to profit splendidly by this, but not without sneering to himself at the confidence reposed in him, which he regarded as nothing less than stupidity. And, as a matter of fact, it is fit material for derision that the Aryan nations, even up to the present day, fail to grasp the situation.

Certainly there has been a silent conspiracy for centuries on the part of School and Church, on the part of the Law and the Press, to mask this situation, but, now and again, sound national common-sense perceived instinctively that the crime, which the ancient Jews committed against the Saviour, outweighed ten times any merit, which their successors might claim, on account of their descent, and the contemporary Jews were taken for what they really were: mysterious beings, alien in blood and country, usurers, dabblers, spies, cheats and voluptuaries.

* * * * *

The complaints of those, who carried on industry in the olden times, are all pitched in the same key, like the reluctant admissions of the clergy, concerning the spoliation of the departing crusaders in the 13th century, whom the Jews deprived of everything they possessed in exchange for bad equipment and faulty weapons. Thus we read — very significant with respect to the mania for dealing, which dominates the Jews — in a complaint from the tradespeople of Hannover in the 18th century: "The trade in manufactured goods has fallen completely into the hands of the Jews. The Jew, by preference, stocks his shop with foreign hats, shoes, stockings, leather gloves, furniture and ready-made clothing of all kinds, and on the other hand, they prefer to export all raw material out of the country" (compare page 42). And again: "the Jews entice away the customers of their neighbours. They lie in waiting everywhere, both for the buyers and the sellers", a practice which had been regarded hitherto as a gross offence against commercial etiquette. In 1685, the gold workers in Frankfort a.M. complained that the Jews had secretly bought up, under their very noses, and carried off by means of their numerous spies, all the available scrap gold and silver. In 1703, the furriers at Königsberg gave utterance to a similar plaint, to the effect that the Jews, Hirsch and Moses, together with their followers, overreached them in the purchase and sale of furs, and caused them great loss (Sombart page 161). "When troops are quartered in the town, they — the Jews — run after the soldiers and officers, and endeavour to entice them into their shops, in order to take away the custom from the other tradespeople." Under their influence also, the pedlar- or hawker-business develops into a perfect nuisance; in 1672 the various trades and professions in the Mark of Brandenburg complain that "the Jews run from village to village, and round the towns, hawking their wares, and forcing the same upon the inhabitants." In Frankfurt on the Oder the complaint was "that the Jews pursued possible customers in all directions — travellers in their hotels, the nobility in their castles, and the students in their lodgings," because they are not content, like the other tradespeople, to lay up goods in their store-rooms, but endeavour by importunity to force the sale of their wares, and thereby to deprive the other business people of their share of the local trade. On the occasion of the great fairs also, the Jews overrun all the restaurants and inns, in order to entice all possible customers to themselves. It is reported from Nikolsburg in Austria that they — the Jews — have possessed themselves of all the trade, all the money, and all the material. They lie in wait for customers outside the town, force themselves upon the travellers, and endeavour to keep them away from the establishments of Christian tradespeople. They listen to every conversation, keep watch for the arrival of strangers, and know how to derive benefit immediately, from every kind of disaster, by hastening to the homes of those concerned with their offers and quotations. Yes, their importunity is sometimes carried so far that it becomes physical compulsion; they attempt to drag reluctant customers by force into their shops, a mode of operation — the so-called "tearing" at a person — which was in full swing on the "Mühlendamm" in Berlin during the "seventies" and "eighties" of the last century. The Hebrews lay in wait at their shop-doors, like spiders in their webs. They stopped any passerby, who appeared to show the slightest interest in their goods, which were spread out even up to the pavement, and tried either to entice, or to tug him by force into the shop. This progeny of Jewish business enterprise has been called "Vermin-picker" business, a fact also cited by Sombart. Yes, the Jewish street-dealers even went so far as to erect their stalls, or to push their barrows, straight in front of the shop of a Christian competitor, in order to deprive him of his customers.

To attract customers to himself, by any and every means, is the sole aim and object of the Jewish dealer, and, in doing so, he does not allow any consideration of decency or shame to stand in his way. The Hebrew was the first to force hostility, as a principle, upon our business life; that pernicious principle, which asserts that the most important task in trade is to alienate the customers of other men, and to regard any and every means as permissible, which can be utilised for trampling under foot all business competitors.[35]

The Hebrew has also carried advertising and soliciting in the newspaper to a stage where it is not only offensive to good taste but outrages public decency as well. Some years ago, the title, "Down with all competition!" was the favourite cry of the Jewish advertisers. The degeneration of newspaper- advertising brought yet another disadvantage in its train, and that was that the public press became more and more dependent upon Jewish mountebanks and quacks, in order not to lose the advertisements of these people, it placed itself completely at their service. And today no public newspaper of importance dares to publish anything derogatory to Jewdom, if it does not wish to lose all Jewish advertisements on the spot, and to be boycotted by the whole Jewish community — a consequence of the unholy alliance between what should properly be the political newspaper, and the advertiser.

---

[35] If there was only some way of making all this known throughout all classes of our community! Then one might indeed expect that the displeasure of all honest people would be directed against such conditions, and that the pernicious stranger would be turned out of our national life for once and all. But, in this respect, the public press fails completely; in fact, it places its services with preference at the disposal of the Jews.

Thus, under Jewish influence, trade has completely lost its original, sound motive of acting as intermediary between producer and consumer, and has degenerated into laying cunning snares for customers. And it is on this account that the complaint of all sound business people in all ages, bears always the same refrain: the Jew ruins trade, because he disregards all rules and refuses to recognise any principle except the acquisition of money.

CERTAIN JEWISH TRADE-TRICKS

An especially questionable kind of trade-tactics, practised by the Jews, consists in taking undue advantage of the difficulties which beset the producers of goods. Thus, the Jews know well how to utilise the occasional embarrassments, both of workman and manufacturer, to force the goods out of them at exceptionally low prices: yes, they also know how to prepare a difficult situation for the producer, and to lead him into the same by all manner of tricks. This complaint is an ancient one. Thus, a report of the wholesale-traders of Augsburg in the year 1803 reads as follows:

"The Jews endeavour to profit out of the universal distress; they force goods out of the man, who happens to be in urgent need of money, at scandalously low prices, and upset and ruin the regular trade by selling these goods again at absurdly inadequate prices." (Sombart page 168). Unfortunately, even the authorities, since the decay of the trade-guilds (beginning of the 18th century) have been short sighted enough to support this essentially Jewish policy. They allowed themselves to become corrupted by the cheap offers of the Hebrews, and never asked by what means the Jew came into possession of the goods, which he could offer so cheaply. A memorandum of the Chancery of the Court of Vienna, dated May 12th 1762, states bluntly: "it is advisable to make military contracts with the Jews, as their quotations are much lower."[36] It is a remarkable fact that, in spite of this, the Jewish army contractors

---

[36] We know only too well, from our experiences in mobilisations since that time, what has been the result of following this advice. Hundreds of thousands of soldiers, belonging to the various European Powers, have had to sacrifice their lives or their health in order to satisfy the profiteering greed of Jewish contractors, who supplied clothing of inferior quality, and adulterated food and medicaments.

have always become rich. It stands to reason that they must have over-reached someone, whether it was the State, or the unfortunate manufacturers.

The ways and means, by which the Hebrew obtains possession of cheap goods, are many; we have already mentioned the spoliation of the producer, who happens to be in difficulties. But the Hebrews also utilise the collapse of business concerns to get hold of parcels of goods very cheaply; they even know how to bring these collapses about purposely, by scheming amongst themselves, in order to transfer the goods from one to the other at a very low price. Levi, who has just opened a new business, knows how to obtain goods on credit. For several times in succession, he fulfils his obligations to the merchant, who supplies him, conscientiously, and by so doing, gains the latter's confidence. Gradually he increases the quantity of goods ordered, and keeps on taking longer and longer credit. The supply-merchants, obviously impressed by the apparent development of the business, are loath to lose such a good customer, and continue to give longer and longer credit. Levi, however, with the help of his compatriots, sells the goods far under the proper price, that is to say, he becomes the middleman for other Jewish businesses, which "cut" prices. He sells the goods to these businesses, at a price, which is actually lower than what the factory charges him; when he has stretched his credit as far as he dares, he declares himself a bankrupt, and the supply-merchants, who have been under the impression that their customer held a large stock of goods, discover an empty nest, and have to satisfy themselves by agreeing to accept from the debtor a meagre percentage of what he really owes them. There is no particular skill or art in delivering goods, or, in other words, selling cheaply, if such means are adopted. The Hebrew, who knows only too well how to reverse the order of things, has, in this case also, reversed the normal business principle: sometimes he does not try to make a profit out of his customers, but makes his gain at the expense of the manufacturers and supply- merchants. He sells the goods actually cheaper than he buys the same, and ends by never paying for the greater part. This peculiar method of carrying on business has actually procured for the Hebrew the reputation of being a philanthropist, because he "helps" poor people to obtain cheap goods — that he makes presents, in fact, to the purchasing public; but only a few are aware that he does this out of other people's pockets. Since time immemorial the Hebrew has been a master of the art of doing good at somebody else's expense.

It is a matter of common knowledge that he is always ready to receive goods, which have been acquired in an underhand and illegal manner. He buys pledged, attached and stolen goods whenever the opportunity presents itself. For preference he endeavours to acquire wares, which are cheaper, either because they have flaws, or, because they have been rejected for some other reason, the so-called "job-lots", which the genuine business-people will not accept on account of small imperfections. The Hebrew reckons on the shallow nature and general lack of any expert knowledge on the part of the public, and knows well how to dispose of such articles to his customers under the guise of genuine wares, which are worth every penny of the price charged for them.

2. LOWERING OF THE STANDARD OF PRODUCTION.

(CHEAP AND BAD)

Sad to say, owing to the influence of Jewish machinations, the manufacture of many products has degenerated. Any notion of quality in goods, has, for the most part, disappeared, and a great demand has sprung up, on the contrary, for the production of cheap and trashy goods. The genuine business people do their best to protect themselves against this unclean traffic, and endeavour to take proceedings against the "cutter", when he tries to pass off his inferior wares as being equal in value to those of better quality. The trade protection associations have frequently brought actions against the "cutters" with satisfactory results; but, in many cases, trade experts have been obliged to concede that differences in the quality of the material, and of the labour are extremely difficult to establish, even when they are responsible for a reduction of from 10—15 per cent of the value of the genuine article. And thus the Hebrew is enabled to keep on reducing the quality of the goods, and to injure the producers as well as the purchasing public.

Our average purchasing public of today is unfortunately far too frivolous to attach value to genuine goods. The Hebrew has carefully trained it, before all things, to seek for and find its satisfaction in "Modernity" and "Appearance", instead of insisting, first of all, on appropriateness and durability, which, in all cases, allow themselves to be combined with a pleasing shape. Most people desire to possess what glitters and dazzles for the moment, quite indifferent as to whether it soon loses its value, and has to be thrown on one side, only to be speedily replaced by some new and equally cheap and showy trash. Thus, not only does the national political economy enter upon a dangerous road, but the national mode of living, and the national morals follow. The delusive arc lights of the great "Stores" are not only destructive to genuine business but are ruinous to the nation itself.

As Sombart concedes, the Jew is the author or originator of the substitute in its most extensive sense, i. e. in plain English: the Jew is the author or originator of adulteration and falsification in trade.

Many goods of inferior value, which have been produced according to the Jewish principle, have actually received the name "Jewgoods." Thus, one speaks of "Jew-linen", "Jew- cotton" and other "Jew-stuff". A particular trick in Jewish business circles, consists in giving less than the proper weight or measure, in the case of goods where weight and measure are difficult to check.[37] When the new system of weights was introduced, purchasers, according to custom, still demanded an extra "quarter of a pound", or whatever the extra amount might be, and the Hebrew knew only too well how to utilise the opportunity by giving only a fifth instead of a quarter. It is also a matter of common knowledge that a "Jew's Gross" is only about 100 instead of 144. If it was formerly customary to maintain in justification of the Jewish method of trading that the Jew could afford to sell and deliver more cheaply, because his way of living was more unpretending and he could subsist on very modest means, this argument is no longer valid. It is notorious that the Hebrews of the present day maintain a most luxurious existence,

---

[37] Women, in particular, are victims of this practice, for, they allow, for instance, "English thread', which is measured by the yard instead of by the metre, to be forced upon them.

and their womenfolk especially endeavour to surpass all other classes — even Royalty and the aristocracy — in luxury and ostentation.

One point must be conceded to the Jews; that by increasing sales for cash to the utmost possible extent they accelerate the turnover. A quick turnover, at any rate, makes it possible for the merchant to content himself with a smaller profit, and yet to maintain the standard of his existence. It is the methods, by which the Hebrew procures the quick turnover, which are for the most part questionable, and which disclose their injuriousness in other branches of the economic life. For, in the last analysis, trade is not the sole aim of trade; the mission of human life is not to produce as much as possible; for enhanced consumption can be injurious to the individual as to the community. Just as excessive nourishment and excessive enjoyment are detrimental to the individual, so are the stimulation and enhancement of the economic functions by no means beneficial in all cases.

The Hebrew turns gladly to the maxim: "Quick turnover and small profits", and utilises it as an advertisement for his particular methods. And, in this case also, it is essentially a matter of discovering a means wherewith he can dazzle and infatuate.

3. DEVIATING MODE OF THOUGHT

The nature of the Jewish mode of thinking is such that it functions quite differently to the normal understanding. The Hebrew thinks, as it were, round the corner; his thoughts travel by the opposite path to the natural one. Whilst the Aryan intelligence directs itself towards production and building-up, the Hebrew is meditating everywhere on confusion and exhaustion, on ruin and dismemberment. He seeks his advantage in the injuries of others, his advancement in the oppression of his fellow-men, who do not happen to be Jews. Jewish thought is always of a negative nature; the Hebrew is the born bacillus of decomposition. Hence it is that a healthy human mode of thinking can only follow the Jewish speculative machinations with great difficulty; and for the same reason, the Hebrew remains an incomprehensible being to the majority of mankind. The Jew is well acquainted with our mode of thinking and feeling, but we know nothing about his. The Hebrew reckons with certainty upon our straightforward conclusions, but we are quite unable to keep step with his crooked thoughts. The Jew, therefore, seldom makes a miscalculation when dealing with a German, but the German almost always, when dealing with the Jew. The Hebrew tries to guide our thoughts into a direction where he can follow their sequence closely — so closely that we are bound to fall into the trap laid for us. He has learnt to think the thoughts of other men in advance; we, however, have not practised the art of following the zig-zag workings of his mind. And thus the Hebrew has acquired an apparent superiority over us which, however, in the final analysis, is only based on a habitual perversion of the natural way of thinking and feeling. His whole endeavour has but one aim, namely, to direct the impulses and activities of others in order to misuse the same. The Hebrew is not a natural being with straightforward impulses; everything in him is diverted and perverted. His warped mind is simply a machine for provoking and harassing. Anyone, who has not gradually learned to know the eccentricity and subtlety of the Jewish mode of thinking by long personal intercourse with Jews themselves — and naturally very few Christians have the opportunity to gain this experience — is quite incapable of pursuing the Jewish train of thought unless he has obtained insight into the true Jewish spirit by reading the Rabbinical writings. Everything there — based on direct denial of reason and morality — is turned topsy-turvy, and is directed against the natural feelings and disposition of humanity. He, who has not studied, in some measure, the books of the Talmud, will never come to a right understanding concerning the Jews.

All the motives and activities of the Jewish brain are directed towards obtaining advantage and material gain. And, in spite of this, the Hebrew imagines that, especially with regard to morality, he is a very exalted being. No one speaks more effusively about ethical values than the Jews, but whoever takes the trouble to examine what they understand by that expression, discovers that they mean the art of seeking their advantage by means of the understanding, under the pretext that they are engaged in some praise-worthy and unselfish effort. If one wished to sum up Jewish morality in one concise phrase, it would read as follows: "All is moral which brings advantage." The Jew is incapable of applying a higher standard to the values in life than that of advantage or profit.

The Jewish perception can be formulated in yet another way: "Morality is the art of over reaching other people, and of creating, at the same time, the impression of a benevolent disposition — in fact, of representing what is in reality an offence against others as an act of charity." (During the recent war, we had ample opportunity of admiring with what masterly skill this doctrine was put into practice by the English statesmen, who had graduated in the Talmudic school.)

Sombart quotes one passage from the "Universal treasure-house of Commerce", which presents the sound morality of a merchant of the old school in the most striking contrast to the present-day Jewish perception. "If you happen to be the sole possessor of a particular class of goods, you are entitled to a fair and honest profit, that is to say, your conscience must be satisfied that you have not exceeded what is Christian- like, and your mind must be at rest upon this point." The Hebrew is incapable of understanding a moral summons like the above; it would, in fact, excite his derision. The religious and moral command had always the first consideration in all Christian business in olden times; it remained for the Jew to chase all morality out of the economic world. He regards everything which brings profit as permissible. He has made the mammonistic idea the dominating influence in our life, with his dogma: "He who serves Mammon pleases God" — for the real God of the Jew is Mammon, a fact which, Karl Marx, himself of Jewish descent, openly admitted.

X

JEWISH TRADE SPECIALITIES

1. PROFESSIONAL BANKRUPTCY

Bankruptcy means to the sound tradesman the severest misfortune which can befall him; in most cases, it spells for him not only economic, but also social and moral extinction. The German tradesman therefore, devotes all his energy, and all his reserves, to avert this calamity; and, just as an honourable captain does not desert his sinking ship so long as he is alive, so many a German merchant has considered himself unable to survive the disgrace of his bankruptcy. In any case, a genuine German tradesman emerges from his bankrupt business as poor as a churchmouse, and shuns the public disgrace. In this respect also, the Jewish morality and mode of thinking, which are of quite a different kind, have brought about a change which, unfortunately, has exercised a demoralising influence upon the conceptions of honour, prevalent amongst the German commercial community. In the eyes of the Hebrew there is nothing dishonourable about bankruptcy, which is to be regarded, in any case, purely as a business accident, and which, on that account, may evoke the sympathy of kindred souls, but which has not otherwise the slightest effect on the social position. No, indeed, the Jewish mode of thinking, which regards bankruptcy as a stroke of good luck, bringing rich profit in its train, is far from being an invention of the comic papers. This is in accordance, not only with the peculiar morality of the Jews, but also with the entire tactic of the Jewish business system or entity.[38]

---

[38] In an article written in the year 1816, it is stated that "the Jew forces trading to a height where the sound Christian merchant grows giddy."

The Hebrew knows well how to begin a business with somebody else's money. According to his solution — often thoughtlessly echoed by people, who are not Jews — "Credit is equivalent to hard cash", and he sets to work to obtain credit from other firms and banks — for preference from those who are not Jewish — assisted in this respect by his racial brethren, who extol his business capacity and reliability with all their might. If the business succeeds, and reaches the stage where a quick and profitable turnover is assured, the Hebrew meets his engagements punctually, and, perhaps, works himself up into the position of a really sound business man. If, however, the site of the shop has not been well chosen, and the right class of customer does not present itself, the owner alters his tactics: he now steers a straight course for bankruptcy, and a bankruptcy, which shall be as profitable to him as possible. He succeeds in this by the following manoeuvre: instead of reducing, or even entirely withdrawing his orders, so as to allow for the deficiency in the sale of his goods, he actually increases them. So long as he still enjoys credit, he intends to make the utmost use of the same. By a steady increase in his orders, he is desirous of creating the impression that the business is in a state of healthy development. He pays punctually for part of the goods received, but lays claim, at the same time, to more and more credit; and this is willingly enough granted to him, for the merchant or manufacturer, who supplies him, is loath to lose so good a customer. The Jew now disposes of the goods, which he has obtained on credit, partly below cost price, in which process, he can always find some of his racial colleagues, ready to lend a helping hand, either by relieving him of large quantities of the goods at half the original price, in order to sell the same at extraordinarily cheap prices in their own shops, or, by selling the goods again as "job-lots" to others, who profess the same faith. The expectant bankrupt takes care to lodge part of the proceeds where it will be safely guarded, and utilises the remainder to continue his part-payments to the manufacturer or merchant in order to retain the confidence of the latter, and to gradually screw up credit to its utmost limit. If he is successful in all this, and is satisfied with the amount of plunder, he finally suspends payment — with the profoundest regret that bad times and unlooked-for losses no longer allow of what was formerly a lucrative business being carried on profitably. The creditors find scarcely any stock and no cash, and have, moreover, the trouble and expense of the investigation. The man is practically safeguarded against any legal proceedings; the books are apparently in order; the selling-off at low prices of the "job- lots" is so far justified by the argument that the goods, in order not to become old-fashioned, had to be got rid of at any price; the considerable sums, which are entered up to the private account, are again justified by heavy expenditure in the household under the plea that, in the interest of the business and its inseparable social connections, it was necessary "to cut a dash". Briefly; it is impossible to get hold of the man.[39]

Made shy by similar experiences, the creditors, for the most part, avoid the costly bankruptcy proceedings, fearing that, in the end, they will have to content themselves with less than five per cent, and prefer to conclude a forced settlement, meagre indeed, but which will leave them at any rate with 25 or 30 per cent of the value of their claims. It frequently happens that a special "bankruptcy sale" is arranged, which is kept going as long as possible, and by which means large quantities of goods, specially ordered for the occasion, are disposed of in the manner described above, so that the whole circle of "business friends" may benefit to the utmost by the favourable opportunity.

Recent legislation has, in some measure, checked this unsavoury practice, which had developed, during the last decades, to an incredible extent, but has by no means put a stop to it: for little as the Hebrew may have invented in other directions — he is a past master in the invention of new ways to circumvent or evade the laws.

The fortunate bankrupt knows well how to start business again — if necessary in another part — and probably on still more lucrative lines; if he considers it advisable, he will carry it on under the name of his wife, or one of his children, in order that his former obligations may not become a source of annoyance to him. And, if again the business fails to become a success, the ingenious fellow

---

[39] One can frequently read in the news-papers that Jewish business people, who have long been in a state of bankruptcy, still continue to live in a very expensive style, and to move in a very expensive social set, until they are at last declared bankrupt to the extent of several millions.

knows how to arrange for a second, and even a third bankruptcy. The money, which is lost in the process, never belongs to him, but always to other people, that is to say, it is invariably the properly of the confiding Goyims.

Wholesale merchants and manufacturers have been plundered systematically in this way for years by Jews, who have made a profession or business of becoming bankrupt; and this particular species of crime has contributed in no small measure to the enrichment of many Jewish families, and, at the same time, to the impoverishment of many honest Germans. For the sufferers by this kind of robbery are not only the merchants, who actually deliver the goods, but also the sound tradespeople, who are squeezed out of existence by this unclean kind of competition. The Hebrew, who has obtained his goods by evil tricks like those described, or who has, perhaps, not paid anything at all, can well afford to sell them more cheaply than the sound tradesman. And thus the "cutting" of prices and unsavoury competition are considerably promoted by those Jews, who have become professional bankrupts.

If complaints concerning these abuses have not been so frequent of recent years, this improvement is only partly to be attributed to the increased severity of the laws, and is due, to a very considerable part, to great mercantile organisations of all kinds, endeavouring to protect themselves against these abuses by uniting to form trade protection societies.

The Jews of today, however, no longer find it so necessary to enrich themselves by such comparatively clumsy methods of deceit; they have acquired money enough in the last few decades, and to use the words of one particular Hebrew — "can permit themselves the luxury of trading respectably" — of course with exceptions!

Many a Jewish business-man has had his task made easy, when engaged in such practices as those just described, by the absolutely irresponsible and ridiculous ease, with which a change of name can be made legitimate in Germany. The official advertisement that, for instance, Hirsch Levi intends to call himself Hermann Winter, or that Aaron Feiteles wishes to be known as Arnold Krause, appears only in the German Imperial and Prussian State Advertiser, a paper, which is not read by anybody outside official circles, so that those interested seldom learn anything about what has taken place until the — for them — unpleasant consequences bring it to their notice. A further advantage is taken by those owning Jewish names, which can be used both for Christian and surname. Thus, Moses Meier Aaron, after his first bankruptcy, can reconstruct the firm as Aaron Meier Moses, to be followed, when necessary, by a third reconstruction as Moses Aaron Meier, and is thus in a position to escape more easily the eyes of his old creditors.

The Hebrew, equipped with principles of this kind, together with a complete lack of even the slightest sense of honour, can engage in any business undertaking with a far lighter heart than a man of another race. It is scarcely possible to find a business opening anywhere, even of the most risky nature, which a Hebrew has not already taken in hand. The costly shop in the newly erected premises at the junction of two streets, a questionable invention, some speculation relying on the folly or curiosity of the public — all are taken up by Jews, while conscientious business people are still carefully considering and weighing the merits and drawbacks of the concern. A decision is actually far easier for the Hebrew than for anybody else, for, in event of a failure, the conscience of the former does not trouble him in the slightest, and he says to himself at the commencement as well: "you are not risking your own money."

The Jews certainly have the reputation of possessing great enterprise — one could also say: of possessing great temerity in business. It cannot be denied that they occasionally help to promote a sound undertaking and that many an inventor would have waited in vain for the realisation of his ideas if the Jews had not come to his assistance. And one may well wish that occasionally our German merchants and capitalists displayed less reserve where new plans and ideas are concerned, and did not leave this field of enterprise so completely at the disposal of the Hebrew. One must, however, take into consideration that the German promoter of any such undertaking not only risks his own money, but very often his own good name as well, whilst, in the case of the Hebrew, neither of these two all-important considerations enter into the question at all.

Moreover, one must not forget a fact, which has already been mentioned; in all business undertakings the Hebrew is assured of the open, or, at any rate, the secret support and cooperation of his racial friends, whereas the German, in such matters, has in most cases to rely upon himself, and even, when peculiar and hazardous enterprises are concerned, has to reckon with the opposition of good friends and relatives, which arises from denseness of perception, and a dislike of novelty. The Hebrew, on the contrary, sets to work with a light heart and in a very different frame of mind: "Risk it! — if you are not successful — well — it is only somebody else who is the loser!"

And further, one must take into consideration that, not only the business world, but that all public life, for the last forty years, has been infected with the Jewish spirit, and has taken on a Jewish aspect. Jewish tendencies are supreme everywhere, and Jewish ideas and views rule the mass of the population, in the towns at any rate. Everything, which is born of the Jewish spirit and pursues Jewish aims, is, on that account, readily assimilated into the current of public life, for it blends with it. The genuine German is completely out of the running; he is as a stranger in this new world; he cannot make himself at home amidst such surroundings. The best things which he can think of, do not seem to fit into this altered world; he is swimming against the stream. This holds good, not only for business, but in equal measure for Art, Stage, Literature and Press. Jewish work is in accordance with the disposition of the times, and the factors of public life, which come under the same influence, further Jewish enterprise. Thus, it is far easier for the Jewish business-man, just as it is for the Jewish author and for the Jewish artist, to "make a name", than it is for the more conscientious, and, for that reason, more awkward German.

The surrounding world is now estranged in many respects from the German mode of thought and action; it is therefore harder for a German to get on than it is for the eel-like Hebrew, concerning whom Franz Dingelstedt ("Lieder eines kosmopolitischen Nachtwächters") (Song of a cosmopolitan watchman) sang in 1840:

"He forces the farmer out of his farm,
He scares the shop-keeper away from the market,
And partly with gold, and partly with his servile wit,
Purchases the pass-word from the Spirit of the age".

If the German does not possess the power to create an environment for himself, suitable for his mode of thought and action, he will be lost in this Judaized world, and Hebbel's words will come true: "The German possesses every qualification to gain heaven, but none to maintain himself upon earth; and thus the time may well come when this people will disappear from the earth."

2. THE INSTALMENT OR HIRE-PURCHASE SYSTEM

In nearly all the larger towns there are business firms, who, by means of brisk advertising, offer, as a special recommendation, that they are prepared to part with their goods on receiving a small preliminary payment, provided that the purchaser pledges himself, by a written agreement, to pay off the debt by regular — generally weekly — instalments. On account of the apparently so favourable offer this kind of business secures many customers, especially amongst small officials, and the more needy of the working-class. People, without any means, look upon these firms almost as benefactors, and as noble-hearted philanthropists because, for instance, they hand over an entire suite of furniture to a young couple, anxious to get married, against an undertaking on the part of the latter to pay a weekly instalment of from 3— 5 marks. This type of business-man knows well how to pose in his advertisement as the friend of mankind. As a matter of fact, there lurks, behind this particular method of conducting business, unparalleled usury — in a shape, admittedly, which the law, as it now stands, finds extremely difficult to deal with. The next point is, that the goods, which are offered, have been hastily made out of inferior material; but in spite of this, the price at which they are invoiced, is high. The willing purchaser, however, pays little heed to the high price for the simple reason that he does not have to pay it at once; he imagines that the comfortable method of payment renders a dispute about the price unnecessary, for it becomes an easy matter to produce the money when the payments are spread over a considerable time. Accordingly, he signs the contract, laid before him, with a light heart, quite heedless of the snare, in which he is entangling himself. It is stated in the contract, amongst other conditions, that the seller is entitled to regain possession of the goods, which have been delivered, without refunding any of the money, which he has already received, if the purchaser does not pay each instalment punctually.[40] The purchaser, who has every intention of paying regularly out of his income, is naturally unable to realise that such could ever be the case, and unhesitatingly attaches his name to the document. But unfortunately it only too often happens that the purchaser — perhaps through loss of his situation, perhaps through illhealth or misfortune — is one day unable to meet his obligations, and suddenly he finds himself robbed, not only of the articles of furniture, which he has taken on this "hire-purchase" system, but also of all the instalments, which he has already paid, and which are irretrievably lost. An appeal to the Law Courts seldom avails, for the written contract has been drawn up in such a manner that, from a legal point of view, the seller is completely within his rights. Year after year large sums of money are sacrificed in this way by people of scanty means, who live, so to speak, from hand to mouth. It can scarcely be a pure accident that these "payment by instalments" businesses are, almost without exception, owned by Jews; they belong to the most objectionable inventions, with which the Hebrew has graced the modern age. The whole operation is based on a well-thought-out plan; it is an important part of the great system to rob the people of their money, according to a carefully thought-out and prearranged scheme. The Hebrew is not content with depriving people of the money, which is already in their pockets; he forces them to pledge their future earnings. The anticipation of the profits of the future is entirely the product of the speculative Jewish mind, which conveys the taint of unreality into the economic life, and builds it up, so to speak, upon air. For an existence, which is founded upon such future values, must, of necessity, undergo shipwreck as soon as the slightest hitch occurs in the tranquil and natural development of affairs. It is said with truth

---

[40] Recent legislation interferes to a considerable extent with the easy operation of contracts of this nature.

in Goethe's Faust: "The Jew will not spare you for he creates anticipations."

We learn that 27 of these great "Hire purchase" or "Payment by instalments" businesses in Germany are united under one control, that is to say, belong to one company, the chairman or managing director of which is said to be one Leskowitz of Dresden. It is further maintained that the yearly income of this man amounts to Marks 800,000 (£40,000). Enormous as this may sound, it is by no means improbable if one takes into consideration that not only must very high prices be paid for all the goods, which these businesses supply, but that those goods, which have been confiscated and taken back in consequence of failure to pay an instalment when due, are "touched- up" a little, and immediately supplied again to a new customer.

In what plight is a community and its legislation when it is unable to check bare-faced plundering of its poorest members by such a system of thinly-disguised usury? Would one not do far better to substitute in the place of these innumerable laws, which eventually prove to be utterly inadequate, and which can be evaded on every occasion by experienced cheats, the healthy sense of fairness, inherent in properly-trained Judges i. e. men of long personal acquaintance with practical life, just like the English do, and which they find answers very well?

3. THE "STORES"

The original of the "Stores" is the eastern "bazaar", which, already more than a century ago, was represented in this land by the country "general-shop", and the latter was really necessary in our remoter districts. Both of these satisfied an obvious need; but even in this direction an alien and degrading feature began to make itself visible in the sound development of trade, in the shape of the 50, 25 and 10 Pfennig bazaars, caricatures of the originals, which were started by the Jews soon after the establishment of the freedom of industry. It is worthy of note that the first "stores", on a grand scale, arose in that most pleasure-loving of all world-cities — Paris — in order to provide the world of frivolous women with a convenient establishment or depot where the hundreds of requirements of an elegant lady could be satisfied under one roof. Their field of activity was then extended into the United States in order to make it possible for the population there, who, though dwelling in the smaller towns and in the open country, separated from one another by vast distances and cut off, for the most part, from traffic, still wished to be "up-to-date". The Hebrews have introduced their imitation bazaars into our larger towns, which were already amply supplied with shopping facilities, without any other justification than that of speculation, based upon the love of comfort, mania for enjoyment, confusion of thought and absence of any critical faculty, which characterise the great majority, especially of women. Not in one single case are our "Stores" necessary in the sense that the eastern bazaars, our country general-shops, and the American "Stores" are necessary, and it is worthy of note that in many countries — for instance Brasil — the erection of these great "Stores" is forbidden in the interests of sound, straightforward commerce, and therefore in the interests of the community generally.

Thus the great, dazzling, central shopping-establishments to be found in all our large cities, and into which the "Stores" gradually develop, owe their existence entirely to a deliberate violation of the practices of sound commerce, which forces a way for itself, regardless of everything and everybody, assisted by and in connection with an extensive association or combination of capital, i. e. great Bank-credit. It is undeniable that these establishments, by reason of the organisation upon which they depend, belong to the most remarkable creations of modern times, and it is quite comprehensible why the purchasing public seems to lose its head over these novelties, and is powerfully attracted by the real or apparent advantages of these establishments. What these advantages are supposed to be, is in everybody's mouth, for the "Stores" themselves have taken very good care that the same should be adequately advertised. It is not so well known, however, that these great bazaars find it necessary to make use of a number of cleverly-conceived manoeuvres in order to attract their public, and to secure a good profit, in spite of the apparent cheapness of their wares.

Chief of all is the endeavour so to work upon the customer by dazzling the eyes, and generally by bewildering the senses with an extravagant and varied display of goods, and further, by enlisting the arts of persuasion and cajolery to such an extent as to make it almost impossible, or, at any rate, extremely difficult for the customer to leave the establishment without having purchased something, whether he actually required it or not. A number of special tricks, as well, have been invented to mislead the customers on the one side, and to exploit ingeniously the manufacturers and merchants on the other. A few examples only of these tricks are given below.

TRICKS TO DECEIVE CUSTOMERS

ARTICLES TO ENTICE

The "Stores" have found that the best means to attract customers is to offer certain articles of little intrinsic value at surprisingly low prices; at prices, in fact, which do not allow of any profit, or may even be less than the actual cost of the goods. They sell many of such articles for several Pfennigs less than the factory price — fully aware that by so doing they are brilliantly advertising themselves. What does it matter after all, if a few Pfennigs are lost each time that reels of cotton, hairpins, goldfish, gloves, buttons, glasses etc. are sold! Customers are drawn in by the enticing prices, and temptation is placed in their way to purchase other articles, the real value of which they are not nearly so well able to estimate. And thus the great emporium is richly recompensed for its small initial loss.

Moreover, it is the intention to create the impression amongst those, who are desirous of buying, that, in a business, where certain articles are so cheap, all must necessarily be cheap. And that is just what they are not. This is one of the most effective deceptions practised by the great "Stores" on the public. For, in the case of the larger and more costly goods, which are only occasionally purchased, and the value of which the ordinary layman is not experienced enough to judge, considerably higher prices are charged than would be the case if the article in question had been purchased at a genuine business of the usual kind, i. e. businesses which specialise in the sale of one kind of goods.

Also, it is worth remarking, that articles, intended to act as a bait, or an allurement, are always objects, which have but little value in a household, and, for that reason, are not purchased to any considerable extent by the public. However, if anybody, in order to take advantage of the cheapness of these goods, endeavours to buy more of the same than is usual, he is almost invariably met with the answer that the stock is sold out.

"Display articles." — One occasionally notices in the windows of the great "Stores" articles of a larger size, which cause astonishment on account of their exceptional cheapness. So far as can be seen, these articles are made of good material and the workmanship is sound. On entering the establishment to buy one of these articles, one is usually shown something of similar appearance but of inferior quality. If the customer detects the difference, he is given to understand that all the better quality has been sold. If he then demands the article, which is displayed in the window, he is told that the same has been sold already, but that the purchaser has given permission for it to remain on display until a new consignment arrives. Certainly the law concerning unclean competition provides — in a measure — a remedy against tricks of this kind, but the customer scarcely ever avails himself of it, and, if he does, seldom with success. The rule is that one simply does not obtain the desired article at the stated price.

"Mixin g of goods." — The following practice is customary in the "Stores" when a quantity of articles are offered for sale in one lot: amongst a number of cheap goods such as articles of clothing, linen, crockery etc, several articles of a better quality than the majority are introduced. These better articles are, for reasons which it is easy to understand, placed on the top, and are handed, for hasty inspection, to likely purchasers. If a sale takes place the salesman endeavours to substitute the inferior article, or, if a large quantity is being dealt with, to mix the inferior articles with the better ones. "Deception-and Exchange-articles." — The "Stores" have introduced the following practice: they buy a parcel of goods of superior quality from a manufacturer of good reputation, and, armed with a sample from these, order articles, deceptively similar in appearance but made of inferior material, to be manufactured at another factory. As they then sell by turns from the superior and inferior stocks (but mostly from the latter) they are in a position to evade the reproach that they deal in inferior goods. Whenever a dispute arises, they simply produce one of the better articles, and assure the customer that this is their normal quality, and that the inferior specimen complained of has been introduced amongst the better goods by accident.

What is related below as having taken place in a large "Stores" has been proved, beyond doubt, to be a fact: the business in question had bought a large quantity of well-made lace, the factory price of which was 10 Pfennigs the metre. Two inferior qualities of lace at the respective factory prices of 6 and 3 Pfennigs the metre, but of exactly the same pattern, were then ordered. The winding cards of these three different qualities of lace, which all appear to the ordinary superficial observer to be of the same quality, are placed, side by side, and are all offered for sale at the same price of 9 Pfennigs the metre. It is easy to understand that those who sold had received instructions to sell as much as possible from the winding-card, which contained the lace, which had cost 3 Pfennigs the metre; it was only when a customer entered, who displayed a certain amount of criticism, and appeared to understand something about the matter, that lace was taken from the winding-card, which contained the superior quality. The lady who, by chance, happened to receive a piece of the 10 Pfennig lace for 9 Pfennigs, would naturally continue for a long time to sing the praises of the superiority and cheapness of the article in question amongst the whole circle of her acquaintances, and, in this way, this particular "stores" recovered by the good advertisement far more than the value of the single Pfennig, which had been actually lost in the transaction.

"Prices which confuse and mislead." The great "Stores" often endeavour, by marking articles at unusual prices (such as 98 Pfennigs, 2 Marks 95 Pfennigs etc.) to create the impression that their calculations are made with the greatest nicety, and that they are satisfied with a very meagre profit. But this is also a delusion, for, amongst the articles marked 98 Pfennigs, there are many, which can be bought in genuine business for 75 or 80 Pfennigs. Moreover, the fact that a customer has allowed himself to be enticed by an apparent saving of 2 Pfennigs is scarcely an event to which he can refer with pride; it is so obviously a speculation of a mean nature, or — generally where women are concerned — is prompted by an absurd idea of economy.

The "Confectionär", which issues the official organ of the union of "Stores" and Warehouses as its Sunday supplement, recently gave its readers the following good advice: "the smaller articles must often be sold at cost price, and sometimes even for less, in order that so much the more may be charged for the larger ones. If a lady is enabled to purchase gloves or soap for a few groschen below the usual price, she is there and then convinced that all articles in that same business- house are cheap, and continues, with complete confidence, to purchase in the same establishment also, mantles and silken garments."

In the course of an action taken by the "Stores" called Stein in Berlin against the "Bund der Handel- und Gewerbetreibenden" ("Association" of Commerce and Industry") a pronouncement was made by the Prussian Court of Appeal, when reversing the judgement of November 14th 1907, as follows: "it is a matter of common knowledge to those engaged in law, that the "Stores" endeavour to attract large numbers of customers, by offering for sale, at absurdly low prices, those particular goods, which are in daily use or consumption by the masses, but that when other goods are sold, far higher prices are demanded than are charged by the small and moderately-sized shops, which specialise in the particular kind of goods concerned."

When a large Berlin "Stores" went so far recently as to offer Imperial 5 Pfennig postcards for 4 Pfennigs, the intention, which was to entice customers into the establishment and to force other articles upon them, was only too apparent. For, finally, the reduced price for the postcards was only granted to those, who could produce proof that they had purchased other goods. But the intention was also present to create the bewildering impression that this "Stores" was making the impossible possible, and was actually in a position to sell the Imperial postcards cheaper than the postal authorities themselves could. The success of this questionable kind of business depends, to a large extent, upon the suggestion that this "Stores", by some incredible means or magic, could actually sell goods cheaper than those who manufactured the same. It is certainly only the most thoughtless, who can allow themselves to be fooled by such unbusinesslike tricks, and the same may therefore be regarded as a speculation in stupidity. Whoever allows himself to be enticed by these "Stores" tricks is certainly not entitled to ask for a certificate stating that he — or she — is capable of sane and independent judgement.

INJURY DONE TO THE PRODUCERS

It can be seen from the practices, which have just been described, how the "Stores" favour, for the most part, the production of inferior goods and thus react very oppressively upon certain branches of manufacture. The method of procedure is usually as follows: the "Stores" buyer puts in an appearance at the office of the factory, and producing a certain article says: "I can order annually large quantities of this article if you can produce the same at from 20 to 25 per cent below the present price. It does not matter if the workmanship and the material are inferior, but the appearance must be the same." When a respectable manufacturer declines to accept this invitation, the "Stores" buyer threatens to take his order to some other firm. Many a manufacturer, apprehensive of being squeezed out of the market, ends up by consenting, and produces the inferior goods, which are desired. One inevitable consequence of the constantly increasing manufacture of shoddy and inferior goods is, that the production of goods of superior quality tends as steadily to diminish.

An expert in the manufacture of china reports: "our factory has worked for years at a loss simply because the demand for a good class of ware, which is worth its price, is gradually falling off. The "Stores" buy only "fourth selection" and flawed goods, that is to say, refuse. They then mix several good pieces among the lot, in the case of plates, for instance, laying them on the top of the others, and the public buys this rubbish unsuspectingly. A sound line of goods, however, waits in vain for a purchaser. There is nothing left but to resign one's self to the manufacture of artificially prepared refuse. On the other hand wages keep on rising, so that it is no longer possible to make the business pay, and this entire branch of industry goes from bad to worse."

Numerous factories in other branches of trade have allowed themselves to be inveigled into manufacturing rubbish, especially for the "Stores", and have found their ruin in the process. It was the invariable habit of the "Stores" buyer to endeavour to beat the price down each time he gave a fresh order, until there was no longer any possibility for the producer to make even the most meagre profit. The customers for the better class of wares had, however, disappeared in the meantime, so there was nothing to be done except to discontinue business.

Another decade like this, and we shall see the greater part of that branch of industry, which is dependent upon orders from the "Stores", ruined likewise.

A sausage manufacturer, when asked how it was that he could deliver his sausages so cheaply to the "Stores" that the latter could sell a pair for 12 Pfennigs when 15 Pfennigs were charged everywhere else, answered laughing: "just measure the things! they are certainly a fifth cheaper, but they are also a quarter shorter." — The purchasing public has no idea whatever of such proceedings, or behaves, at any rate, as if it had no such idea; it is bewitched by the fascinating and bewildering life of the great "Stores", and does not pause to consider to what an extent the entire economic life is being undermined by such a questionable form of development. For, not only is industry reduced to producing rubbish, but also those sound businesses in the towns, which confine themselves to the sale of high-class specialities, are being ruined, because the "Stores" are gradually depriving them of their customers. In the vicinity of the "Stores" one good business after another disappears; in Berlin, for instance, in the year 1913, no less than 18,000 separate shops were standing empty. Development of this kind can only end in a gigantic economic catastrophe; and we shall be indebted for this to the magnificence of the "Stores", as well as to the incredible shortsightedness of the public, which allows itself to be enticed into such man-traps, and which stifles every feeling of responsibility with arguments, which are prompted solely by its own laziness and vanity.

A lowering of quality in the type of all articles available for trade. — As the "Stores" have use only for great quantities of articles as much alike as possible, they endeavour, as far as they can, to reduce the number of the various samples and types. The whole of the Art-Industry suffers especially thereby, as it is wont to grant both fancy and personal taste as large a field as possible. The "Stores" like to have a suitable sample reproduced a thousand, or even a million times, and this naturally causes other good samples to be forced out of the market. The Art-Industry loses its individuality; all becomes mass-manufacture for mass-taste.

As inferior material is almost invariably introduced where the above course is practised, the Art-Industry suffers degradation and cheapening in every respect.

The French political economist, Trepreau, characterises the development in the following words: "This change is causing the taste for what is good and beautiful, which formerly obtained such a good reputation for French trade, to disappear, and is substituting for it the mass-production of rubbish, which is degrading our industry, and the sequel of which will be the disappearance of all specialities of artistic handicraft in the immediate future".

In the case of jam and preserves, for example, the factories were compelled, in consequence of the pressure, to reduce prices and to produce special lines of preserves for the "Stores" alone, whereby not only did the quality suffer but the difference between gross and nett weight was increased by improper filling.

Many textile fabrics are reduced, not only with regard to the quality of the yarn and the closeness of the mesh, but actually with regard to the breadth, customary in the trade. Thus velvet was woven 42 centimetres instead of 50 centimetres broad — a fact which quite escapes a hasty inspection. To what an extent the contents of the balls and skeins of yarn, thread etc, mostly stated in English yards instead of in metres, differs from what it ought to be, is seldom ascertained by our thoughtless women, although, in this case, the difference in money is considerable.

But enough; the manufacturers, whether they like it or not, are compelled to help the "Stores" to deceive the public, although they destroy their own business in doing so.

THE OVERPOWERING AND MONOPOLISATION OF ALL
ECONOMIC MEANS

A further danger menaces our economic and social relations, arising from the circumstance that the "Stores", by gradually concentrating the retail trade into their hands, have almost obtained a monopoly of the same. This can make it as bad in the future for the purchasing public as for the manufacturers. As soon as the "Stores" have driven the majority of competing shops out of the field, they will not find it necessary any longer to entice customers with cheap prices, because the public will simply be compelled to buy many things from the "Stores" on account of the total disappearance of the sound old businesses, which confined themselves to one kind of trade and specialised in the same. When this time comes, the "Stores" will raise the prices as high as they like, and this will be made all the easier for them, as they have already formed themselves into a trust, and are codifying their rules and regulations. And there is no doubt that the purchasing public will eventually have to pay the reckoning for the apparent favours which it enjoys today.

At the present day the great "Stores" exert a kind of monopoly-domination over the manufacturers. They claim the right to take all kinds of discounts — special "Stores"-Bonus etc — which the manufacturers are powerless to resist, as they are placed more or less at the mercy of these great undertakings, who can give or withhold orders. When a special tax of 2% was imposed on the "Stores" in Prussia, the "Stores" immediately passed it on to the manufacturers and merchants, by deducting 2% from all their accounts, even before the tax actually came into force. Thus it is clear how the monopolising nature of these great "Stores," which is steadily increasing, is creating and inflicting a state of servile dependency upon the manufacturers, which, in its turn, will gravely endanger not only the economic but also the civic freedom — to say nothing of objections from the moral point of view. And it is not only the employers, who suffer, but the employees are threatened with the same evils and to the same extent. All those, who patronise the "Stores", should make a note of this.

As a matter of fact the "Stores" and the great Banks, which work in close alliance with them, are obtaining, in consequence of the continually progressing concentration of the economic life, a dominating power, which gives cause for the gravest apprehension. They have the power to crush every smaller competing business, and to make the manufacturers and producers absolutely dependent on them. This means nothing less than steering a direct course towards an economic "right of the fist", which is an end to every conception of justice and morality. Every kind of compulsion, which hurts the feeling of justice and wounds social sensibility, must of necessity lead to an undermining of public morality, and finally to anarchy, and consequently cannot be tolerated in any well-organised community. Since the great "Stores" already form an international trust, they are in a position to subject the citizens of any country to international machinations, and to interfere to such a degree with the means for upholding authority that they seriously menace the economic freedom and independence of the inhabitants.

This calls for objection and opposition. The state cannot sanction that private persons or companies should have a monopoly of commerce, and consequently of profiteering. But this is precisely what any further development of the "Stores" system will lead to.

Least of all, however, can an economic predominance of such a nature be tolerated, when it endeavours to attain its ends by questionable means, when it makes use of trickery and deceit, and thereby endangers public well-being.

MORAL AND PHYSICAL HARM

The great "Stores" endanger not only the economic existence of the smaller and moderate-sized businesses, as well as the steady and regular production of goods, but are harmful to the public morality. It is a well-known fact that, side by side with the evolution of the great "Stores", certain new and disquieting features have made their appearance in the moral attitude of the public. A new category of offences has come into being; the seductive influence leading to an improper appropriation of goods, the pathological appearance of that class of theft, which is peculiar to the "Stores". Experience shows that this particular type of larceny is not confined to the poorer class of people and professional thieves, but is practised by individuals drawn from all stations of life, and more especially by females, even when the latter belong to the most prosperous grades of society. The phenomenon is accounted for by the peculiar nature of business as conducted in the great "Stores". Everything is designed to excite cupidity, to bewilder and to ensnare. The whirl of business and the multitude of impressions raise excitement to such an extent that the senses become quite confused. Weak characters succumb entirely to these influences, and lose control of their will-power. They are tempted, when they feel that they are not observed, to appropriate something, and steal occasionally even from their fellow-customers. They are, however, nearly always caught, for the proprietors of the "Stores", well aware of the insidious charm of their "shows", keep a special staff of detectives to watch those whom they attract. Numerous cases have already occurred, where ladies of good position have been escorted into a private office, and have been subjected to the indignity of a personal search. It is easy to imagine what scandals develop out of such incidents.

But even if it does not lead quite so far as punishable offences, the influence upon the character of the public of the peculiar method of trading introduced by the "Stores", is altogether bad, for the simple reason that it induces many to buy more than their circumstances warrant, and to spend money on useless things. The whole system connected with this method of trading is designed to create the impression on the customers that they are guilty of neglect if they do not at once recognise and utilise the opportunity to make a cheap purchase, or, in other words, a bargain. The cheap rubbish also, made to look like something better, seduces simple people into buying articles quite unsuited to their position in life; by so doing they accustom themselves to a mode of living, which far exceeds what their circumstances and means justify. One of the great "Stores" advertised for a considerable period with reference to one of their brands of cheap Champagne: "Champagne must become a popular drink!" — a phrase that one of the Social-Democratic members of the Reichstag actually made his own particular slogan.

The demoralisation, which arises out of the peculiar method of trading adopted by the great "Stores", extends not only to the purchasing public, but even more to the staff or personnel of the "Stores", to the salesmen and saleswomen who labour under the steady und unvarying influence of the lax morale prevalent in these establishments, and who are compelled to help to deceive and overreach the public. To the above remarks may be added some foreign criticisms, in order to show how the objectionable features referred to have already acquired an international significance.

The physical injury caused by the unceasing strain of the service is considerable, and this reacts on the character. D Paul Berthold says concerning it:

"The assistants live in unhealthy surroundings, in badly-ventilated apartments, which are crowded with people. In most of the great "Stores" the number of cases of illness and of actual death is appalling, so much so, that those, who work for several years in these establishments without acquiring tuberculosis, form the exceptions."

In addition moral perils arise from other causes. Dr. H. Lambrecht, Director of the Ministry for Public Works in Brussels deserves recognition for having published in a memorandum concerning "Stores and Cooperative Societies", a number of facts dealing with these matters — facts which are all the more striking for having been scientifically corroborated. He makes inter alia, the following remarks with reference to this subject:

"This penning-in of a number of young females, and making them absolutely dependent on a person of the opposite sex, whether the latter may happen to be the shop-walker, inspector or manager, constitutes already a gross moral danger, which is all the more marked, when one takes into consideration that the saleswomen are drawn from the very class, which is most susceptible to the enticement of luxury and social pleasures".

He goes on to express his opinion about the questionable "friendships", which the great "Stores" offer both sexes so many opportunities of making, and which are utilised, not only by the salesmen and the saleswomen, but also by the customers. We have neither space nor time to refer further to the chapter dealing with this delicate subject. Lambrecht continues:

"The danger, however, is still further increased by the inadequate payment of the young girls employed, by bad advice, and by bad example. In these great businesses, in each of which several hundred people are employed, some of the older ones always find the means to dress themselves better than the others, and to visit the theatres and the restaurants after business hours, and soon the little girl apprentice, with her salary of 20 marks a month, allows herself to be deceived by what she imagines to be the brilliant prospect in store for her".

J. Hennigsen (Hamburg) after portraying the questionable moral relations, which evolve out of the "Stores" system, remarks:

"I am convinced that if all this could only be published, far and wide, no German woman, who still preserved a spark of sympathy with her fellow-women, would ever set foot again in one of these "Stores".

And Baroness Brincard, after describing the same conditions, observes:

"Generally speaking, women are sympathetic beings, whose hearts are touched by all suffering. Therefore they do not act intentionally when they profit grossly from the misery and distress of other women, but unfortunately it is just the women of the well-to-do classes, who know nothing of these matters, who neither see nor think..."

The great "Stores" are responsible for the production of a new nervous disease, a fact which Emile Zola has portrayed in his book "*Au Bonheur des Dames*". The French physician, Dr. Dubuisson, has chosen as a theme for his book ("*Les voleuses des grands magasins*") the injurious effect which the "Stores" have upon neurotic people; he says therein:

"It is impossible, even for people of the strongest constitutions, to spend any considerable time in these gigantic establishments without experiencing a peculiar feeling of nervous debility — of mental langour and bewilderment".

In the case of neurotic people this condition amounts to a complete confusion of the senses, which, to a certain extent, deprives them of the control of their actions, and brings in its train mental and moral disaster.

Dr. Laquer in "Der Warenhaus-Diebstahl" ("Thieving at the Stores") says:

"Thieving at the great "Stores" is very extensively carried on, and it is a matter of urgent importance that this fact should be made widely known, especially as children are taking a large part in it. The unguarded display of goods without any compulsion to buy, is a great temptation to those, who are deficient in will-power; for this reason alone it should be restricted. Whether this deficiency in will-power (notably in the case of women in an interesting condition), when brought face to face with the allurements of the great

"Stores", is to be regarded as a malady, must be decided by the evidence of medical experts in the Law Courts... "

In any case, the "Stores" contribute to an enormous extent to undermine the morality of a generation, whose conscience is already blunted, and to multiply to a serious extent the already numerous social evils. The determining factors in the State ought to seriously consider, whether the trivial advantages of making one's purchases under these luxurious conditions are sufficiently valuable to be placed in the scales against the economic and moral welfare of the population. And, before everything else, if it is consistent with the duty of those, who are in authority, to see that justice is enforced and that the interests of the commonwealth are guarded, that the brute force of money, combined with boundless selfishness, should be established as a system to enslave the whole nation. The evasion of our social politicians, who maintain that these results of modern life are inevitable, and must be "surmounted", is equivalent to the consolation, given to a man, who is unable to swim, that, in any case, he would also have to learn how not-to drown.

PREMIUMS FOR THOSE EMPLOYED AND THE COST INVOLVED IN CARRYING ON THIS METHOD OF TRADING

How thoroughly unsound the business principles are in the great "Stores", is shown by the evidence of Dr. Josef Lux, who maintains that many of the "Stores" have different prices for certain customers and for certain times of the day.

A salesman, who had been employed in a "Stores", informs us that the employees were instructed to exploit the weaknesses and inattentiveness of the public. A leading principle was that, if possible, no one should be allowed to leave the building without making a purchase. If a certain article was too dear for a customer, after several ingenious attempts had been made to persuade him or her to take something else, the same article would be produced again at a lower price under the pretext that it was of a different quality. Further, that salesmen and saleswomen were instructed, if the opportunity presented itself, to charge more than the goods had actually been priced at. In this case they receive special premiums for the excess profits, which they have been instrumental in obtaining.

How often the employees at the "Stores" are tempted to purloin the goods is only too well known. The Law Courts are incessantly engaged with cases of this kind.[41] Several years ago in the Berlin Courts, in one case alone, 54 salesmen and saleswomen as well as the head of a department out of the same "Stores", received sentences.

The idea, that the working expenses of the "Stores" are lower than those of other businesses, is erroneous. The peculiar conditions, under which these great businesses are worked, call for all kinds of arrangements, which can be dispensed with in sound businesses.

In order to protect themselves in some measure against thefts, both by employees and customers, most of the great "Stores" engage and maintain a number of detectives, secret agents, inspectors and searchers, whose business it is to keep both the public and the staff under continual observation and control; and daily a number of the staff, as well as of the customers, are detained at the exits, and are conducted to a room, where they must divest themselves of their clothing in order to be thoroughly searched. The moral effects of this bodily examination need only be hinted at. It is by no means excluded that a perfectly innocent customer might have suspicion deliberately directed against her, and would consequently be exposed to a search of this kind.

In any case, the "Stores" are bound to maintain a large staff of people, whose sole duty consists in dealing with the moral damage, which follows as a matter of course in the train of this novel method of conducting business, and this, of course, increases the expenses enormously. If one also takes into account the continuous and costly advertising, which the "Stores" are quite unable to do without, it ought to be sufficiently clear that these modern

---

[41] In No. 182 of the "*Hammer*" there is an article entitled: "34 Summonses in one "Store", and in No. 239 an article under the heading: "Morality in the 'Stores'".

undertakings cannot spell progress from an economic point of view, and that they are not at all in the position to deliver genuine goods at lower prices than other businesses. They are only able to keep themselves going by deceiving the public, and by lowering the quality of the goods.

Moreover, they have a devastating effect upon the economic existence of the middle-class, and, in this respect also, bring again a whole row of social evils in their train.

Trepreau ascribes the appalling falling-off in the number of marriages in France to the herding-together of the unmarried of both sexes in the enormous business barracks, which are called "business emporiums" or "stores".

It is just the women and girls, who never think that by supporting the "Stores" they are sinning against their own sex. If one only pauses for a moment to consider that, owing to the growing power of the great capitalistic "Stores", the possibility of a man of the middle-class ever establishing himself in a business of his own is quite precluded, marriage becomes more and more remote for many men, and more and more women are consequently driven to seek some means of making their own livelihood, one is finally bound to admit that, by reason of the development of the "Stores" system, the woman-question has become considerably more acute.

Thus it is the women themselves, who help to destroy their own social position when they give their custom to the great "Stores".

* * * * *

Lambrecht thus sums up the result of his investigations: the system of concentration in retail-trade offers no social advantages, which are not far outbalanced by other great disadvantages. The latter are leading towards a social condition full of danger, and which must be regarded as less advantageous and desirable when compared with the soundness and many-sidedness of the smaller businesses, each of which confines itself to one special branch of trade.

Regarded from the social point of view, it is the ethical forces, and not the economic, which must decide the issue.

Already all the older civilisations have gone to ruin because they would not recognise this truth about the accumulation of all wealth in a few hands, and the consequent impoverishment of the masses. What leads to decay cannot be called progress. For us, however, material self-enrichment must not be carried on to the detriment of morality, and the general welfare must not be sacrificed in order that profiteering shall flourish. The mission of the truly moral system of government remains unaltered, viz, to respect and protect the economically-weak man, who, at the same time, can well be the best man when judged from the physical and moral point of view. A particularly valuable social quality of the middle-class is moderation in all its needs and requirements, even in its aspirations after honours and riches; for, only in this case, can there be a fairly good distribution of prosperity, and a cheerful state of well-being be made possible for the community. The entire mechanism of acquisition, which has been placed at the absolute disposal of an unrestrained lust for gain, has not increased either the health, or the safety, or the happiness of human individuals.

The social consequences of an evolution along these lines are: monotony, degeneration, and a gradual disappearance of the aesthetic sense and taste; degradation of personality and of the individual, and lack of an appropriate field of activity; suppression of the artistic industry. This whole series of appearances are the forerunners and symptoms of the decay of a nation, and of its culture.

It is almost superfluous to add that the great "Stores", in all parts of the world, are almost exclusively in the hands of Hebrews, and that it is in this particular domain that the Jewish business spirit celebrates its questionable triumphs.

* * * * *

A press, which represents every political party, and is always at the service of the great "Stores" on account of the rich harvest, which it derives from the advertisements of these establishments, has, up till now, helped to present these modern bazaars of rubbish in the most favourable light, and to write all manner of nice things about them. It has, in any case, refrained altogether from exposing the terrible nature of the economic, social and moral damage which is inseparably connected with the management and working of these great emporiums. Thus, for the sake of money, a grave crime is perpetrated against our nation.

When women, in particular, in the attempt to justify their patronage of these establishments, offer the excuse that it is so convenient to do their shopping at the "Stores", they should be reminded that convenience is a property or quality, which ultimately can be used to justify any kind of indolence and carelessness, and that it becomes an absolute vice when it is referred to as an excuse for supporting dubious undertakings. This much-praised convenience is, however, as all genuine frequenters of the great "Stores" will, without exception, admit, inseparably bound up with an incalculable expenditure of time, and with many other drawbacks as well, so that in reality, double as much inconvenience is experienced as if one had made the purchases in separate shops. The dawdling about in the "Stores" is already recognised as one of the modern feminine vices, which the Hebrew knows so well how to foster.

If all the facts, which have been portrayed above, were only sufficiently known, the great "Stores" would soon lose their fascinating splendour in the eyes of all thoughtful people. Most of all, it is to be hoped that the conscience will awake in our womankind, and will ask itself the question, if it is consonant with decency and morality to support, with their custom, these questionable emporiums of trash, and thus to condemn whole classes of our nation to economic and moral ruin. It is fully time that the customers realised at last their social responsibility. Whoever, for the sake of a paltry and often merely an apparent advantage, supports businesses founded on questionable principles, whoever shows favour to an unwholesome and immoral development, must not be surprised when the consequences of his ill-considered trading finally turn against him; for the morbid principle, spreading always further and further, endangers the social order and moral welfare, and helps to establish conditions, which most seriously menace social and national stability. Our cultured ladies have opportunity enough to observe and deplore the growing laxity of public morals; it never seems to occur to them, however, that they themselves have helped to undermine the spirit, which makes for order and morality, by the support, which they give to these questionable business-undertakings, which pander solely to fashion. It is more especially the possessing and cultured classes, who ought to be conscious of their social duties, and who ought not — sometimes out of stinginess, and sometimes out of a lust for spending — to give their custom and support to these dubious trading concerns, and thereby to set a bad example to those below them in the social scale. The principle of the great "Stores" is uneconomic, unsocial and immoral; and out of these great lanterns of modern times, erected to attract and dazzle, issues a spirit, which threatens to poison and demoralise all society from top to bottom: the spirit greedy for gain at any cost, the spirit of vain boastfulness and of pleasure-seeking, the spirit of frivolity, of bodily and spiritual sickness, in fact of megalomania.

Whoever has regard for our nation and its future, whoever has not already made it a habit to barter his moral consciousness for momentary enjoyment and momentary advantage, ought now to understand clearly, in which direction we are bound, if we continue to give our support to lax morality in business affairs, and other paths of life; for, all offence against good sense and morality, by destroying both state and society, attacks finally both us and our posterity.

XI

MORAL PRINCIPLES IN TRADE

Many people consider themselves very clever when they impart the advice to the merchant, who complains that he is unable to hold his own against the Jews: do the same as the Jew! In reality, this amounts to the following: do not recognise any religious motives whatever in your mode of doing business, and descend to the level of a low money-grubber and voluptuary. The economic principle of the Jew threatens to trample under foot, in our time, all other higher principles of life. That, however, is no evidence of its superiority, but of the contrary — its moral inferiority; for, the supposition that, if all forces have free play, the better and the nobler must win, is erroneous. On the contrary, what Goethe said, remains true for all time:

Nobody should complain about what is base, For it remains all-powerful, whatever people may say.

So far as ordinary, everyday life is concerned, what is low and devoid of scruple wins invariably, if it is allowed free play — just as surely as the manners of the quadruped prevail over those of the civilised man if both are compelled to live in the same room, and to feed out of the same trough. The task assigned to anyone, who has a desire to promote real culture, consists in subduing or eradicating what is vile, in order that it may not smother what is noble, before the latter can arrive at full development. Whoever is desirous of rearing choice plants in his garden, must wage incessant warfare against weeds and insect pests. Unfortunately in our time, the morality, belonging to the higher culture, has been neglected and forgotten, namely, the wil l to control , and the right to control , which is the prerogativ e of al l that is noble. When one no longer dared to think, and to act like an aristocrat, everything became vulgar and plebeian; and the Hebrew is the leading dancer in the Cancan of vulgarity. He calls this descent into vulgarity "Progress", and designates, on the other hand, everything of an aristocratic or noble nature, as out-of-date or reactionary.

Society, in former days, possessed an organic structure; it separated itself, practically automatically, into classes, whose rights and duties were conscientiously defined and graduated. Thus, a genuine social and moral order came into being, which secured to each man such prosperity as he was entitled to, and assigned to him his due share of rights, as well as duties. The Hebrew has shattered this ancient moral order to pieces. He has absolutely no perception for a moral structure of this kind; to his eyes it appears merely a jumble of disconnected fragments; he is incapable of understanding the purpose of all this regulated coherence. He regards every restraint as a fetter, and as an interference with his liberty. In addition to his greed for gain, the Hebrew is, for this reason, driven by an irresistible impulse, before all other things, to dissolve all old-established associations, and to break up all arrangements, which are the outcome of social organisation. He calls for "Freedom" and "Equality", but whether he does so out of pure calculation, or reacts in response to some dark instinct, it is difficult to say; at any rate, he knows for certain that, on the dissolution of all social bonds, he and his fellow-conspirators will gain the upper hand in the ensuing chaos. Thus, it is that he demands — loudly and incessantly — "Free play for the exercise of every kind of power", which, in reality, amounts to: "Privilege for unscrupulousness, and domination by those, who conspire in secret."

There is no doubt whatever that the phrase "Freedom and Progress" has provided the Hebrew with a slogan, which he has known how to make his own particular property, certainly not to procure freedom for others but to procure license for himself, and to unsettle and seduce others to desert the firm union of time-honoured organisation, so that, disorganised and isolated, they may, all the more easily, fall into his power. In spite of this, it is his constant boast that, by breaking down the old restrictions, he has introduced a desirable and beneficial freedom into the economic life;

and, to a superficial observer, this may well appear to be true. But, in reality, a ruthless campaign of all against all has been instituted, which has certainly produced, as its first and immediate result, a release of all kinds of forces, and a stimulating and goading of the economic life to an alarming extent, but which must eventually exhaust the most valuable activities in a nation, and end in a complete victory for those, who are most ruthless and dishonest.

In former times, there were also no lack of stimulating competition; it was, however, of quite a different kind. The competition then, was in the good quality of what was produced; whoever sold the best goods, secured the most custom. The Hebrew, by "cutting" prices, has reversed the nature of the competition; for today, the low value of the goods produced is the principal object of the commercial rivalry of the world. Whoever can manage to offer goods at an exceedingly low price — without any consideration for the quality, or, at any rate, only with the appearance of quality — is assured of success. And, whoever makes use of deception, in addition, can rely upon brilliant results. Unclean competition has usurped the position, once occupied by sound and straightforward commercial rivalry.

There is no doubt whatever — as has been stated already on page 99 — that the ancient guilds, which the Hebrew invariably abuses as a reactionary system, possessed their good features. They not only required proof of the capability of each craftsman, but they tested also the quality of what was produced. Each master had to answer for the genuineness of the goods, which he produced, and the guild- or hall-mark furnished the article produced with evidence of its soundness. At the time spoken of, there still existed a morality in business, which, at the present day, has dwindled away to such an extent, that only some pitiful traces are still to be found, here and there. That mutual "hunting-down" of customers, which was formerly regarded as dishonourable, is, today, the special boast of the Hebrew. In those days there was a maxim: "No one must force his way into the business of another, or push his own business to such an extent that another citizen is ruined thereby." This amount of morality, this amount of regard for one's neighbour, this amount of social sense are unknown in the business-life of today. The announcement that one would accept lower prices than one's competitors, was regarded, in olden times, as the lowest degree of commercial impropriety. The Hebrew, with mental machinery of an entirely different kind, has no sympathy with such dignity and propriety. These appear to him merely as irksome restrictions, which make it more difficult to earn money; for this reason he rejects them. An inevitable sequel to these modern business maxims and views is the relaxation of all morality, and of all social ties throughout the community. One looks around and asks one's self, if humanity indeed has made any moral or social advance since those olden days.

Whilst the merchant of former times knew how to preserve the dignity of the independent man, and in the course of trading, never sacrificed his self-respect in order to obtain business, the Hebrew, on the contrary, has degraded the entire domain of commerce, and has cast honour and shame to the winds, simply to create business. He has introduced into the economic life that degrading hurry and scurry, which wears the soles off the boots in order to steal a march on a competitor, and sacrifices self-respect and decency sooner than allow any business to go elsewhere.

Only the grossest form of self-deception could enable anyone to imagine that this kind of mutual "hunting-down" is of the slightest value from an economic point of view. In reality this excessive activity is accompanied by a crazy waste of energy. Formerly, as now, the merchant found his customers, but the whole process was carried on, and completed itself, in a peaceful and dignified fashion. The merchant could wait until the customer came; and the customer came, surely enough, for there was nobody interested in alienating him. Thus all business traffic pursued the even tenor of its way, without haste and without excitement, and a man could obtain a decent subsistence without infringement of his self- respect. At the present day, business people harry one another to death, for each has the feeling that a potential robber is lurking in ambush, in his preserve, ready to waylay his customers and to take their money if he does not come up quickly to prevent it.

This hurry and nervousness, peculiar to present-day business, first made their appearance when the Jewish traders assumed the ascendancy. Sombart says:

"The world, well-arranged as it used to be, with all its ancient soundness and solidity was simply taken by storm by the Jews, and we behold this people, stride by stride, thrusting back the former economic order and economic mode of thinking."

Actually, this assault by the Hebrews on our Aryan world is not only an attack on our economic arrangements, but is simultaneously an attempt to undermine the very foundations of our moral system. Sombart certainly gives it as his opinion, that transgressions against the precepts of rectitude and morality are part and parcel of human nature. We protest against such a conception. Certainly there have always been individuals, who have not known how to remain within the limits, appointed by rectitude and morality, but they were invariably denounced as bunglers and disturbers, and regarded accordingly. Respect for the restraints of law and sound morality must be set down as a fundamental and marked feature of the Aryan or Nordic mode of living and thought; and if, at the present day, we are scarcely aware of the possession of this quality, we at any rate know, that it was bad example and dire necessity, which compelled us to cast it from us. He, who wishes to compete on equal terms with the Hebrew, must descend to the moral level of the latter.

This dire necessity has forced itself upon the German merchant, at an earlier date, than upon his brother traders in other countries, as Germany, on account of its political disruption, has fallen an easier prey to the Jew than any other of the ancient lands of culture. Two hundred years ago, the German name already laboured under the misfortune of being used as a cloak by the Jews. When the Jewish business people began to come into prominence, an English writer (1745) expressed his indignation, that there were certain people, who publicly announced their readiness to sell their goods at lower prices than their fellow-traders. He stigmatized this unseemly "cutting" of prices, as shameless. In England, "Dutchmen", that is to say, taken literally, "Germans", were regarded as being the instigators of this practice. It was really the inhabitants of Holland, however, who were meant, and who, up till the year 1648, belonged politically to the German Empire, and were then, as now, called "Dutchmen." It is these people i. e. the Dutch Jews, whom we Germans have to thank for the unpleasant fact that, even now, the English and Americans refer contemptuously to the Germans as "Dutchmen." The Dutch Hebrews, who arrived in England at that time, were the real originators of under-bidding, and of the traffic in shoddy merchandise. The Jews also, who were hunted out of Spain, and fled, for the most part, to Holland, made their sinister influence felt upon the destinies of us Germans. Soon after 1700, they had already begun a system of predatory culture in a recovering Germany; the book-trade serves as an instance, upon which particular business they conferred the questionable benefit of sales, on a gigantic scale, at book-auctions, a practice, which they had introduced in Holland, because the profit by the old-fashioned method of selling volume by volume was acquired too slowly to suit their taste. In modern times also, it is much to be regretted that the German merchant has accustomed himself to, and definitely accepted, all kinds of unseemly practices, which were formerly the monopoly of the Hebrews. Sombart allows that Jewish ethics differ from those of mankind in general, and that those offences on the part of Jews against public morality cannot be laid to the account of any individual in particular, but arise rather from those general ideas regarding life and business morality, which are implanted in the Jewish nature. He asks (page 153):

"What really then was specifically Jewish? And is one entitled to assume, in general a peculiar idiosyncrasy in the attitude of the Jew towards all enduring arrangements? I believe so; yes, and I believe that this specific Jewish characteristic of infringing the law, expresses, before everything else, the idea that the Jews regard their offences against right and morality, as not being the particular concern of any individual amongst them, but rather as being the discharge of a code of commercial morality, accepted by and current amongst the Jews, and that their business habits are only those, which are sanctioned by the majority of the Jewish business people. We are bound to conclude, from the general and continued practice of fixed customs, that the Jews do not at all regard their irregular mode of trading as immoral, and consequently as unpermissible, but are convinced, on the contrary, that they are acting in a perfectly moral manner — the "correct" right as opposed to a ridiculous conception of right and morality."

As a matter of fact, our moral perception of things is "senseless" so far as the Hebrew is concerned; it is too lofty for him. If there is any pronounced feature about Hebrewdom, whereby it can at once be distinguished from the rest of humanity, it is precisely this absence of moral sensitiveness. In reality the Hebrew is a lower type of being, in whom all those qualities are wanting, which confer a real dignity upon mankind—honour, a sense of shame, a conscience and moral consciousness. As our entire existence is confined within these barriers, we are naturally not so free to carry on the competitive struggle, whether it be of a spiritual or economic nature, so effectively as the person, who declines to recognise any such restraints. Just as a cleanly being steps aside to avoid a foul mire, into which a swine plunges with satisfaction, so does a man, with clean instincts, revolt against following the Hebrew into the swamp of moral degradation. If he tries to do so, either he or his better nature is ruined.

And this is the peculiar difficulty of the present time, that we have allowed ourselves to be overcome by the swinish predilection of the Hebrew, that we have descended from our moral altitude, in order to scuffle with him in the mud and mire for our daily fodder. It is vain to hope that one will ever be able to elevate the Hebrew to the plane of nobler manhood; for at least three thousand years, he has shown himself to be incapable of improvement, and he will always remain so. It is a fallacy to maintain that this moral deficiency made itself so glaringly conspicuous in the Jew, owing to his compulsory detention in the Ghetto, and would leave him as soon as he was permitted to move freely in a moral community. This fond expectation has been bitterly disappointed by the actual facts: the Hebrew, with his insensibility for higher moral values, will invariably drag down the rest of the community to his own low level, whenever he is permitted full scope for his baneful activity. The same presumption has shown itself to be false also, in countries, where the Jews have enjoyed unrestricted freedom for centuries, such countries for instance, as England, the Netherlands and the United States. In these lands, as well as in France, where they have had complete civic rights since the end of the eighteenth century, and now are the undisputed masters,[42] their nature has not altered by one hair-breadth.

Sombart speaks in the highest terms of a certain Jewess, the so-called "Glückel von Hameln," who lived from 1645 to 1724, and wrote her own biography. But, in spite of his praise, he added the significant remark: "All the aspirations and endeavours, all the thoughts and feelings of this woman centred themselves on Money. For the whole 313 pages of her memoirs, she speaks of nothing else but money, and of acquiring riches." (Page 156). And it is this trait especially, which proclaims the lower nature, and which predominates in the Hebrew; for we are entitled to maintain with confidence, that the man is by so much the more spiritual and moral, the less his thoughts are influenced by material considerations. The noblest spirits, taken from any period, have seldom been good managers. The interest concerning money did not occupy their minds to any considerable extent, and was regarded as a secondary consideration. It was the noble Nazarene, who announced: "You cannot serve both God and Mammon." The more idealism, the more spiritual purity and dignity, and the less regard for money.

The Hebrew endeavours to substitute cunning in the place of the idealism, in which he is so conspicuously lacking, and to compensate for his deficiency in moral feeling and in deep instincts, by a more subtle understanding. The intellect — the cool power of calculation — belongs, by no manner of means, to the higher spiritual functions; invariably it forms but a poor substitute for the deeper spiritual forces, which are wanting, for the feeling and perceiving discernment of things and connections between things. Just as the Hebrew endeavours in the economic life to substitute the mere possession of money for the ability to work and create, in which he is so deficient, so does he endeavour to conceal his lack of

---

[42] After Martin, Levy is the name, which occurs most frequently in the French business world, a fact which the well-known Dr. Bertillon has established by reference to the various address-books. (T-gl. Rundschau, Nr. 291 of 1913).

the deeper, spiritual capacity by a veneer of sham culture. It is, for this reason, very questionable praise, when Sombart refers again and again to the "pre-eminent intellectuality" of the Jews; In reality, all that he means is the mental cunning, the subtle process of calculation, which is peculiar to a low order of intellect.

DEVIATION IN THE TREND OF JEWISH LIFE

Now we will occupy ourselves for a short time with the economic side of the matter: the Hebrew desires to possess riches in order to obtain mastery over others, and to oppress them; and it is in this particular, where there is a great difference between the acquisition of money by Jews, and the acquisition of money by other races. Certainly there are plenty of business people amongst Aryans and Christians, whose inclination is predominantly towards making money, and people, enough and to spare, who do not pay much attention to the moral side of the question, and regard all means and methods as equally good, provided that money can be acquired thereby. But, in one respect, they impose a restriction on themselves; they content themselves with guarding and enjoying their wealth; they do not begrudge others, besides themselves, the opportunity to acquire wealth and to enjoy it. It is quite different where the Hebrew is concerned. It is, as if he is consumed by an inappeasable hatred towards all, who happen to possess something; as if he felt himself alone entitled to claim all material possessions in this world for himself and for his people; as if he could not rest so long as goods and money still remained in the hands of those, who are not Jews. This frame of mind finds unconcealed expression in the Talmudic-Rabbinical writings. One finds there, for instance: "God created the world solely for the Jews, and accordingly all property in the world belongs to the Jews." The Talmud therefore declares: "The possessions of those, who are not Jews, are equivalent to possessions without an owner and the first, who seizes the same, is entitled to them."

This is no theoretical interpretation; the Jews take it, and act on it in deadly earnest. They regard it as their special mission in life to travel all over the earth in order to acquire all the possessions of the Goyim. They do not consider that they have fulfilled their duty to their God, Jahweh, until all the riches in the world are in their hands, so that they can lay the same at the feet of their idol. It is for this reason that the real Jew is animated by a feverish restlessness to dispossess the Goy of his property. It is, as if he suffered mental distress, so long as there remained any property in his vicinity, which he had not yet acquired. It is precisely this behaviour, which draws such a sharp dividing line between the Jewish and "Christian" business and usury practices. The Hebrew does not only desire to gain, but to ruin and enslave others as well. The young deputy Bismarck, speaking in the Landtag of 1847, furnished a classical proof of this contention:

"I will give an example, which contains the whole history of the relations existing between Jew and Christian. — I know a rural district where the Jewish population is numerous, where there are peasants, who cannot call a single object on their farms their own property, where the entire furniture, from the bed to the stove, belongs to the Jew, and where the peasant pays a rent for each separate piece of furniture; the growing corn and the corn in the barn belong to the Jew, and the Jew sells the corn for bread, seed and feeding purposes back to the peasant again, by the peck. I, at any rate, in the course of my professional duties, have never come across nor even heard of a Christian practising usury comparable with this."

Anyone, who is acquainted with the activity of the Jews in Bavarian Franconia, in Hesse, in the north of Würtemberg and other places, can provide more than enough instances of a similar kind.

The Jew, when doing business, is always impelled by a double motive: not only does he desire advantage for himself, but he wishes, at the same time, to cause damage to the other side. It is for this reason, that he will not reject a piece of business, that brings him in nothing, so long as it serves his purpose of weakening others. His aim is to sweep all competitors away. "He does not ask", says Sombart, "if a profit can be made or not, or if it will be necessary to work for a time without making a profit, simply in order that, later on, he may make all the more profit". This is the "great", startling innovation, which the Jew has introduced into business life, and which celebrates its economic triumph in the form of the great "Stores". At the back of the Jewish fighting tactic, is always lurking the idea of monopoly — of sole domination — the desire to annihilate all competitors.

A dark instinct for disturbance and destruction, for confusion and dissolution, all of which facilitate the plundering of others, is the most marked feature in the Hebrew; for, in the universal ruin, the richest booty falls to his share. In this respect he resembles the vulture, which, scenting its prey, hovers over the battle-field. The ruin of others brings him his surest spoil. Whilst the merchant of former days willingly restricted his activities to dealing in one speciality, in one particular district, the Hebrew, by preference, deals everywhere with everybody. The former division of trade, according to specialities, had the great advantage of enabling the merchant to acquire a far more thorough knowledge of his goods, and, at the same time, to provide, in his particular line, the greatest variety of choice. The Hebrew, on the contrary, whose original business-occupation was always in the old-clothes shop, in which secondhand articles of all kinds were to be found, has not been able, even at the present day, to free himself of his preference for a medley of second-hand rubbish: he preserves the character and atmosphere of the old-clothes shop, even in his emporiums of trash and his great "stores"; yes, and even into his great industrial undertakings. Even Sombart perceives in all this, what he describes as a characteristically Jewish touch, and acknowledges that the great "stores" are almost exclusively in Jewish hands.

Sombart mentions with pride, that the Hebrews are the fathers of the "hire-purchase" business; and this may well be the case. (Compare page 117). One must not run away with the idea, which is for ever being trumpeted forth in the advertisements of these business, namely that sympathy with the small man was the motive, which originated them. A far different tendency is at the root of the movement. Just as the Hebrew buys up the harvest, for a mere song, from a peasant, who is short of money, or is in other difficulties, while the grain is still on the stalk and even before it is ripe, so does he secure for himself, by means of the "hire-purchase" system, all the wages of the poor man for weeks and months in advance. In Faust the Jew is spoken of as follows:

"Er schafft Antizipationen—
Die Schweine kommen nicht zu Fette,
Verpfändet ist der Pfühl im Bette,
Und auf den Tisch kommt vorgegessen Brot."

(Goethe)

["He creates anticipations...
The swine are never left to fatten
Pawned is the pillow in the bed
And the very bread, which is placed on the table,
has been eaten in advance."]

The Jew knows how to prevent the unfortunate people from taking their money elsewhere, by binding them over in a legal agreement, to assign the proceeds of their labour to him for a long time in advance. The "hire-purchase" system is therefore a particular and valuable link in the chain of business operations, by which the Jews suck up the money in circulation. It prevents the saving of money by those, who are not Jews, and quickens the return flow, even of the smallest stream of money, into the reservoir of Judah. Certainly all these Jewish practices have introduced a novel and peculiar atmosphere into modern business life, but it is certainly not a healthy and beneficial one. The final injurious effects of this kind of commercial activity upon the economic life are not immediately apparent, for the excessive stimulation of the economic life produces, with its colour, variety and movement, a positively dazzling effect. But it is no less certain that this Jewish tendency, in the economic life, is continually bringing public morality to a lower and lower level, and is destroying all regard for the general welfare of the community. The principle of ruthless selfishness has obtained the mastery, and the right of the individual to enrich himself, by any and every means, has established itself, even if the rest of the community suffer grievously thereby, and both state and morality are sacrificed. Social harmony has been replaced by mutual enmity, everybody fights everybody, and this can only end in universal destruction. It is no longer a cause for wonder when active business people break down prematurely from nervous exhaustion in their best years, and when all manner of insidious diseases and social disorders arise out of this mad state of affairs. We are being continually and insistently informed that all this must be so — that all this is inseparable from progress. We perceive, at any rate, that the physical and mental powers of mankind are giving way, under these malign influences, to the verge of complete extinction.

This method of destruction must be opposed by a wise and sensible discipline, whereby all the material requirements of life can be satisfied without impairing the constitutive powers of mankind. This disciplinary system must adopt, as its standard, the principle that the preservation and elevation of mankind are of more importance than the mere increase of business, and the accumulation of world riches.

XII

THE HEBREWS AS SUPPORTERS

OF CAPITALISM

S ombart advances the question as to whether the Jew possesses a special capacity for capitalism. It appears most extraordinary to us that such a question should ever have been propounded. Capitalism is not an activity, which calls for a special kind of capacity, but a condition, the cultivation or administration of which, calls for certain qualifications. Even, in the case of the Hebrew, capitalism, for its own sake, is not regarded as the main object, but rather as a means for increasing his own power, and for enslaving those, who are not Jews.

Thus, the question will take the following shape: does the Hebrew possess a special talent for amassing capital, and for giving a capitalistic formation to the economic life? Nobody has ever been in doubt concerning this fact.

Sombart claims for the Hebrews the merit of being the founders and upholders of modern world-wide commerce, of modern finance, of the Stock Exchange, in fact, of the commercialisation of the entire economic life; of being the parents of free trade, and of free competition, of being the exponents of the modern spirit in the realm of business. We will cheerfully concede all this, but, at the same time it is perfectly clear to us, that this modern spirit is by no means a good spirit, for it is the spirit of the disintegration of political economy, of the destruction of the productive nations. The explanation of the idea of capitalism, which, according to Sombart, is as follows, seems strange indeed to us:

"Capitalism is the name we give to that organisation of economic intercourse, by which two different groups of the population — the owners of the means of production, who, at the same time, carry on the work of directing, and the ordinary work-people who own nothing — cooperate, so indeed that the representatives of Capital (i. e. of the requisite store of the necessary goods) are the real economic subjects, that is to say, hold the power of deciding the nature and direction of the economic management, and bear the responsibility for the issue, whatever it may be" (page 186).

According to this, Capitalism characterises itself as the economic method of the proletarian state, which is ruled and guided unresistingly by a few financial magnates, as a new edition of slavery in its most acute form. In actuality, this is the ideal of the Hebrew, to whom it has been promised in the Talmud, that a time will come when every Jew will possess 2800 slaves. The only question is whether the other nations regard such a state of things as desirable, and are willing to help to bring it about.

This might be expressed in a somewhat more general fashion as follows: the capitalistic economic system regards the formation of capital as the principal aim of economic activity. According to this system, capital, and not man, is of most importance. This system places man and his spiritual needs on a lower plane than the accumulation of capital. Money-making is regarded as the first principle of life. And the object of this creation of capital? — the domination and exploitation of mankind by means of loan-servitude.

Formerly the earning of money was a side-issue in the economic life; the other, and more important object was: on the one hand, the satisfaction of human needs by the production of the requisite goods, and the guaranteeing, on the other hand, of the possibility of an existence for the producer, as well as for the business or middle-man. The man, and the possibility of his existence, were always the chief consideration. According to the capitalistic system of the Hebrew, the matter was regarded in a very different light. Sombart is of opinion that:

- Out of a systematic direction of economic affairs, for the purpose of making profit, which thereby provides the incentive for the effort to expand continuously all kinds of business activity, arises, as a natural consequence, a conscious guiding or directing of all trading activity towards the supreme reasonable method of establishing and maintaining economic relations."

It is certainly true that the economic life receives a very marked warp or distortion in one particular direction, if one enquires every moment what profit can be made, but we certainly cannot recognise the method just described as the "supreme rational"; it is rather supremely irrational, because it is so busily engaged in the mad accumulation of capital that it entirely disregards the aim of all culture: namely the preservation and elevation of mankind.

In olden times the economic method was grounded firmly on the principle of organic growth and building-up, but the modern Jewish economic method aims at a ruthless extermination — at the so-called predatory culture. It drags riches together, from all directions, at the cost of human welfare; it produces wares, which, to a considerable extent, serve but one purpose, and that is simply to entice and trick money out of the pockets of the people; it creates a few rich by the indebtedness and impoverishment of the masses. But, above all, it uses up human energy to such an extent, that it must soon end in the exhaustion and decline of the nation.

It is characteristic of this capitalistic system that it is unable to realise the effects of its own action — that it is actually killing the goose, which lays the golden eggs. Impelled by the short-sighted greed for amassing money, it wrecks the organic foundations of national life. Is there perhaps design behind all this? Is this Jewish-capitalistic economic method perhaps the means to the end of fulfilling the ancient commandment: "Thou shalt eat up all nations?"

Sombart asks the question:

"What is the meaning in the capitalistic sense of a successful stroke of business? Naturally that this activity, with its terms and conditions, should be followed by a good result. In what way however, is this successful result to be gauged? Certainly not by the quality of the performance. Just as little by the quantity. All the more, simply and solely, if. . ."

The reader expects now to hear: whether, under the operation of this beneficial, capitalistic system, Culture and Humanity are to be conducted to a still higher plane, or: whether Morality and Social Arrangement are to show a gratifying advance?

- Oh, dear no; completely erroneous! According to Sombart, the beneficial result of this economic method is to be gauged solely as follows:

"If, at the end of an economic period the advanced money is again in hand, and has brought with it something additional, which we call profit" (page 188).

The sublime blessings, to be derived from this economic system, could not be stated in a more pertinent manner, and one must infer that Sombart is a man, with a very keen sense of sarcastic humour, who, under the pretext of recognition, is desirous of exposing, in these words, the utter barrenness of capitalism. Even the question is not asked, whether an improvement in the production of goods is the result of this economic method — no: "the sole consideration is, that at the conclusion of the transaction, the gain in money or property remains in the hands of the capitalist, who took it in hand." — Mankind, you have no need to be alarmed; capitalistic Jewdom is conducting you towards a splendid goal:

"... so that the debit and credit of the ledger shall be closed with a balance in favour of the enterprising capitalist. In this effect are included all the successes and all the transactions, undertaken by the capitalistic organisation." (Sombart p. 188)

What is then an undertaker or contractor in the capitalistic sense? "He is a man," says Sombart, "who has a task to fulfil, and sacrifices his life in fulfilling it."[43] Certainly there are undertakers or contractors of this kind but, for the most part, they are not of Jewish origin. Certainly there are men, who, with the sacrifice of their entire physical and mental energy, devote themselves to some great work and who can be described as actually sacrificing their lives for these objects. Great industrialists, such as Krupp, Borsig, Schichau, Hartmann and many others were men of this stamp, but we certainly do not find Hebrews amongst them. The Rothschilds, Bleichröders, Guttmanns, Hirschs have accumulated hundreds of millions, in a few decades, but we search in vain for any great and astounding work, which they have accomplished; we see, at the most, that they have known how to exploit, in the most cunning fashion, other men, who have been the real producers, in order to amass enormous riches for themselves; we are unable to perceive that they have in any way hazarded their lives, while engaged in this kind of business. They were the money-lenders and speculators, who finally pocketed the entire benefit accruing from the work of others, without themselves accomplishing anything worth mentioning. If Sombart means, that the real promoter of undertakings must be a combination of producer and dealer, it does not say much for the Hebrew capitalists as far as the promotion or origination of undertakings is concerned, for, as a rule, we find nothing of the productive element in them, only the dealer. And the latter Sombart defines in the following manner:

"The dealer is a man, desirous of lucrative business, all of whose ideas and feelings are concentrated upon the value in money of conditions and negotiations, and who therefore consistently regards all phenomena in terms of money; for whom the world is a great market of supply and demand, of crises and occasions, of possibilities of gains and losses, who is always asking: How much does it cost and what does it yield? And whose incessant questions in this respect resolve themselves into the final momentous one: What does the world cost?"

---

[43] A strange formulary! Just as if the official, the officer, the doctor, the workman etc had not also tasks to fulfil, and might not with equal right be said to sacrifice their lives in fulfilling the same!

Truly, the character and behaviour of the Hebrew, as dealer, could not be better portrayed, and we have a strong suspicion that Herr Sombart is, in reality, a cleverly disguised opponent of the Jews. With still more exquisite irony, he characterises the Hebrew actually as "discoverer" — namely as the discoverer of fresh possibilities of "doing business", who knows full well, how and where to discharge his goods, when there is not the slightest requirement nor demand for the same, and who, in order to excite new needs, provides Esquimos with bathing- drawers and niggers with hot-water bottles. And Sombart also knows full well how to portray the tenacious importunity of the Hebrew, when he characterises the specifically Jewish talent for dealing, as the art of,

"Acquiring a pair of old trousers by cunningly wearing out the patience of a needy cavalier, to whose apartments he may already have been five times without accomplishing his purpose, in order, later on, to talk some peasant into buying the garment, by exercising all his powers of persuasion."

According to Sombart, amongst the other requirements of the Dealer, must be included a power "to see with a thousand eyes, and to hear with a thousand ears", and this accomplishment has been brought to perfection by Jewdom, by means of the organisation and consistent cooperation of all Jews. The German business-man can only see with his own two eyes, and only in exceptional cases has other eyes at his disposal, to help him to extend his vision. Jewdom, however, has been organised into a Hydra with a thousand heads, which are all attached to the same body, and which all follow the same instinct. This Jewish "dealing" organisation, with its thousand senses, spies upon the artless nations, never lets an opportunity slip of "doing business", and knows how to arrange matters so that the profit always falls to its share.

According to the sound, old, time-honoured ideas, trading or dealing was an honourable exchange, in which one gave either goods for goods, or goods for money; and the sense of fairness regulated the proceeding to mutual satisfaction. In the case of an honestly conducted transaction both sides might well derive advantage and profit therefrom, because the object purchased might be worth more to the purchaser than the price paid, and, at the same time, the seller might secure a profit. It is quite different according to the Jewish perception. Sombart's opinion is, that trading or bargaining means "a struggle with mental weapons", and, in reality, all Jewish trading and bargaining is made up of persuasion, overreaching, false representation and imposition. He is not desirous merely of satisfying a want but, in addition to endeavouring to secure an excessive profit for himself, he attempts to do the other side as much harm as possible. The Hebrews, as a nation, which, for thousands of years, has practised nothing but haggling, usury and overreaching, have developed the art of persuasion to the highest possible point. How often does one not hear simple-natured people, who have been talked into buying the goods of some Jewish pedlar, excuse themselves by saying: "I had to buy something from the man because I could not otherwise get rid of him". Yes, it is impossible to ignore the fact that many Jews — at any rate when they come into contact with artless and ingenuous people — possess an almost demoniacal power of suggestion, and of infatuating simple natures, so that the latter follow unresistingly the intentions of those, who are fooling them. We shall return to this particular theme in chapter XVI: "The influence of the Jew upon Womankind." —

"One of the most effective inward means of coercion, which the Hebrew is in the habit of applying, consists in arousing the idea, that the immediate conclusion of the business in hand will prove advantageous."

Thus speaks Sombart, and the Hebrew knows full well how to utilise this means to the very utmost. It is actually a fact that some Jewish pedlars are in the habit of intimating to possible customers, that the goods they offer, are stolen property, or are taken from a bankrupt's stock, and must, on that account, be disposed of as quickly as possible, and at almost any price.

Sombart rightly refers to the peculiar position of isolation, which the Hebrew takes up in the midst of the other national communities, as a circumstance, which confers exceptional advantages upon him in the midst of the other nations. He emphasizes that the advantages, enjoyed by the Hebrew, are rooted in the following circumstances: 1. in their extensive dispersion, 2. in their alienage, 3. in their half-citizenship, and 4. in their wealth. Unfortunately Sombart has omitted the most important items, namely, 5. the open and the secret connection amongst themselves, and 6. the Jewish morality, which is especially adapted for trading and for deceit.

1. THE EXTENSIVE DISPERSION

The Hebrews, thanks to their extensive dispersion over all lands, are enabled, by means, of their international and domestic connections, which they attend to with the utmost assiduity, to maintain an accurate survey of all economic occurrences in distant, as well as in adjacent territories. By this means they are enabled to secure, at all times, the earliest reliable information concerning the prospect of the crops, concerning the production and sale of goods, concerning stocks of goods in hand, concerning the forwarding of goods, both by land and water, and concerning the circulation of money and any local deficiency of money. It is also known for certain that they mutually exchange most valuable information and hints with respect to these matters — not only by means of the reports in the Press of the various markets and exchanges, which reports are, almost without exception, under their control - but also by means of private letters and dispatches in cipher. Important facts like these, are far too little known and appreciated at their full value in our time. Anyone, who has an inkling of these matters, cannot be in the least surprised at the success of the Jews; he, at any rate, will not gaze upwards with amazement and admiration at the supposed eminent and unusual faculties for trade, possessed by the Jews, because these faculties rest on very ordinary foundations. There have always been men with keen insight, who have seen through these inner workings; but, unfortunately the wisdom of olden times seems lost to the present generation, and it often appears to us as if our teachers and spiritual pastors, as well as our political leaders of today, put on smoked spectacles, so as not to see what is happening before their eyes.

Even in the year 1698, a report from the French Ambassador at the Hague, is devoted to a description of the activities of the Dutch Jews, and of the machinations of these people on the Amsterdam Exchange.[44] Amongst other things, mention is made therein of the secret brotherhoods (Congregations), which the Jews maintain, and which stand in the most intimate connection with one another. For instance, the "Fraternity of Saloniki, which rules over their nation in both those other parts of the world, and is surety for it," and that of "Venice which, together with that of Amsterdam, holds sway over all the northern parts." Mention is also made that these "brotherhoods" are only tolerated in England, and have to be kept secret in France. The result of the intercourse between these "brotherhoods" is, that the Jews are the first and the best informed concerning anything connected with trade, or of a novel nature, and out of this liaison they build up their system (The Speculation), and meet weekly on Sundays for consultation, while the Christians are occupied with their religious duties. The ambassador continues:

"These speculative schemes, which are of a most subtle nature, and have been prepared in accordance with the intelligence, which has come in during the preceding week, are sifted and refined by their Rabbis and learned men, and are then, on the following Sunday, handed over to their Jewish brokers and agents, who are selected for their exceptional craftiness. After the latter have consulted with one another, each of them circulates, on the same day, the news, which is specially adapted to serve their purposes. The next day, they at once set to work buying, selling, exchanging and dealing in shares. As they always have large sums of money and stocks of goods at their disposal, they are always in a position to judge correctly when the right moment has arrived to carry out their "coups", whether at the top or at the bottom of the market, or simultaneously in both directions." (Sombart, page 202.)

This has been, in very truth, the secret of the Jewish brokers for centuries, and it is nothing less than astounding how neither our merchants, nor our learned political economists, nor our politicians, nor our statesmen can see through these secret machinations, and still cling to their naive belief that supply and demand determine the

---

[44] Revue historique. Vol. 44 (1890)

price. In reality, the Hebrews, combined internationally, form a clique for exploring all opportunities, and for systematically influencing all market conditions. Even at the present day, similar conspirators and instigators of the same unsavoury plotting and scheming are to be found amongst the Rabbis, and one can soothe one's self with the reflection that, on occasions, matters are dealt with in the Synagogues, which have nothing to do with the service of God, but which, on the contrary, exhale the very essence of trade and the money-market (compare page 74).

This Jewish system of espionage, and the secret machinations in the synagogues and on the Stock Exchange, place the Hebrew in a position to obtain quicker and more reliable information, concerning all matters, than anybody else in the country, not excepting the Governments. And thus it comes to pass, that the latter, in their naiveté and artlessness, frequently imagine that they must make use of the Hebrew, not only for the purpose of obtaining important news from abroad, but also in order to exert diplomatic influence in all directions. They forget that by doing this, they are putting the cart in front of the horse, and that it is Jewdom and the money-market, which derive thereby all the benefit from any new political move.

Anyone, who is desirous of obtaining a correct idea of the methods and extent of Jewish interference with and intrusion into the higher political circles, should read what Emil Witte, formerly commercial counsellor under v. Holleben at the German Embassy in the United States, has to say in his book "Aus einer deutschen Botschaft. Zehn Jahre deutsch-amerikanischer Diplomatie" (*From a German Embassy. Ten years of German- American diplomacy*). This work is rich in disclosures concerning the nature of, and the position occupied by the two telegraphic agencies of Reuter (London) and Wolff (Berlin), to whom has been assigned the chief rôle of making known important political news to the public by means of the Press.

Whilst dealing with this subject, the following remarks will be of interest, as they afford glimpses into the career of a Jewish adventurer. The founder of the "Reuter Bureau" was born in Cassel of poverty-stricken Jewish parents, and his real name is Josaphat.

After an obscure and apparently turbulent youth, Reuter became partner in a bookseller's business in Berlin; he left this position on account of certain "irregularities", and soon afterwards founded the Reuter Bureau in London, in company with a fellow tribesman, Dr. Engländer, one of those numerous men of honour, who, by their assumed German names, bring everything connected with that country into disrepute abroad, and who was, at the same time, a pronounced Anarchist. With the help of Oscar Meding (Gregor Samarow) the well-known Guelphic author and political agent, he was successful in inducing the blind King George V of Hannover to grant the concession of a telegraph-cable from Lowestoft to Norderney, which he disposed of, in 1869, for a profit of more than £200,000 (over four million marks) to the British Government. Raised to the grade of Baron by Duke Ernst of Coburg-Gotha, he earned large sums of money by acting as impresario to the Shah Nasr-el-Din of Persia, and paid the latter's travelling expenses all over Europe. By so doing, he secured from the Shah, every possible concession, which Persia had to impart.

In order to put a stop to the mutual competition, engendered by the founding in Berlin in 1865 of the telegraphic bureau of Dr. Wolff — also a Jew — Reuter purchased a part share in the same, so that since then the same genius has held sway over the two bureaux. What the nature of this spirit or genius is, can be ascertained later on in this book, at the appropriate place. Here it will suffice to say, that the owner of the R. Bureau — Baron de Reuter — is portrayed as a man, possessed by a demoniacal ambition, who is enabled, by his position and his enormous wealth, to play a pernicious part on the political stage, even though it takes place behind the scenes. A man, moreover, utterly unscrupulous as to the means he employs to enrich, and to advance himself — one can read a great deal more about him in Witte's book — and who was turned out by Bismarck on account of the hostile tone, which his news service always displayed towards Germany. The German Baron had his revenge for this, by securing a dominating influence in the direction of Wolff's Bureau, which is supported by Prussia and Germany, and since then has taken his part in shaping politics in both of these countries by the method peculiar to him. How and when this takes place, the public has never been allowed to learn, although it is a fact of common knowledge in all our newspaper offices, that Reuter's Bureau is the heart and soul of all the foreign animosity towards the German Empire.[45] Thus, this institution, which exists to feed half the world with news — in other words to influence vast masses of people — is connected by the "most intimate ties" with the telegraphic bureau of Wolff, which is domiciled in Berlin. What that means, is expressed by Witte, on page 118, in a quotation from an article in *"Black and White"* by a former Times correspondent—Charles Lowe — concerning the bills of exchange transactions between Reuter and Wolff, as well as the inner organisation of the telegraphic bureau of Wolff:

" "Wolff" is a joint-stock company, composed of some of the first Jewish bankers in Berlin, and, naturally enough, the members of this association claim the privilege for themselves of having the first look at all important telegrams, a privilege, the prodigious significance of which, for the twin worlds of international politics and international finance, is immediately apparent.

The W. T. B. is a semi-official arrangement, the recognised organ of the German and Prussian Government. "Do ut des" (I give in order that you may give) or, "quid pro quo" (nothing for nothing) is the principle, which regulates its relations to both governments, of which it is, at one and the same time, henchman and mouthpiece. Many contemptuous expressions have been used concerning the "Reptile" Bureau in Berlin, but, as a matter of fact, such a Bureau does not exist, or, at any rate, only in the shape of the above-mentioned telegraphic bureau. This is not to say that Wolff receives a subsidy in money out of the "Reptile" fund of the Government. In the case of a newspaper, or a similar undertaking, however, payment, in the form of important news, is just as valuable, if not more valuable, than payment in hard cash. What does the payment to Wolff consist of? First of all, in the precedence, which the Government accords to all messages received by or emanating from Wolff's Bureau, in order to assure to that office, whenever possible, priority in the publication of its announcements, a consideration, which is naturally of the utmost importance to a telegraphic bureau.

---

[45] Anyone, who is desirous of tracking down the instigators of the World's War, must certainly not pass Reuter by unnoticed.

Moreover, the Government makes use of Wolff's Bureau as its channel of information and mouth-piece, when it wishes to publish a "dementi" to influence public opinion, or to communicate certain information in a certain form to the world — especially to that part, which lies outside Germany; this last can be very comfortably accomplished thanks to Wolff's international connections."

The W. T. B. is an institution, founded by Bleichroder, and for which Louis Schneider, formerly non-commissioned officer and later courtier, the well-known reader to King William I, was successful in obtaining the favourable notice of his august master. In his letter to Dr. Wolff, in which he praises the Doctor's intention, the King, in 1865, announced his expectation that "patriotic financiers like Messrs Oppenfeld, Magnus and Bleichröder" would support Wolff's undertaking. What the shareholders in Wolff's Telegraphic Bureau understand by "patriotism", is disclosed by the activity of this institution, which Bismarck distinctly referred to in his famous aphorism "to lie like a telegram." The principal shareholders according to Witte, are the chief of Bleichröder's Bank, Dr. Paul von Schwabach, English Consul-General, and Herbert v. Reuter, chief of the English telegraphic bureau, whose enmity towards Germany is an established fact. Amongst other shareholders are the banking- houses of Mendelsohn and of Warschauer.

Similar agreements to that between the Bureaux of Wolff and Reuter exist also between these two institutions and official or semi-official telegraphic agencies in other European countries, of which the best known are the French "Agence Havas" and the Italian "Agencia Stefania". All these are in the hands of Jews. One must pause to reflect what it really means, when one learns that by means of contracts, in which high penalties have been mutually agreed upon, each of the above-mentioned "Bureaux" engages to communicate to the Press in unaltered form (that is to say without any regard for the truth) any message, received from any other agency belonging to the Union or Ring of telegraphic news-agencies! Of the two competing American telegraphic news-agencies "Associated Press" and "Laffan Bureau", the former enjoys, thanks to the "smartness" of its representative, without any reciprocation on its side, official priority for the quickest dispatch of its news from Berlin — because one believes here in Germany that by this complaisance a "Good Press" is manufactured in America. One must read Witte's book, in order to learn from the actual facts of the World War, what astounding success has resulted from this policy.

Witte continues: "the men, who are interested in the telegraphic bureaux, know no fatherland, think and feel internationally. — War, and danger of war provide, as far as they are concerned, the most favourable opportunities for fishing in troubled waters. It has already repeatedly come to light in the Law Courts, and there is documentary evidence to confirm the statement, that Wolff's Bureau has suppressed important news in the interests of its shareholders, so that the "patriotic financiers" (to whom King William I addressed himself) might be enabled, thanks to the exclusive information, to transact profitable business on the Stock Exchange. It was established, moreover, that the Foreign Office communicates the Speech from the Throne of the Kaiser, at the opening and closing of the Reichstag, to Wolff's Bureau, several hours before it is made known to the Reichstag and to the Press." (Page 121 — 122).

This "national" Telegraphic Bureau was not ashamed to receive subscriptions from private individuals for the quickest possible telegraphic information of the death of the Emperor William II during the life of this monarch. Already for years (Witte wrote his book in 1907) the number of such subscribers had reached 5000.

One asks one's self: are the representatives of the German Empire unable to discover any means of protecting themselves against this "patriotic" Telegraphic Bureau and its dark machinations by instituting themselves a self-supporting independent news-service, which would ward off from us the insidious peril, which threatens the whole German Empire by the prejudicing of its outlook and opinions for the sake of Jewish money- interests?[46]

---

[46] Even during the World War the W. T. B. was allowed to have a monopoly of the news-service! Who can wonder now at the way in which the war ended.

Sombart can also tell us something about similar secret methods of the Jews. He says:

Their method in High Finance has frequently been the following: they first of all made themselves useful to the prince or ruler, as interpreters, by means of their knowledge of languages; they were then sent as negotiators and agents to foreign courts: then the prince or ruler entrusted them with the management of his property (which opportunity, it may be remarked by the way, was skilfully taken advantage of to lead the prince or ruler into debt, and to become his creditor), and by these means they became masters of the finances, and, in more recent years, of the Exchanges (page 203)."

The Jews work always according to the same old receipt. It is already sketched out in fullest detail in the history of Joseph of Egypt's behaviour towards Potiphar and Pharaoh; and thus the Hebrew does not find it necessary to develop any particular intelligence in order to repeat the same old artifice daily — especially as the Christian nations are brought up in complete ignorance of such tricks, and repeat, in good faith, the Jewish lie that the Egyptian Joseph was a pious, virtuous man and a national benefactor. Even in the earliest times the Jews played a leading part at the courts of the German princes; thus, for example, Isaac at the court of Charlemagne, and Kalonymos at the court of Otto II. Frederick Barbarossa was surrounded by an entire staff of Jews, just like Rudolph I. — Maximilian I, being an unbusinesslike man, was heavily in debt to the Jews. During the extensive German wars in the 17th and 18th centuries, espionage was carried on by the Jews, in all directions, to an enormous extent; even during the Prussian-German wars of liberation in 1813 and later (compare the Kreuzzeitung 1913 No. 209) more than half the traitors, who served the French as spies, were Jews.[47] The Jews were to be found in swarms at the various Courts until the monarchs fell. The latter were blind enough to take the most dangerous enemies of the monarchy

---

[47] This much is certain: the Jewish boast, on the contrary, concerning the participation of Jews in the battles of liberation, was proved already in the year 1819 to be a lie. That the same lie flourishes today, and even to a greater extent than formerly, so that one Jewish Journalist even goes so far as to claim Eleonore Prochaska — the Potsdam heroine - as a Jewess, is only in accordance with the usual Jewish falsification of history.

to their bosom, and to place implicit trust in them. The collapse of the monarchs is not undeserved; stupidity is a crime in rulers; there was no lack of warning.

In modern times, the notorious Bernhard Maimon provides a typical example of the Jewish intriguer behind the scenes on the political stage. On account of frequent thefts of documents from the Foreign Office in Paris, in 1911, various arrests were made, and Maimon, who was eventually unmasked as the leader of an extensive system of espionage, was included amongst the thieves. Concerning this talented political adventurer one could read as follows in a Jewish paper:

"Bernard Maimon, who is perhaps sixty years of age, is, without doubt, one of the most interesting adventurers of the present time, truly a modern Casanova, who, just like his famous (Jewish) predecessor, is constantly and universally engaged in politics, works simultaneously for and against all parties, brings the greatest financial operations to successful issue, negotiates the most difficult state loans, and still has time and inclination to engage in most daring love-adventures." — Bernhard — or properly Baruch — Maimon is a Gallician Jew, which has not prevented him from playing, sometimes the Christian, sometimes the Moslem. He was well versed, not only in the Talmud, but also in the Koran and in the Bible, and understood, to a remarkable degree, how to make the most of this knowledge. The Hebrew paper full of admiration, relates further:

"His extensive public, and still more extensive secret relations with the British Embassy were in constant rivalry with his mysterious connections with other Embassies, and especially with the palace of Abdul Hamid. Tachsin, the first secretary at Yildiz Kiosk, was literally a mere tool in the hands of Maimon. And whenever Maimon stayed away from the palace in his own hotel, there was an uninterrupted exchange of letters and messages between Yildiz and Maimon, by night as well as day.

Apparently Maimon gave the first consideration to the interests of England, but it is quite certain that he had other irons in the fire. He was a spy for the whole world, and it flattered his vanity to play with the first diplomatists of the day like a cat plays with a mouse, and to converse with monarchs, in their private apartments, concerning matters, which their ministers only learnt about for the first time much later on in the day. The Winter Palace on the Neva was open to him, and Abdul Hamid had the greatest personal regard for, and placed the blindest confidence in him, in spite of, or just because Maimon was on very friendly terms with the Young Turks. Whenever Maimon was staying in Constantinople, Abdul Hamid took counsel with him daily concerning all international questions, and when he was at a distance from the Bosphorus, his advice was often sought and given by telegraph. And, at one and the same time, Bernard Maimon was the counsellor — even the friend of King George of Greece, and his adviser during the Turco-Grecian War. He put in an appearance at Crete, accompanied by an entire staff of the leading French and English war-correspondents, and even the renowned American photographer, Underwood, was not wanting, for pictures of the most memorable episodes had to be provided for the great illustrated papers of both hemispheres — and Bernard Maimon naturally as the central figure in each case! The political adventurer, Bernard Maimon, travelled only by special train from one residence to the other, and lived only In the best hotels. — So much for the wisdom of the old governments, and so much for the wisdom of their diplomacy! Who can wonder that they suffered ship-wreck!"

* * * * *

The distribution of the Hebrews over all lands is particularly advantageous for their system of reconnoitring, and one can take it for granted that the distribution represents a carefully- spread net, so that every important centre has its appointed spy or scout. When Governments so frequently gave the preference to Jews in the case of army-contracts and similar business transactions, it was always justified by the argument that the Jews, thanks to their far-flung net of agents, were in a far better position than other merchants to "assemble" rapidly provisions and other materials in large quantities — thanks again to the connections, which they maintained from town to town. In a book with the title "Über Judentum und Juden"

(*Concerning Jewdom and the Jews*) [1795] the author, von Kortum says: "The Jewish contractor has no need to be scared by difficulties. He has only to electrify the Jewish community at the right place, and in a moment he has as many helpers and helpers' helpers as he requires." Then again, how he emphasises the fact: "formerly the Jew never traded alone as an isolated individual, but always as a member of the most extensive trading company in the world", and there is also a noteworthy petition of the merchants of Paris, in the latter half of the 18th century, which states: "they (the Jews) resemble drops of quicksilver, which disperse themselves and run about in all directions, but which, on the slightest shock, reunite themselves into one mass."

The fact that the Government gives the Jews still further support for their business espionage, by entrusting them with the consular representations, belongs to those incomprehensibilities, of which our administrative wisdom furnishes so many instances.

THE "FOREIGNNESS" OF THE HEBREWS

The fact that the Hebrew is a foreigner in all countries is of great use to him.

The Jew never identifies himself with the interests of the country in which he lives. He has his own peculiar nationality, and constitutes, with those of his kind, an international nation as it were; and the interests of this nation are supreme with him; they form, literally, the base of his religious faith. Why should he break away from a community, which is not only united by the double tie of consanguinity and religion, but represents as well a gigantic business association, which, simply owing to this adherence to one another, is able not only to maintain its own existence but can guarantee an existence to each individual Jew as well! And an alien business association of this kind, with an alien religion, will see to it that its interests are sharply separated from those of other nations, and must accordingly confront the latter both as foreigner and enemy. The leaders of the Hebrew nation recognised this fact thousands of years ago; and, for this reason, they drew up the rule: "remain a stranger in the land, for you go there to take possession of it." And, as Professor Adolf Wahrmund very appositely remarks, the Jews, even at the present day, regard their journey across the world as a warlike expedition, undertaken for the purpose of conquest — certainly not by displaying courage, sword in hand, but by the weapons of financial and mental enslavement, with which they overreach and infatuate the different nations, and impose usurious spoliation and moral disturbance on them. Just as Jacob, the ancestor of Jewry, defrauded the honest peasant Esau of his rights as first-born, and, by a trick, sneaked into possession of what should have been another's inheritance, so, even up to the present day, Jewdom remains the professional "sneaker" of inheritance among the other nations. The Talmudic doctrine announces: "The possessions of those, who are not Jews, are to be regarded as property without an owner, and whoever is the first to seize the same is entitled to it."

One must certainly concede that the Hebrews have acquired to an uncommon degree agility of mind, business circumspection, and a penetrating judgement as regards relations and persons. These capabilities are the inheritance of a race, which, for thousands of years, has not practised anything but trading, usury, espionage and overreaching of honest people. It was, by no means, the external pressure of his environment, which converted the Hebrew into a usurer and a deceiver; he has never been anything else. This can be seen from his primordial laws and doctrines, which — apart from meaningless stories and forms of ritual, scarcely touch upon anything except how to exploit and befool that part of humanity, which is not Jewish. It must also be taken into consideration that Jewdom, which is for ever on the move, impelled by the lust for roving, and which represents the nomadism of modern times, is enabled, by constant change of relations and surroundings, to develop a keener insight into affairs, than those who never move from the spot where they were born. The Hebrews are intruders everywhere, who were obliged to capture a place for themselves by means of cunning, and who, for that reason, have always practised, in a masterly fashion, the requisite artifices. "New-settlers" as Sombart, not very appropriately, calls them, "must keep their eyes open, in order to make themselves quickly at home in their new quarters, must be careful how they proceed, in order that they may, at any rate, make a livelihood under the new conditions. While the long established inhabitants are resting comfortably in their warm beds, they (the Jews) are standing outside in the chilly morning air, and must first of all endeavour to build themselves a nest! There they stand — regarded by all settled inhabitants as intruders."

And the alienage of the people of Juda, as even Sombart allows, is not only of an external but of an internal nature as well. He says:

"Israel, however, was alien amongst the other peoples since time immemorial in quite another one might almost say psychological-social sense, in the sense, of an internal contrariety to the population surrounding them, in the sense of an almost partitioned-off seclusion from the economist nations. They, the Jews, were conscious that they were something out of the ordinary, and were, in turn, regarded as such by the economist nations."

That, in the last analysis, is the secret which stigmatises Hebrewdom: this alienage and contrariety, which they, as guests in foreign countries, feel and display towards their hosts; and it is the chief defect of our education, that not only are these peculiar relations not made clear to us, but we are actually deceived concerning them! While the Jew never allows himself to forget for one moment that he must regard us as strangers and enemies, whom it is business to exploit and overreach, we are brought up under the false impression that the Hebrew is a harmless member of the human community, just like the members of any other nation. And even more; we actually befriend and favour the most dangerous enemy of our economic and national existence, in consequence of the unlucky associations which Church doctrine has most erroneously derived from the traditions of Jewdom.

The Church ascribes a moral and religious importance to the Jew, which he simply does not possess. Out of this fundamental error on our part, Hebrewdom draws its main strength; our blindness and foolish trust provide him with the most favourable opportunities. Whilst he—certainly with the demeanour of the innocent friend of humanity — lies in wait for each opportunity to overreach us, we advance towards him with open arms, open heart and open pocket, and make his task of exploiting and harming us a very easy one. Viewing the situation, as described above, one may well ask if the Hebrew really is in need of a special intelligence department, and of superior business ability, in order to gain an economic advantage over us, when the secret alliance of his racial companions and our unlimited trustfulness have already made the game so ridiculously easy for him.

We have already seen, in section V, how the Hebrew, in his compartment-like seclusion, recognises no moral obligations of any kind toward us; and how he considers himself entitled to abuse our trustfulness in any and every way.

One must realise that the whole culture of civilised humanity rests on a foundation of mutual trust. The co-operation of a great, civilised community is only rendered possible by each honestly fulfilling his duty, and thereby justifying the reliance and confidence of others in him. The Hebrew knows nothing of fidelity and trust — at least as far as "strangers" are concerned. He knows only of a compact with his own clique, which is more of the nature of a conspiracy, and which is indispensable for the successful issue of his plans for overreaching others. As regards strangers, however, he considers himself freed from any moral responsibility whatever. Sombart says:

"The mere fact that one had to do with a 'stranger' has sufficed in all times, which had not yet been tainted by humanitarian considerations, to relieve the conscience and to loosen the bonds of moral obligation."

And this is the position taken up by the Hebrew even at the present day; all of us are strangers in his eyes, fit material for exploitation, whom it is his duty to injure, for the greater honour of Israel and of his idol Jahwe. These relations of the Hebrew with the stranger are the antithesis to the attitude and behaviour of the

German under like conditions. Overstrained conceptions of humanity prompt us to display especial consideration and obligingness towards those, who are not Germans. We have had to pay dearly for this unpatriotic indulgence in the past; and to nobody more than to the Jews.

3. SEMI-CITIZENSHIP OF THE JEWS

The Semi-Citizenship of the Jews, which has already been mentioned, proceeds from their alien nature. They are semi-citizens amongst us, because their allegiance to our national community is only feigned and superficial, for secretly they retain their separate Jewish civil community, and their separate nationality. This causes them, however, in another sense to become double-citizens, for, according to the law, they belong simultaneously to two nationalities and states; amongst us they are, at one and the same time, German and Hebrew; they are amenable to two systems of law, and can claim protection from both; for they have the option of invoking, at one time, the German, and at another, the Jewish code, selecting whichever system appears to be most advantageous. They acquire thereby privileges over all other citizens of the state, and it is only a trait of their ancient mendacity and presumption, when they behave as if they were not treated with full justice in our country. As a matter of fact as double citizens they enjoy double rights — are actually privileged. Fichte has already called attention to this:

"Through almost every country in Europe a mighty, hostile state is extending itself, and is engaged in constant warfare with all the other states: its oppressive tyranny causes grievous suffering to the citizens of all the other countries, and it is called Jewdom. I do not believe that this fearful state of affairs has come about because Jewdom forms a separate and exceedingly compact community, but because it is founded upon hatred of the whole human race.[48]

It has gone so far, in his (Fichte's) opinion, that:

---

[48] J. G. Fichte: "Urteile über die französische Revolution" (Opinions concerning the French Revolution) [1793] Extracts are to be found in the "Handbuch der Judenfrage" (*Handbook of the Jewish Question*). 26th Edition, Pages 63—65.

"In a country where even the King may not, of his own free will, deprive me of the cottage, which I inherited from my father, and where I have my legal rights against the all-powerful minister, the first Jew, nevertheless, who takes it into his head, can plunder me with impunity," and he then continues:

"You are all aware of this and cannot deny it, and utter words sweet as sugar about tolerance, the rights of man and civic rights, and the whole time you are inflicting injury on our chief rights as men Cannot you recall in this case the instance of the state within the state? Does not the intelligible thought ever occur to you that the Jews, who, apart from you, are citizens of a state, which is more firmly founded and more powerful than all of yours, will, if you once give them citizenship in your own countries, tread you, the original citizens, under their feet?"

The assertion that, in olden times, the Jews were denied entry into the honourable industries, and consequently were forced to resort to usury, is contradicted in the most emphatic manner by Sombart. He cites, amongst other proofs, an order of the Cabinet, dated 1790, which permitted the protected Jews of Breslau to carry on all kinds of mechanical crafts, and mentions also that, amongst these Jews, besides those who were tolerated, there were privileged and universally- privileged ones, who were allowed full exercise of all Christian rights in the ordinary course of life. It is quite certain that some Jews enjoyed special privileges, which were hereditary in their families.[49] Sombart also lays stress on the fact, that if the Jews neither obtained nor sought for admittance into the corporations and guilds, this was to be attributed mainly to the Christian character of these organisations; the crucifix repelled them. The Jews, moreover, already in the 12th and 13th centuries, were not only on a completely equal footing with the great merchants, the shopkeepers and the leading people as regards freedom of the markets (Freitag: "Bilder a. d. Vergangenheit" II *Pictures out of the past" II*) but they

---

[49] "Amongst themselves the Jews lived (during the 10th-12th centuries and later) according to the Mosaic-Talmudic Law, from which, later on, many legal ideas have crept into the common law of the community. In each town the Jews formed a special community by themselves" — that is to say the Ghetto — "under a Jewish bishop, who was appointed by the King at their suggestion, and who exercised judicial powers amongst them in all cases of dispute."

actually had the privilege over their competitors of being protected, together with clergymen, women and pilgrims, against all action under feudal law (Schröder's Rechtsgeschichte. I *History of Law. I*). In olden times the religiousness of the Christian, and the alienage of the Jew himself, operated to the latter's advantage, just as German cowardliness and "culture" do, at the present day. Owing to their alienage the Jews possessed one peculiar advantage, namely, that there was no need for them to take part in the quarrels of other nations, and could, on that account, all the more easily derive benefit from political complications — at the expense of the two conflicting powers. Sombart says: "national conflicts became actually the principal source of Jewish acquisition." Espionage might also be included (compare page 156). Besides this, one must not forget the farming-out of the privilege to mint money, which the German Emperors, since the 13th century, had made over to the towns and to the large landowners, who, in their turn, had handed it on to single tenants — amongst them many Jews. Up to the middle of the 18th century these people secured enormous profits for themselves from debasement of the coinage alone. "Outwardly good and inwardly bad, outwardly Frederick but inwardly Ephraim"[50] was the derisive comment of the people of Brandenburg concerning the badly silvered-over groschen, issued during the Seven Years War.

4. JEWISH WEALTH

The ancient complaint about the oppression of the Jews in olden times, contradicts itself alone by the fact of their indulgent mode of living, and their display of luxury. We have already mentioned how they inhabited the most magnificent mansions, not only in Holland and London, but also in Paris and Hamburg, and Gl-ckel of Hameln discourses in the same strain concerning the princely splendour displayed at a rich Jewish wedding in Amsterdam. Sombart furnishes long lists of the names of rich Jews in England, Hamburg and Frankfurt, during the 17th and 18th centuries, and the amounts — stated in figures — of the fortunes of

---

[50] The Jew Ephraim (Itzig & O) was the head of the mintage-farmers, of whose services Frederic the Great was compelled to avail himself when surrounded with difficulties.

these people are a sufficient refutation of the ancient fable about the "poor, oppressed Jew." He says:

"The peculiar and interesting fact, that the Jews were always the richest people, has continued unaltered for centuries, and remains as true today as it was two or three hundred years ago. It anything, it is still more pronounced and universal at the present time than formerly.[51]

We possess sufficient explanation of this mystery, when we have once become acquainted with the means, by which Jewdom acquires its riches. Only we must once more oppose the erroneous idea, that the riches of the Jews, who live in our midst, are part and parcel of the national wealth. The Hebrews, of their own accord, place themselves outside the pale of the nation; their riches, therefore, are not to be included in our national wealth. On the contrary, the Jewish riches are the sum of what is lost to us in prosperity. These riches, at the present moment, are in the possession of a foreign and hostile nation, which is using them in order to oppress us. All the mighty banking foundations and gigantic Stock Exchange speculations of the Hebrews are, in reality, consummated mainly with ou r money. In the case of all Jewish activity there is no suggestion of the creation of sound economic values, but only of a crafty shifting of ownership. An honest Hebrew, one Conrad Alberti (Sittenfeld), acknowledged as much when he wrote as follows in the "Gesellschaft" of 1889 No. 12:

"No one can dispute that Jewdom takes a leading part in polluting and corrupting all relations. A characteristic of the Jew is the stubborn endeavour to produce values without work, and this being a matter of impossibility, it simply means that these values are artificially produced by swindling and corruption, by manoeuvres on the Stock Exchange in conjunction with the Press in order to spread false rumours, and by other and similar methods. These artificial and fictitious values are then acquired, unloaded and exchanged for

---

[51] Sombart's book is especially recommended to the notice of Social Democrats, in order that they may learn who are the originators of the capitalistic system, which they pretend to hate so much, and who are the real oppressors of the people. Perhaps then they will begin to reflect whether they are justified in selecting their leaders and advisers out of this particular circle.

genuine values, produced by real work, only to melt away and vanish in the hands of their new owners like Helen in the arms of Faust. The representatives of corruption on the Exchange, in the Press and in the Theatre in my novel "The Old and Young", representatives of that class who strive to enrich themselves without working, are therefore Jews."

When Sombart says: "Capitalism is born from the money-loan", I should like to add to this: Capitalism actually exists only in the money-loan; for, under the expression "Capital" in the narrower sense, I understand only Loan-Capital, that is to say the kind of capital which is utilised, not to generate productive activity, but solely to win interest. It cannot be disputed that the dangerous capitalism of the present day arises solely from the loaning of money, for the productive fortunes of our great industrialists must not be compared in this respect with the usury-capital of the Rothschilds and their associates. The productive capital of industry consists, like that of the large land-owners, preponderatingly of landed property, buildings and industrial investments, and only gives a return when inventive intelligence, organising power and hard work are also brought into active operation. The distinguishing feature, however, of loan-capital — "speculative capital" — is to bring in a return without doing any work for it. Productive capital gives opportunity for work and wages simultaneously to hundreds and thousands, but loan-capital is only a steady drain on the return earned by others, taking often the lion's share; for it makes sure of its percentage whatever happens, even when adverse circumstances or the failure of the harvest wipe out all profit.

When certain people make the simple masses believe that the farmer and the large land-owner — the hated "Agrarian" — are the real oppressors and plunderers of the people, they omit to mention that very frequently this "Agrarian" himself is grievously oppressed, and is on the rack from year's end to year's end, to raise the money to pay the interest on the mortgages. The workman in industrial service, or in possession of a handicraft, always remains a free man, who receives an honest wage for honest work, and who can, if he chooses, give notice and change his employer. But whoever finds himself in the bondage of Loan-capital and doomed to pay interest, is seldom, if ever, able to shake off the fetters. The landowner, burdened with mortgages, is far less free and far less of a master than the youngest proletarian from the factory. All his life long he, and often his children and grandchildren as well, are chained to the same piece of soil, which claims all their labour in order to raise interest for Loan-capital. How crazy it is then, to direct the envy and hatred of the town- bred proletariat against these supposed tyrants! In reality, many of these so-called owners — even the large landed proprietors — are themselves "owned" by the Loan-capitalists.

A new kind of secret serfdom has come into being, which is invisible to the ordinary public, and which consists in allowing the slave to retain the outward appearance of lord and master, whilst it condemns the much-envied owner to a kind of bondage.

This bondage is rooted finally in our wrong arrangement of our interest system. It is opposed to common sense, in the case of a sum of money lent on interest once only, to make, not only the recipient of the loan, but his children and children's children liable to pay interest for all time. This "eternal interest" is, on the one side, the curse of the productive classes, and on the other, the fertile soil in which are rooted the power and dominancy of that oppressor of the nations — Judah. The interest system invests the money- lender with a relative might which, in reality, is more oppressive than the dominance and despotism of the olden times. The despot of earlier times invariably took the part of his bondmen, and protected them against dangers from without, because their preservation and his own economic interest were inseparable. The lender of money does not recognise this personal concern for the welfare of those who pay him interest; he chases them ruthlessly from hearth and home when they are no longer able to pay him tribute. He also enjoys the advantage that the unpledged portion of his debtor's property falls, in this manner, into his clutches as well. Sometimes he acquires, under a forced sale, the entire possessions of his debtor in satisfaction of his claim, and thereby gains that part of the property, which had not yet been pledged. He then introduces a fresh "interest-slave" into the property, and proceeds to treat the same, who perhaps has increased the value of the property by his personal energy, in precisely the same manner should he fall into arrears.

Between the "interest-master" and the "interest-slave" all human relations have ceased; the connection between the two has become purely mechanical; it has become unhuman and soulless. On the other hand, the activity of the receiver of interest does not call for the slightest intellectual or physical exertion. The knight of olden times protected his bondmen with spear and shield against their foes; the lord of capital has divested himself of all such responsibilities. The accumulation of capital also has become a purely mechanical process. Interest and capital accumulate in accordance with the purely mechanical law of mass-attraction — an absolutely imbecile proceeding devoid of any organic sense. Sombart says:

"With regard to the lending of money, economic activity as such has lost all meaning; the occupation of lending money has ceased to be a sensible activity of either mind or body."

There is one, and only one object: the material result i. e. the acquisition of fresh capital, and therewith the extension of the power of the lender of the money.

In this manner loan-capital gains power over other men, and has forced itself into a dominating position, which is founded neither on physical, nor on intellectual, nor on moral superiority. This position depends entirely upon a fictitious power, and one which is devoid of any human element, namely the conception or notion of capital. It is enabled by means of eternal interest, extending into immeasurable time, to make foreign labour subject to itself, and to overpower and crush all spiritual and moral effort. The formation of capital out of interest is something automatic and spiritless, for it can be consummated just as well in the hands of an idiot as in the hands of a being destitute of all morality — simply by a fiction, by a false economic view.

"The possibility of earning money without any personal exertion by an economic transaction, makes its first distinct appearance in the lending of money. The possibility also, of getting strangers to work for one without physical compulsion, is immediately apparent."

Thus writes Sombart on page 223; it seems to us, however, that the "scooping-in" of interest is scarcely worthy of the name of "economic transaction."

After such illuminating reflections, it seems very extraordinary to us, that it is precisely in the capitalistic Jewish press where a bitter hatred is unceasingly fomented against the domination of olden times, and against anything which refers to, or recalls the same. Feudal-domination, Knighthood, Nobility are mediaeval ideas, and as such are exposed to incessant attacks from the so-called "liberal" press. With what right and for what purpose? Simply with the object of not allowing the infatuated population, who are ignorant of history, to wake up to the fact that they are languishing and wasting away under new tyrants, the interest-despots, who set to work in a far more selfish and brutal manner than was ever the case even with the most ruthless Feudal-Lord of the Middle Ages.

XIII

Business and Religion

Sombart speaks mockingly of the "fearful maxims" which Pfefferkorn, Eisenmenger, Rohling, Dr. Justus and others have culled from the religious books of the Jews. It would have been a good thing if he had submitted a sample of these "horrors" to his readers, for, often as these "maxims" have been examined by other conscientious scholars, they — the maxims — have invariably retained the same aspects. And, when the explanatory artifices of the Jews are brought into play, according to the receipt given in chapter V, one is in a position to understand that the Hebrew can interpret entirely different, and far worse meanings out of those doctrines, than the conscientious Christian translator is capable of. The same Sombart, who reported to us some time back, how, owing to the Talmud, the entire Jewish spiritual world had declined into impotence, and how every minute point, every letter, every word had its own important meaning, goes so far as to say light-heartedly a few pages further on:

"naturally in the course of so many centuries these particular doctrines have altered entirely in meaning."

This is untrue. All that is correct is, that in the Talmud with its commentaries, the most divergent opinions of the Rabbis find utterance, and that the doctrines and expositions contained therein, frequently contradict one another; that, however, is only equivalent to saying that it is open to every faithful Jew to accept as authentic whatever doctrine and exposition may best suit his purpose for the time being. Thus, when one passage reads: "you must not lie to, deceive, or rob the Goi", and another Rabbi says: "under circumstances you may do so", more latitude is allowed to the conscience of the Jew who believes in his Talmud. He can act either in this way, or in that, and will still find himself in agreement with the law, will still remain a pious and orthodox Jew.

Out of the mass of inconsistencies and contradictions contained in the Rabbinical writings, arises that cheap form of diversion which the Rabbis have always carried on at the expense of those who do not happen to be Jews. If anyone calls attention to a passage in the Talmud, which states: You may do the Goi an injury, the Rabbi can at once turn up another place where it says: You must not do this. The morality of the Talmud is like a conjurer's box with a false bottom, from which the moral and the immoral can be produced according to wish. It is therefore, trifling on the part of Sombart when, referring to the serious scientific study which Christian Scholars have made of the Talmud, to speak of the "downright silly game, which the Anti-Semites and their Christian or Jewish opponents have been playing ever since the recollection of man". The only question is, which side is playing a silly game. Sombart himself is engaged in a game of harassing and mystifying when he says with reference to these matters:

'So far as the religious writings are read by the laity themselves, it seems to me essential that, generally speaking, a settled opinion should be expressed with regard to any particular question. It is a matter of indifference if, at the same time, the contrary opinion is also represented; for the devout man, who has been edified by these writings, is content to accept the view which coincides with his own interests, so that he is thereby in a better position to defend the same."

According to this logic one might well believe that Sombart had also attended the Talmudic School, for this is a genuine specimen of the Rabbinical expression of opinion: one particular view or manner of understanding suffices if it exactly suits the reader! — capital. But if there happen to be two entirely opposite opinions, the devout man has the opportunity of selecting whichever one pleases him best. And one is bound to admit this is a very empty kind of morality. Sombart adds: "since everything, in this case, is divine revelation, one passage is just as valuable as another."

Quite correct! here we have the morality with the double bottom — openly defended by a scholar who does not desire to be a Jew!

The Rabbinical writings, which most certainly have been written by the most intellectual amongst the Jewish people, actually prove that, amongst the Jews, the feeling for true morality, for the ethical consciousness, is entirely wanting. There is no good and evil for them; everything is gauged by momentary advantage. A naive ponderer, like Friedrich Nietzsche, saw with admiration in all this, a "higher form of morality," and felt tempted to write his "Jenseits von Gut und B-se" (*"The other side of Good and Evil"*). He had no conception how his action smoothed and prepared the way for unmoral Jewdom. There is no "other side" to good and evil for constructive and productive people, for nations of real culture; these require stern standards and accurate balances to determine what is constructive and what is destructive, and to show what preserves and what demolishes. It is only the Hebrew, who does not construct anything, who can allow himself the luxury of an "other side to Good and Evil."

Sombart is more honest when he confesses:

"I find in the Jewish Religion the same leading ideas as those which characterize capitalism: I see that the former is filled with the same spirit as the latter."

In reality, the conscienceless predatory spirit, which distinguishes modern Capitalism in its worst form — Mammonism — fulfils also the Talmudic Rabbinical doctrine. One must be grateful to Sombart for this admission. He proceeds to say — and this statement must also be approved on account of its honesty — that this religion "has not arisen from an irresistible impulse, nor from the deep fervour of the heart of those, whose souls have been mutilated, nor from the religious ecstasy of adoring spirits, but from a premeditated plan like a carefully-considered proposition, resembling a diplomatic problem."

He designates it as a work of the understanding, calculated to break up and enslave the whole natural world. How strangely does

this opinion correspond with the perception of the derided Anti-
Semites, who have been saying the same for decades!

Undoubtedly the Jewish doctrine arises from the
understanding, warped with vanity, which has lost all touch with the
fundamental laws of natural growth or development, and would like
to convert life, devoid now of soul and reason, into a sum of
arithmetic. The word, Rationalism, which one would like to apply to
this particular frame of mind and this mode of regarding life, is not
appropriate here. Ratio always means reason, i. e. thought that is in
harmony with natural laws; reason is not merely understanding, but
is, at all events, understanding united to instinct or feeling, being
endowed with a keen sensibility as to the essential nature of things.
Mere understanding is simply arithmetic, without instinct, without
feeling. And the Jewish mode of thinking must be placed in this
category. If, according to the popular belief, the devil is to be
regarded as stupid, then this points out very pertinently the purely
intellectual nature of the calculation and scheming which arise out of
Evil. For this calculation, devoid of instinct, invariably ends by
deceiving itself for the simple reason that no allowance having been
made for Nature, the calculation rests on a false basis. When
Sombart says: "Rationalism is the principal trait of Judaism just as it
is of Capitalism," he means the mere mechanism of the
understanding — soulless calculation. And when he goes on to say:
"the Jewish religion does not recognise anything of a mystic nature,"
he might have said still more correctly that it did not recognise
idealism, nor true morality, nor anything ethical. When he further
maintains that the ancient religions were always ready to attribute
any deed, which aroused a sense of shame or remorse, to the
Divinity, it is the Jewish doctrine alone that entirely justifies the
accusation. Already, in the time referred to by the Old Testament, all
kinds of disgraceful deeds, perpetrated by the people of Judah
against other nations, were undertaken, always ostensibly at the
bidding of their God Jahwe or Jehovah; and the same diversion is
continued in the Talmud. Jahwe not only approves of all manner of
evil things, but he himself, as personification of the Jewish entity,
tells lies and deceives. The philosopher, Ludwig Feuerbach, has
already designated the so-called Jewish religion as nothing more
than a business contract between Judah and its God. Nothing is to

be found in these laws and doctrines, which does not hint at some material benefit for the children of Israel. Jahwe demands obedience from his people, and promises them in return: riches and long life. "Utilitarianism profit — is the predominant principle of Jewdom" says Feuerbach. "The Jews have retained their peculiarity up to the present day: their deity is the most practical principle in the world: egoism, and egoism in the form of religion." Ernest Renan says the same thing (Hist. des lang. sém.).

Sombart is no different with reference to Jewish doctrine: "There is no kind of compact or partnership between God and man, which is not consummated in the form that man performs something that is agreeable to God, and is rewarded by God correspondingly."

But even Jahwe does not do anything for his chosen people except for cash down. He is no God of the self-sacrificing love, but is an out-and-out business man like the Jew himself; and thus, throughout the whole Jewish religion, there is no higher moral guiding star. There is nothing to raise man above himself, no unselfish sacrifice, no inspiration for ideals. Always only

"A constant weighing-up and comparison of the advantage or disadvantage, which any action or omission to act may entail, a most complicated kind of book-keeping in order to keep the debit side of each individual's account in order."

Such is Jewish piety according to Sombart. And, just as according to the Jewish mode of thinking, everything resolves itself into action and reaction, into payment and acquisition, so, in the so-called Jewish religion, is the acquisition of money regarded as the supreme and sole object of life. The Jew introduces the huckster's spirit even into his divine services, and Sombart reports that these ceremonies have, in many cases, developed into nothing less than formal auctions. Thus, for example, the official posts of the Thora in the Synagogue are sold by auction to the highest bidders (Sombart page 249). He also confirms that the Rabbis were, for the most part, prominent business people, (compare also page 73) and therefore we are bound to acquiesce when he hints that the Jewish religious system has greatly assisted the capitalistic career of Jewdom. In other words, the so-called Jewish religion is nothing else than the wrapping-up of sharp business practices in a religious garment.

A nation certainly has nothing to be proud of in having invented and retained in favour, even up to the present day, a code of morals which in truth is devoid of all morality. But why should not the Hebrew cling tenaciously to this traditional doctrine; for, thanks to its help, success is on his side! Why should he not cherish his Jahwe, who has been such an excellent adviser to him in all business matters? It is a fatal weakness of the other nations that, up till now, they have not been able to perceive what their real relations to the Jews are, and have not been able to discover the ways and means by which the Jews enrich themselves. So the Jew still retains the fantasy that not only is his intelligence of a higher quality than that of other men, but that his religion is also superior to theirs. He will only become sober-minded when the other nations at last settle accounts with him, and when he discovers that the accountant, Jahwe, unmasked and hurled from his throne, is no longer in a position to help him.

* * * * *

Indeed, there cannot be any more striking contrast than that presented by the intense, unearthly idealism of Christ, which disregards the material world, and the rabbinical spirit which is directed entirely towards material advantage and earthly enjoyment. Sombart says:

"In this respect the Jews stand in the most striking contrast to the Christians, whose religion has endeavoured to its utmost to embitter all joy in this world. Just as often as riches are praised in the Old Testament, are they cursed, and poverty extolled, in the New Testament." It is therefore illuminating, why the devout Christian and the pious Jew play such very unequal parts in the acquisitive life. The Christian seeks to acquire in order to gain his living; the Jew is desirous of heaping up riches in order to control and to enjoy. And, at this juncture, the question arises: Has not the unworldly religion of the Christians perhaps been the unconscious agent to fasten the golden fetters of Jewdom on the Aryan nations? — But while the views taken of life, and the moral obligations of the Aryan nations have, in the course of time, altered and become freer and more humane, the same cannot be said of Jewdom. Its law remains rigid and unchangeable up to the present day: in the course of 3000 years Jewdom cannot record any moral advance. What stands written, stands written, and is just as valid today as on the first day, when, according to the legend, it was dictated directly by Jahwe to Moses on the summit of Mount Sinai. Jewish law is built up on a faith of sheer and literal acceptation, with exclusion of all common sense and of all unfettered judgement. It reduces its adherents to dumb slaves. Jewdom is, in reality, the religion of servility. Whenever the fable is repeated that the Jews were our instructors in moral and religious matters, and presented us, as it were, with a religion, the repetition discloses either complete ignorance of the subject, or a deliberate perversion of facts. The people of Judah were never moral and pious in our sense of these words; they do not possess any faculty of perception in this respect. And whoever regards the blind subservience of the Hebrew to literalness as the highest degree of piety, is incapable of recognising the spiritual and moral nature of the genuine man. The really religious man is he, who untiringly searches for the deepest and most intimate associations between natural and moral occurrences, who is constantly extending his knowledge, who surveys and judges of his own actions according to their effect, and who does not cling blindly and incapable of judgement to mere literal forms. Lagarde says appositely: "A religion only lives as long as it is cultivated." In reality it is only the constant striving for moral perfection and the constant seeking for and deepening of moral insight, which form the essence of true religiousness. Where these are wanting, there is no religion; and they are wanting in Jewdom. The slave to literalness, who conforms to the time- worn doctrine without passing any criticism, and who, at the best, endeavours to thread a way by means of cowardly subtlety between the various precepts of the same, is wanting in nothing so much as in religious consciousness. And thus, from this standpoint, the Jewish doctrine cannot lay any claim to the name of religion.

Sombart says with respect to the "Thora" of Israel:

"The commands and prohibitions of God contained therein must be observed most strictly by the pious man; whether great or small; whether they appear sensible or senseless to him; they are to be fulfilled in the strictest sense of the word, just as they stand, for the simple reason that they are the command of God."

Thus, common sense and individual reflection, individual moral feeling and conscience are excluded — of necessity — in order to equip Jewdom for the particular task, which has been assigned to it as its world mission: viz. to ruin the other nations morally and physically, and to seize their possessions. The Jewish nation is the soulless tool of an abstract idea, which has been exalted even to Divinity, and whose ultimate aim is the plundering and annihilation of honest mankind. The driving force in this struggle is the hatred of mankind, a disposition hostile to life, the evil spirit.

From a superficial point of view, that is to say the point of view of all those to whom the essence of true religion is unknown, the Jewish doctrine may certainly appear as a model religion because it concerns itself with the lowest functions of life (for instance, with one's behaviour in the w.c.), and represents all such precepts as direct commands from God. Moreover, the Jewish language possesses a peculiar pathos, a fact to which Goethe has already called attention, and readily avails itself of extravagant expressions. But we must not be le d astray by the high-sounding words. It is frequently the case in ordinary life that the person, who has the richest vocabulary and the most touching phrases at his disposal, has a cold heart, whilst another, whose soul is almost choked with overpowering emotion, is unable to utter a word. Both the written and the spoken language of the Jews use occasionally extravagant expressions for what is actually base, worldly, and even immoral, and by this means the semblance of religiousness is aroused, where, in reality, nothing of that nature exists. On the other side, blind obedience raises itself, which slavishly follows the letter of the law, which constitutes the might of the business managers of this "religion," namely the Rabbis. And thus it is intelligible if the apparent piety of the Jews appears exemplary to priests, who are greedy of power.

In reality, the Hebrews have borrowed many devout words from the religions of older and more deeply-feeling nations, in order to act as a cloak to their selfish and worldly aspirations. When a comparatively honest Hebrew, like Dr. Jacob Fromer, maintains that in Jewdom everything is ethical,[52] all that he means to say is: everything therein is regarded from a practical point of view: for the conception of morality is foreign to this man also. I should feel inclined to believe that the Hebrew meant Art when he said Ethics, so as to give to all bargains and transactions, even of the lowest description, a decent appearance, and to invest the same with a mantle of piety, although the pretence could not be extended beyond representing that the transaction in question lay within the province of God. For instance, a Hebrew, who was about to rob a man, actually went so far as to clothe his intention in the following words: "My Lord God, thou hast given thy servant power over the goods of the stranger, and see, I hasten to execute thy divine Will." — In this manner the Hebrew has introduced an element of untruthfulness and hypocrisy into the life of mankind, that is devoid of all naturalness and morality, and which is intended to detach the rest of humanity from any dependence on Nature and common sense. And this hostile principle works with amazing results, and is, at this moment, steadily and irresistibly dragging mankind down that stairway of degeneration prepared for it by the Jew.

One may say: Jewdom is an attempt to tear the existence of mankind apart from Nature, and to mould it into a kind of calculating and exact comprehension. This is what is understood by the much-praised "Intellectuality" of Hebrewdom. To say no more about it, a life without dependence upon Nature cannot continue for any length of time; and just as the Hebrew with his disintegrating intellect has never succeeded in maintaining a state of his own, has never succeeded in creating an independent, self-contained, and self-supporting society and culture, so does he convey the spirit of disintegration into the midst of those nations, who believe in culture. From whatever point he is regarded, the Hebrew displays the features of the parasite. He does not derive his means of

---

[52] See Dr. Jacob Fromer: "Das Wesen des Judentums" ("*The Essence of Jewdom*"). The author has been fiercely attacked by many of his co-religionists on account of his frank and frequent criticisms.

existence directly from Nature — from the soil — but only by means of an intermediary system of living, the essential members of which he sucks dry. But it is the custom of the parasite, if not checked, to entirely consume the juices and energy of its host, and then, if it is unable to migrate to a fresh source of sustenance, it perishes together with the host. Accordingly there is little that can be regarded as rational in the nature of the parasite, but there is, on the contrary, a blind and greedy stupidity, which finally destroys the foundation of the parasite's own existence. The Jews, therefore, are not, as Sombart is of opinion, "rationalists," but short-sighted beings, wanting in sensibility, and nothing better than spongers. His aversion to everything natural does not allow the Hebrew to feel any unfeigned pleasure in the simple expressions of Nature. A lovely flower, the song of a bird, are meaningless to him; he is scarcely aware of them.[53] Human emotions, such as affection, and sympathy with other beings, which would impede his cold and calculated pursuit of what is advantageous, appear to him mere folly. The Talmudic doctrine has no room for such. Rabbinism is a stern schooling for the Jewish soul, which finds its counterpart, perhaps, only in the arts, principles and practices of the Jesuits. Everything is calculated and adapted with the object of making the pupil the hard tool of another's will. A good heart and a gentle disposition must not be tolerated, because these would prejudice the object and purpose of trade. Sombart calls the Jewish doctrine a "Mechanism of means to carry out a purpose."

Certainly a great deal of what is contained in the Rabbinical Writings sounds very fine and virtuous; especially the unceasing zeal manifested towards unchastity, which even goes so far as to spurn womankind and all natural pleasure derived from the senses. "Let not thine eyes lust after women, turn a deaf ear to their voice, avert thy gaze from their form. Thou shalt not even look upon the garment of a woman with approval!" And so it continues in the same strain; but how does all this agree with what is actually practised? From time immemorial up to the present day the Hebrews are known to us as the most shameless pursuers of

---

[53] Heinrich Heine's classification of plants, as those which one eats, and those which one cannot eat, is an excellent instance of the Jewish perception of nature.

women. And anyone who undertook to write a history of Jewish unchastity, would have to extend it into countless volumes.

If the Rabbis of the Talmud are so zealous in warning their people against unchastity, the principal cause for this would appear to be fear regarding their own peculiar weakness. Even Sombart admits that, in the case of the Jews, we have to deal with a people strongly disposed towards sexual excesses, whom Tacitus has already described as a "projectissima ad libidinem gens." Just as the Hebrew is unnatural in everything else, so is he unnatural in this respect; his sexual inclinations and desires exceed all usual bounds and are quite without restraint.

THE SEPARATION OR SHUTTING-OFF OF THE JEWS

We will now return to the affinity between the Jewish religion and Capitalism. Sombart also allows that the object of the Jewish doctrine is: to conduct a life, contrary to Nature or alongside nature, in order to develop an economic system, which likewise builds itself up alongside nature and in defiance of it. And, he is of the opinion that the religion of the Jews must be the means of accomplishing this.

"In order that Capitalism could develop, it was first of all necessary that all the bones in the body of the industrious and forceful, but neutral man should be broken, that a specific psychology or mechanism of the soul, equipped solely from the intellect, should be substituted in the place of the original and natural life, and that a subversion, as it were, of all the values of life should be introduced. The "homo capitalisticus" is the artificial and artful creation, which finally emerges from this subversion."

One is now entitled to ask: what was then the motive for such an extraordinary object? What natural man could entertain the desire to renounce and subvert all his natural inclinations?

Here it is not the case as Sombart thinks, and is generally believed, of the Hebrew being the product of a cunningly thought-out doctrine of life, but rather as follows: the strange doctrine arises from, or is the product of the Hebrew himself, and his attitude towards honourable society. The conjecture holds good that Jewdom originated amongst the expelled elements of the ancient, civilised, oriental nations,[54] and one must bear in mind the Tschandala of the Indians, composed of the degenerates and criminals excluded from the honourable castes, in order to find an enlightening explanation of the peculiarity of Hebrew mentality. Those who had been expelled, despised by all the other castes, revenged themselves by deriding and reversing all moral conceptions. What was sacred to others, they made a mockery of; they praised, on the contrary, those attributes and dispositions which other people despised. "Amongst these people everything is profane, which is sacred in our eyes; and, on the other hand, what appears abominable to us is permissible to them", thus characterises Tacitus the Jews. In reality the very essence of Jewishness is a subversion of all the views of moral humanity. Whether it happens unconsciously or is undertaken deliberately, it still remains a fact that the Hebrews, in their nomenclature, reverse the names of many things; thus, for example, those who have been expelled, they call "the chosen". Out of this compulsory segregation — the Tschandala were not allowed to dwell amongst the honourable castes — they established, in the course of time, a voluntary separation; and finally raised their segregation to the status of law, and in their turn — like the gipsies and the wandering people of the Middle Ages — looked down with contempt upon all who stood outside their circle, that is to say, upon all honest people.

The seclusion of the Jews from the rest of humanity, to which it is customary to refer as if it were the result of some cruel despotism, has always been voluntary; they were not driven into the Ghetto, but united of their own free will to form it, in order to practise their own peculiar customs without interruption, and also because their law forbids contact with the rest of mankind. It was therefore an advance on the part of the public authorities, when they allowed the Hebrews to erect separate quarters for the Jews. Many

---

[54] See Fritsch: "Handbuch der Judenfrage" (*Handbook of the Jewish Question.*) 27 t h Edition page 236, and *"Origin and Essence of Jewdom"*, *"Jahwe or Jehovah Book"*, second edition pages 176—193.

Jewish historians admit this frankly, and also the proved fact that it is precisely the Ghetto life, which is mainly responsible for preserving the Jewish national existence. Sombart says:

"The Jews themselves created the Ghetto, which originally, from the non-Jewish point of view, was to be regarded as a concession or privilege, and not the consequence of a hostile attitude. They wished to live apart because they regarded themselves as superior to the common people surrounding them; because they felt themselves the chosen — the priestly people Their disposition, which is hostile to every foreign element, their tendency towards seclusion, extend far back into the ages."

Already, at a very remote period, they were forbidden to contract mixed marriages with other nations; and the Old Testament is full of outbursts of contempt for the surrounding nations — Edom and the Canaanites. The reproach, so often raised by people prone to sentimentality, that the Jews have become what they are, in consequence of the scorn and exclusion which they have experienced from the other nations, is thus quite beside the mark. It was far more a case of the Jews excluding themselves from other nations; they regarded, themselves as a peculiarity, high above all other peoples upon whom they looked down disdainfully. "The Jews desired and were obliged to live thus in accordance with their destiny, which was their religion," is the opinion of Sombart.

The economic nations have often approached the Jews with goodwill and trust: they — the Jews — enjoyed, during the Middle Ages, not only all rights, but often actual privileges, particularly under the government of the crosier (compare page 20 and following). A bishop, named Hausmann, built a well-fortified town, especially for the Jews, at Speyer in the 11th century, from which they used to undertake veritable pillaging excursions into the surrounding country, without anyone being able to intercept them. They were not obliged to restore any stolen property, which might be found amongst them, or could, at any rate, charge any price which they liked to set upon the same.

"The important consequence of this segregation and concentration of the Jewish population, which were effected by religion, as far as the economic life was concerned, was just that foreignness of which we have already recognised the importance: namely that all traffic of the Jews, as soon as they emerged from the Ghetto, was a traffic with foreigners."

In such a strain writes Sombart. Foreigners or strangers, are, as we have learned from our examination of the Talmudic writings (Section V), outlaws, beasts, fit material for exploitation. In the case of such strangers, usury was not only allowed, but ordered to take precedence of every thing else, and if there are perhaps passages in the Talmudic writings, which seem to teach the contrary, these are only variegations customary in Rabbinical Jewdom, which are intended to obscure the real sense. Even Sombart concedes this much:

"I am inclined to think that a great part of these discussions serve the exclusive purpose of obscuring, by all kinds of sophistry, the extraordinarily clearly defined situation, which has been created by the Thora." Thus, according to the Jewish doctrine, you may practise usury at the expense of the foreigner (5 Moses 23, 20); and plainly stated, the larger the amount of undeserved wealth, which the Hebrew amasses during his life, the greater the complacency with which he looks back on that past life; for, by so doing, he has rendered his God supreme service — that God, Jahwe, who so ardently desires the spoliation and extirpation of all the other nations of the world. "Whilst the pious Christian", continues Sombart, "who has practised usury, is seized with agonies of remorse on his death-bed, and is ready, before the end comes, to divest himself of all his property because he, at this moment, regards it as unjustly acquired, and it weighs upon his soul; the pious Jew, on the contrary, in the evening of his life, surveys with gratification the well-filled trunks and chests, crammed with Zechins, which he has succeeded, throughout his long life, in squeezing out of the wretched Christians. This is a spectacle upon which his pious heart can regale itself with the utmost satisfaction, for every groschen which lies there is, as it were, an offering laid before his God." (Sombart page 287).

Sombart is of the opinion that only ignorance or malice could deny that the position of the foreigner, as far as Jewish justice is concerned, is an exceptional position, and that the obligations and responsibilities of the Jew refer always and only to the "neighbour" i. e. to the Jewish racial companion. And he adds:

"But the fundamental idea, that you should have less consideration for the stranger than for the racial companion, has not altered from the time of the Thora until the present day."

This is a most important admission, and can always be brought forward as a challenge to those people, who are of the opinion that the Jewish doctrine is, at the present day, no longer efficacious, and that the Talmud contains views, which have been overcome. By these very words, Sombart at the same time, contradicts his opinion expressed above, that the Talmud doctrine has altered in the course of the centuries.

"This completely vague perception: that you are not committing any sin, and that it is permissible in the course of business with a stranger to tell him that odd is even, became firmly established wherever that formal Rabbinism developed out of a study of the Talmud, which was the case in many districts of Eastern Europe. (Sombart page 289)."

Even the Jewish historian, Graetz, who otherwise certainly cannot be regarded as impartial, confesses that:

"Distortion and perversion, the trickiness of the lawyer, affectation of wit and precipitate rejection of whatever might not be included in his range of vision, are the essential features of the Polish Jew. Honesty, and a sound mode of thinking have deserted him, as well as simplicity, and a desire for and an appreciation of truth."

We certainly are of opinion that, so far as moral negligence in the case of the Jew is concerned, it is not a question of the loss and disappearance of moral qualities, but is, on the contrary, to be attributed to a primitive and hereditary defect; for we discover this trait, not merely since the origin of the Talmud, but already even in The Old Testament. One need only call attention to the treacherous behaviour of the sons of Jacob, who persuaded the honest Hevites to undergo circumcision, and then attacked and slew them while suffering from the effects of the operation. (1. Moses 34).

It is worthy of note how the Rabbis in their Talmudic writings concern themselves in a most intimate manner with all kinds of business practices; and again, it is only in accordance with the principles of the Talmud, that warnings should be issued ostensibly against immoral business practices, whilst later on, the prohibitions are withdrawn and the selfsame practices are declared permissible. Rabbi Jehuda speaks thus in one and the same breath:

"The grocer shall not present the children with cakes and nuts, for, by so doing he attracts them to his shop — the Sages, however, allow it. Further, one must not cut the price — the Sages, however, are of the opinion: the precept is worthy of remembrance (i. e. it would be a praiseworthy habit). Abba Saul has decided that the split beans are not to be picked out — the Sages, on the contrary, allow it."

Here we find the contradictory and discordant morality of the Talmud expressed in the sleekest manner — apparently without consciousness that it is a doctrine of nonsense and immorality. That is to say: everything is forbidden and everything is allowed; see which suits you best. However, the compilers of the Shulchan aruch, without any attempt at concealment, have made this question perfectly clear; they say in Chochen hammischpat 228, 18:

"The shopkeeper is permitted to make presents of nuts and suchlike to the children who buy from him, in order to attract them to him; he is also in the position to sell more cheaply than the market-price, and the people on the market are unable to raise any objection."

Unrestricted license in underbidding and competition form the very life-breath of the Jewish existence, everything is permitted, which makes business easy; everything is allowed, which puts the

Jew in a position to over-reach and fleece others. For this reason, Sombart says at the conclusion of this chapter: "God (i. e. Jahwe — English Jehovah) desires free-trade, God desires freedom of industry! What a motive to make the same effective *in* the economic life."

The references of Sombart to the accordance of English Puritanism with Judaism are interesting, and Heine, in his time, made fun of this association by calling the Puritans "pork- eating Jews". A fact, which Sombart lays stress upon, is that the Jews in England, especially among the Puritans, enjoyed during the 17th century a respect and reverence, which are only to be described as fanatical, and many writers of the period vied with one another to prove that the English were direct descendants of the Jews. At all events, certain pietistic circles in England were at great pains to copy the Jews in their mode of living, nomenclature and other externals. This symbolism was carried so far, that the Christian clergy and even the Christian laity studied the Rabbinical literature for preference. Sombart refers to a "droll little book", which appeared in 1608, under the title of the *"Calvinistic Mirror of the Jews"*, and which, amongst other things, treated of the relations subsisting between Puritanism (Calvinism) and Judaism. The following quotation out of this book is worthy of note: "the Jews penetrate into every country to cheat the inhabitants."

In the Netherland and German pietistic circles also, (Wupperthal, Swabia etc.) one encounters reminders of the English Puritanism in the form of nomenclature, intense veneration of the Sabbath, and so forth. These form, without doubt, the strongest props of that fateful validity which the Old Testament possesses in the German Protestant Church. There are even Protestant clergy, who are ready to represent the Jews as the pattern of religiousness, and — perhaps unconsciously — to work more for the cause of Jewdom than for that of Christianity.

XIV

THE RACE PROBLEM

1. IN GENERAL

Sombart gives himself great airs in his Xllth chapter, where he treats of Jewish peculiarity when regarded from a racial point of view. He is of opinion — obviously with a side thrust at the wicked Anti- Semites — that the racial problem and national psychology have become the plaything of caprice and dilettantism, and that in particular the portrayal of the Jewish entity is "undertaken as a kind of political sport by coarse individuals with gross instincts". It certainly cannot be denied that, in the course of the Anti-Semitic movement, many people and tendencies have started up, whose origins and pretensions will not bear investigation; but, at the present day, even these people, who can never inflict enough pain by the derision, which they cast upon the opinions of others, refuse, in a superior manner, to listen to anything Anti-Semitic. And yet, a very considerable number of leading spirits and estimable characters have belonged, and still belong to the spokesmen of this movement. We do not wish here to dwell upon the fact that great men in all times, that philosophers from Giodarno Bruno and Voltaire to Fichte, Herder, Schopenhauer and Feuerbach, that statesmen like Frederick the Great, Napoleon I and Bismarck, that artists like Richard Wagner and Franz Liszt must be included amongst the opponents of the Jews.[55] The more modern Anti-Semitic movement also includes in its ranks as spokesmen, individuals like Paul de Lagarde, Eugen

---

[55] A collection of extracts from the writings of these men is to be found in the "Handbuch der Judenfrage" (*Handbook of the Jewish Question*) 27 edition, pages 12—117. — The racial question is dealt with exhaustively by the well-known geographer Rich. Andree in "Zur Volkskunde der Juden" (*Popular information respecting the Jews*) Bielefeld 1881.

Dühring and Adolf Wahrmund, whose profound erudition cannot even be approached by any of their opponents however much it may be belittled or ignored by the public press, itself completely under Jewish domination. However, before everything, it must not be forgotten that it was the wicked Anti-Semites, who first tackled the Race-problem and aroused racial consciousness again among the nations. If, at the commencement, it was only the difference between Aryan and Semite, which engaged their attention, it is nevertheless due to their initiative that the whole of the modern racial movement has come into being, and has built itself up upon the fundamental views of the Anti- Semites. If, now and again, objectionable behaviour puts in an appearance in the course of the Anti-Jewish movement, and epithets are applied to the Hebrews, which are not exactly flattering, there is no cause whatever for undue sensitiveness in this respect on the Jewish side. One has only to recall how low-class Jewish wits, in the so-called comic papers, which are founded almost without exception by Hebrews, let themselves go concerning other nations, classes, privileges and political opponents. Scarcely anything is low and foul enough to enable the Hebrew to give full vent to his hatred against those, who differ from him in their opinions, and for this reason there is little or no justification on his side for a display of moral indignation and extreme sensitiveness on hearing an expression of opinion concerning himself, which is often remarkably appropriate.

This assumption of indignation collapses in a ridiculous fashion, if the fact is disputed, from a purely Jewish point of view, — like a certain Friedrich Hertz and others attempt to do — that there are such people as Jews at the present day. This is more than droll. So long as the so-called Jewish religion continues, so long will Judaism, as a compact hostile force, live and operate amongst the other nations. But even if it were possible to extirpate this religion, the racial peculiarity of the Jew, which has acquired an extraordinary tenacity by incessant inbreeding, would long continue to function.

Sombart then honourably takes pains to put an end to those chatterers, who wish to deny the existence of a Jewish race and a Jewish peculiarity. But he himself is certainly not clear in his own mind concerning the racial entity when he says: "On the other hand it is senseless to give the name of "Jew" to an Israelite of unmistakable origin, who has succeeded in throwing off the fetters of Esra and Nehemiah, in whose mind there is no longer any thought for the law of Moses, and whose heart no longer feels contempt for other races."

In the next place it is doubtful if a Jew can ever completely free himself of the views, derived from his racial peculiarity, which were being prepared and established from the time of Moses to that of Esra and Nehemiah, and which, later on, under the influence of Talmudic Rabbinism, were extended and expanded until they became a gross exaggeration. But even if he is capable of emancipating himself, Jewish instincts will survive and function in his offspring. So long as we have no experience of a Jewish business-man causing his son to become a farmer, a conductor, a carpenter or a sailor, it is certain that no one will seriously believe in the transformation of the people of Judah into genuine human beings. We are in agreement on this point with our own most excellent Fichte, who also did not believe that the Hebrews were capable of being converted, unless "all their heads were cut off in one night, and other heads were substituted in which there was not a single Jewish idea." These words describe most aptly the indestructibility of the Jewish racial entity.

The study of the racial problem has taught us that an indissoluble bond exists between the blood and the mental disposition of mankind. It is said in The Old Testament that "the soul of a man dwells in his blood," and that means, that the mental nature of man is inseparably united with his blood. This fact we must ultimately learn to accept in all its seriousness. We have long been accustomed to attach value to the blood and stock amongst animals; we do not desire that a poodle should become a sporting-dog, or that a horse from Brabant should develop into a racer. We know that advantages, just like disadvantages and defects, are transmitted with the blood.

We have no intention of conveying the impression that all good and bad characteristics must be transmitted with unchanging fidelity from generation to generation, that the children of a clever father must be, without exception, geniuses, and that the offspring of a criminal is invariably criminal; but we perceive a certain constancy in the transmissibility of average qualities, whereby only those deviations and variations crop up, which Nature allows herself everywhere as a diversion. If the constancy in the transmissibility of qualities is comparatively insignificant as regards the present-day generation, this must be attributed to the excessive intermingling of tribes and races, which has been taking place for centuries — even for thousands of years. The pure races certainly have almost completely disappeared, and only mongrel descendants surround us. In spite of this, one must not straightway deny that the racial entity has ceased to operate. The frivolous doctrine, that all men are equal, has caused unspeakable disaster and has actually introduced degeneration into the human race. We Germans of today have certainly no reason to boast of our race, for its worth is seriously depreciated, both blood and intellect having been dulled. But this should not restrain us from appreciating to the utmost the importance of the racial entity, and from endeavouring, by means of racial culture, to restore what has been sacrificed by an irresponsible racial lottery.

It is a fact — and it is about the only reputable thing which one can say about Judaism — that racial consciousness is fostered to a greater extent among the Hebrews than among any other nation, whether consciously or unconsciously, by the rigid law which enjoins that everyone, who does not belong to the race, must be regarded with hostility and contempt. Thus the irrefutable fact remains, that the racial entity amongst the Jews is today of greater validity, both physically and mentally, than amongst all the other races. The Hebrew, almost everywhere, can be recognised amongst other races both by his external appearance and, if anything, still more by his mental cast. And this racial constancy asserts itself, even when mingled with other strains.

The Jewish Professor Eduard Gans expresses himself as follows: "Baptism and interbreeding are of no avail; we remain, even in the hundredth generation Jews, as we were 3000 years ago. We never lose the odour of our race — not even by tenfold crossing.

And, in every case of cohabitation with every woman, our race dominates: young Jews result."

Whoever, in face of facts like these, still persists in denying the existence of a Jewish race, cannot have much regard for truth. But we can very well understand why it is so distasteful to the Hebrews to see racial recognition and racial consciousness awakening among other nations. In the moment when this comes to pass, the alienage of the Jew will, for the first time, make itself apparent to all, and this will, in every respect, make the Hebrew's business more difficult. Up till now, the Jew has been able, in an inimitable manner, to mingle with other nations, and to delude them into believing that he really belonged to them — a circumstance, which rendered his overreaching operations extremely easy to carry out. As soon, however, as the other nations become aware of their own particularity, and of the value of their own especial gifts, both moral and intellectual, they will soon recognise in the Hebrew the disturber of their domestic peace and of their harmonious development, and will endeavour to keep him at a distance.

2. THE PSYCHOLOGY OF THE JEWS

The Hebrew certainly possesses a great adaptability, but it would be erroneous to expect from his external adjustment to the habits and customs of other nations that the Jew is absorbed and disappears. The Jewish peculiarity differs far too much from the nature of all other nations to allow a complete fusion to appear even probable. In the last analysis it is the Jewish view of life, and the Jewish moral law, which do not admit of any permanent association with other nations.

Sombart makes a vain attempt to sum up the Hebrew entity in precise ideas. He sees, amongst these, only a few of a disagreeable nature, and is unable to connect the same with fixed characteristics. The distinguishing features of the Jew enumerated by him, appear to me to be insufficient. I believe that I shall meet with but little opposition, when I characterise the average Jew as follows: sharp at business and glib of tongue, greedy for money and of a saving disposition, cunning and addicted to dissimulation, averse to bodily labour, sensual and shameless, vain, cowardly and impudent. There are but few Jews in whom the majority of these characteristics cannot be detected. When Sombart speaks incessantly of their "prominence in intellectuality", it is clear that he means only the calm, calculating intelligence of the Jew, generally speaking, the mere operation of the cold understanding as opposed to the sensibility of deeper and more emotional natures. This much-praised intellectuality of the Hebrew is, in reality, only the outcome of necessity.[56] How could otherwise a people, devoid of all capacity for production, maintain their existence unless they unceasingly made use of cunning and deception, and knew how to fool others into furthering their own secret plans? It cannot be denied that Hebrews have occasionally distinguished themselves as clever physicians, scholars and barristers, but only so far, in these professions, as the possession of a coldly-calculating and subtle understanding permitted them to advance. And, in this respect, they have frequently been actually favoured by their own low standard of morality. Moral laxity frequently gives the Hebrew an advantage over other people. Whoever is not particularly scrupulous concerning his moral duty towards mankind, has a much freer hand on many occasions than those, who are restrained by their conscience and consideration.

Just as the Jewish business-man, thanks to his moral laxity, outstrips competitors in commerce, so is it in many other departments of life. For sense of duty, conscience and honour have but little value in the eyes of the Hebrews when compared with intellectual capacity. The Jew is desirous, at all costs, of passing as clever; everything else is a matter of comparative indifference to him. There are a number of Jewish proverbs, which regard stupidity as being far worse than any other mental or moral defect. All of these are centred on the idea: you may be a rascal if you only show yourself sly. Whilst the civilised and honour-loving nations attach the highest value to moral character, and to the emotional side of

[56] The well-known oriental traveller, H. Vámbéry, (originally Bamberger) confirms this fact, amongst others, in his report concerning the Jews of the Orient, 1879, in which he states that it is a delusion to assume that the Jews in Europe possessed higher intelligence than the nations who acted as their hosts, for, to take Middle Asia as an example, the Jew, when confronted by the Hindoo and the Armenian, invariably came off second best.

human nature, the Hebrew appraises a man merely according to his mental adroitness. Whoever is clever, is therefore worthy of admiration, even if he uses his cleverness to the detriment of others — perhaps, for that reason, all the more to be admired! It is often to be observed in the Jewish Press how the attempt is made to find a certain measure of excuse for grave crimes on the grounds that considerable intellectual capacity has been displayed in committing the same. This confusing and disordering of moral ideas by the introduction of intellectual standards, are to be included amongst the most dangerous means, by which Hebrewdom is seeking to destroy the other nations. Unfortunately, the moral sense in many classes has already been considerably weakened, because its power of discrimination has been injuriously affected by the fact that thanks to Jewish example — admiration is frequently accorded to the criminal. It thus happens, that when a crime is being discussed, one can often hear good-natured men mitigating their abhorrence somewhat as follows: "But, after all, he showed himself a very sharp fellow!" — Indeed a sign of the Judaization of our mode of thinking.

Sombart characterises the Jewish — and probably at the same time his own — perception with the words: "the highest humanism is supreme intellectualism" — an appraisement, to which we feel ourselves compelled to object. For, measured by this standard, the most accomplished rogue and swindler would, under circumstances, represent humanity's supreme ideal. The heroic nations have an assured conviction of another ideal. They seek it in the direction of self-sacrifice of the individual for the general welfare, or, for an idea — for freedom or for honour — but, above all, in the complete subjugation of selfishness. The hero of our dramas, whose fate rivets our attention and affects us deeply, is not a sly customer, who, thanks to his crafty alertness, knows how to dodge all dangers, but is, on the contrary, an upright, inflexible character, who accepts his recognised duty courageously, and who does not turn aside from the path of truth and justice whatever menace may stand in his way. He thinks little of his own advantage, but all the more of duty and honour. A real hero of this type will appear to the eyes of the Jew as no better than a fool; — "better a live dog than a dead lion" is a

Semitic proverb. This indicates the deep chasm, which exists between the Jewish and the genuinely human mode of thinking.

However, the understanding which merely calculates, proves itself generally inadequate for dealing with all serious matters in life. There is something higher than the intellect. A man of fine character allows himself to be swayed more by innate and instinctive feelings than by cold calculation. And these instinctive feelings which, in reality, indicate an intimate spiritual and emotional insight into the connection between things, are a far surer guide to mankind than all the speculations of the intellect. Where the guiding instinct is wanting, we see the intellect straying into all manner of blind alleys, clambering too high on its own artificial structures, which have lost all touch with reason and nature, and at last, for this reason, failing completely. The Hebrew, a being, who is not of immediate natural origin, and who, for that reason, makes his journey through life without any intimate connection with nature, is devoid of instinctive feelings. He endeavours to replace them by conscious intellect. This may confer a certain apparent superiority on him so long as he moves in artificial surroundings, which depend, more or less, upon intellectual foundations. He is, however, completely at a loss, and feels helpless immediately when he finds himself in a situation where the relations are entirely natural. A Robinson, alone on a desert island, can contrive, with scant resources, to keep body and soul together; a Hebrew is incapable of doing so. The Jew is a second-rate man, whose existence depends upon all kinds of artificial assumptions. He is Nature's step-child, and cannot get on with this mother. He is always in need of some man, who has grown up in touch with Nature and who is full of natural impulse, to carry him — the Jew — through life.

And when Sombart believes that he can perceive the acme of genius in freedom from all natural law, and in tearing one's self loose from all natural instincts, he betrays, in spite of himself, his own Jewishness. The opposite is correct; genius stands — unconsciously in most cases — in closest relationship, in inmost feeling with the natural laws of being and becoming! It draws from a source, whose deepest spring is scarcely known to itself. It is only for the reason that the internal and eternal obedience to law, of all natural things and occurrences, resides also in the creations of genius, that the latter are eternal and inextinguishable; and it is also for this reason that they stir the emotions of mankind, so long as men do not close their ears to the voice of nature.

The conspicuous intellectualism of the Jew is direct evidence of his weakness and of his inferiority from a human point of view. It is only when the natural feeling fails, when the instinct is no longer a safe guide, that the calculating intellect begins in its distress to strain after artificial remedies, and seeks to create artificial conditions, which are agreeable to it. The Jew can only flourish in an artificial world. In reality, the mental speculations of the Hebrew are confined to comparatively narrow fields of activity, where it is a matter of obtaining an advantage and of misleading and confusing the opponent. Only there is he a master; everywhere else, where it is a case of penetrating more deeply into artistic, technical and exact scientific knowledge, the intellect of the Jew does not suffice. And therefore, the Hebrew is never inventor and artist in the grand style. Whoever follows up the refined subtleties of the Rabbis in the Talmud, can often observe how their petty, short-sighted, calculating spirit leads them into incredible imbecilities. According to the popular opinion, the devil is a professor of slyness. But also, according to popular tradition, there are all kinds of legends, showing how the peasant gets the better of the devil; and from this popular notion emerges a deep meaning. The peasant may appear to be awkward and helpless in the external affairs of life, especially when he is brought face to face with the artificial conditions of town life; he possesses, for the most part, however, although it may be only by means of his feelings, a deeper insight into natural things than many a learned townsman. And the devil, for all his arithmetic, always miscalculates when he encounters natural cleverness, and when the unalterable laws of nature break through his web of deceit. Yes, after all, the devil is stupid, and so is his cousin, the Jew. Place him face to face with Nature, with no creative men to assist him, and all his lordly intellectualism will suffer a miserable shipwreck — will not save him from starvation.

On the other hand, the Jew has known how to confer an extraordinary power of attraction on the modern towns with their artificial and refined methods of traffic and intercourse; he entices the simple villagers away from nature into these modern paradises of vice, where everything is cast in an unnatural and artificial mould. Jews, and Jewish mentality reign supreme in the large towns, and the natural man feels that he is a stranger there, more like a child, straying helplessly into the traps of the Jews, which are laid for him on every side. Therefore, whoever wishes to escape from the Jewish illusion must fly from these places, and seek refuge again on the maternal breast of Nature; and, just as surely is he doomed to certain ruin, who imagines that he can continue to live as a child of Nature in the meretricious and false world of the Jew.

Even Sombart admits as much:

"We frequently find in the case of the Jew that all instinctive feeling is stunted, just as if all sensibility and sensitive relations to the rest of the world were foreign to his disposition."

Here, however, it is conceded that the Hebrew himself stands forth as both foreign and contrary to Nature. He moves in the midst of Nature as a dull and insensible being; he certainly sees things separately, but he passes over the causal connection of the natural phenomenon and the inward obedience to law of all life, without paying the slightest attention to the same. For this reason, he is unable to judge what the final effects of his scheming and plotting will be; he is always directed merely by the advantage of the moment. He hankers after the goods and chattels of the peasant; he knows how to get hold of the same, and to drive the peasant from hearth and home; but he neither stops to reflect, nor does he care, what will become of the village, when all the peasants have been plundered in this fashion and driven away. He sucks the last drop of blood out of the workman and the small employer of labour, and dispatches them to ruin, without asking: what will become of the world if we weaken the productive classes in this manner? He entangles the various countries in debts and loans, and hands them over to ruin, without taking the trouble to think that these operations will eventually cause human society itself to collapse — that society which nourishes him with its flesh, and out of whose body he derives his parasitic existence. We see here the same fool, who saws off the branch on which he is sitting, and who kills the hen, which lays golden eggs for him. Accustomed to the constant provision of new hunting-grounds and fresh objects of usury by an inexhaustible Nature, and by the indefatigable industry of the nations, he is unable to conceive that the world-dominion, for which he is striving, would mean simultaneous world-ruin. The vain nature of his understanding, which does not look beyond to-day and to-morrow, operates destructively and suicidally in all directions.

Hence only powers can work constructively, which stand in organic relation to Nature; and the profoundest essence of natural things can only be comprehended by means of sensibility. The intellect is not sufficient to sound the well of life. The Jewish mode of thinking is inorganic, and is, for that reason, incapable of creative operation. For that reason also, the Hebrews are incapable of forming a state of their own, for, in the last analysis, the state is of an organic nature, and endures only through organic laws. Society, in a well- ordered state, requires organisation of the classes, a rational constructive policy, and internal connections — i. e. sound relations and ties with one another, which enable the concern, taken as a whole, to prosper. The Hebrew has no understanding for all this. He regards individual men merely as objects to be turned to profitable account, and is incapable of comprehending why these same men are desirous of retaining a scale in their social order, why they band together in organic associations the better to fulfil their duties as men and citizens. All this appears to him as foolish prejudice and antiquated institution; he would like to alter, loosen and dissolve everything in order to find an easy and convenient field for his profiteering operations. He is, therefore, hostile to all organic social creations: the guilds, the trade associations, the nobility, the army. These are like a thorn in his eye. He would like to disrupt and atomise them, and to isolate the members. He is guided in this policy by the calculation that he can deal better with the individual, and can more easily make him subservient to his aims than he can the compact whole. He calls this disruption of all organic structures, "bringing freedom", "liberalising"; he knows how to delude men into believing that their organic connection is a barrier, which must be broken down, a fetter, which must be shaken off, in order to attain to true liberty — the liberty of the wolf amongst sheep.

Sombart remarks very appositely:

"The Jew is very sharp-sighted, but he does not see much. In the first place, he does not perceive that his environment is a living one. And, for this reason, feeling for what is singular in life, for its entirety, for its indivisibility, for what has organically developed, for what has grown naturally, is lost to him. Consequently all conditions and relations of dependence, which are built up on personality, such as personal rule, personal service, personal sacrifice, are foreign to him. The Jew, from his very disposition, is averse to all chivalry, to all sentiment, to all nobility, to all feudalism, to all patriarchism. He is also incapable of understanding a community, which is built up on the above relations. Everything to do with class or rank, everything incorporative is hateful to him. He is political individualist."[57]

And yet he is individualist only in a restricted sense; he is himself the slave of a rigid principle, of a law of compulsion, which, in the place of a natural tie, binds him together with his kind. The Jew himself possesses no individuality; he is invariably only the more or less successful repetition of a Jewish pattern. The Jews, amongst themselves, resemble one another in their national characteristics to a much greater extent than the men of other nations; and the extraordinary limitation of their disposition is rooted in the above fact. The Hebrew is, as it were, an automaton, trained and adjusted to carry on definite social activities; he fulfils exactly the same functions in all grades of society. For this reason a Hebrew is easily replaced by another Hebrew, whilst the same cannot be said of men of other nations.

The Hebrew is now desirous of transferring this systematic constitution of the Jewish league, i.e. this mechanical placing together of elements all equal in value and devoid of individuality, to other social creations, and even to the state. He is unable to understand why organised society is on the defensive against this subjugation to one pattern, and he denounces this opposition to his endeavours to break up and dissolve, as "Reaction". In reality, this

---

[57] We are justified in supposing that this train of thought on the part of Sombart was set in motion by the "*Hammer*", which, ever since it was founded in 1902, has often thrown light upon the "Jew Question" from this point of view.

reaction is the natural and healthy resistance, which an organised society evolves against the efforts of the Hebrew to introduce decay and dissolution; in other words, it is the instinct of self-preservation.

The actual and harmful reactionary is, on the contrary, the Hebrew, who checks the natural growth of national life by his plan to reduce all to one emasculated pattern, and who desires to force this life back into its primordial state — the struggle for existence of all against all. It is he who hinders natural development, and thereby disturbs the even progress of life.

This fact, to our unspeakable misfortune, is only recognised by a few. The enormous liberation of energy, caused by the speculative principle of the Hebrew, and the enormous development of the external life caused thereby, deceive everyone as to the true state of affairs. The glitter and gleam all around us appear to many as the veritable light of life, but it is, in reality, only the phosphorescence of corruption. The Hebrew, by inciting to that wild struggle for existence, has forced into action the last reserves of national energy, and thus the national life itself seems to have experienced a tremendous stimulus; and yet it is only the waging of a desperate battle for mutual destruction, which must end suddenly from exhaustion.

But what does the Hebrew care about that! As a man who depends upon the momentary fluctuation of affairs, he derives his chief benefit from such conditions, and that is enough for him. Sombart says:

"The Jew brings everything into relation with his "I". The questions, which have first claim on his interest, are: Why? To what purpose? Where do I come in? What do I get out of it? His real living interest is the interest for success. It is unJewish to regard an activity as an end in itself, to live life itself for its own sake, without purpose in accordance with destiny; it is unJewish to rejoice harmlessly in Nature. (Sombart page 230-31)."

And just as he is himself, so has the Jew devised his God. The Jewish God stands outside the pale of Nature as a despot, who alters the course of affairs arbitrarily to suit his purposes. He allows all kinds of miracles to take place, which are contrary to Nature, and arranges everything so that it turns out to the advantage of his favourite people.

3. APPARENT JEWISH SUPERIORITY

When Sombart expresses the opinion: "At the present day, the Jew of Western Europe no longer desires to retain his faith and his national peculiarity; he wishes, on the contrary, so far as national consciousness has not again been aroused in him, to allow his peculiarity to disappear as completely and quickly as possible, and to adopt the culture of the nations who act as host to him," we must ask circumspectly: where are the proofs of this suggested effort? Who authorises Sombart to assure us of this? For our part, we perceive and know just the contrary.

It may well be conceded that, at the present day, the Hebrew is occasionally uncomfortable under his skin, since observant men have begun to make a practice of observing his activity, and are now revealing his tricks; it may well be the case at the present day that many a Jew no longer wishes to be recognised as such, and would prefer to change his appearance; the fact remains that it is simply impossible for the Jew to be absorbed by other nations, even if it were his wish. His distinctive nature is far too different from that of other nations, and moreover his self-esteem is too great. He has no intention of resigning his privilege of being regarded as a "chosen people." But the aversion also of the other nations, so far as a healthy instinct is still alive in them, will protest against any such fusion. Certain sections of society, which have already completed their resemblance to the Hebrew, represent types of degeneration doomed, in any case, to disappear. It is only the degenerate who shows inclination towards the Hebrew; the former, by the loss of the finer instincts, has sacrificed his real manhood, has been discarded by nature, and sinks into that swamp of corruption represented by Hebrewdom — the dregs of culture.

The following judgement concerning the Jews testifies that Sombart, in his scientific positiveness, is gradually working round to our perception, even though it may be in a circuitous manner:

"His intuition has not grown out of his innermost being, but is a product of the head. His stand-point is not the level earth, but an artificial building in the air. He is not organic original but mechanic- rational. He is not rooted in the mother-soil of sensibility — instinct."

All this is covered by the perception expressed a long time ago by the Anti-Semites. Only, at the same time, it must not be forgotten: the Jewish entity, and its inward perception of life, is certainly an artificial creation of the intellect; but, in the course of thousands of years, it has become so ingrained in the Hebrew — has entered so thoroughly into his flesh and blood, that he is actually less capable of changing his skin than the representative of any other race. He certainly possesses adroitness enough to adopt superficially the manners, and even the mode of thinking, of others; he has sufficient powers of dissimulation and of acting, to make us believe that he is a being very similar to ourselves; but, in the end, the unadulterated Hebrew always comes to the surface again. This pliancy, this outward adaptability, this talent for representing one's self as something different to what one really is, might appear admirable to us, if it was not at the same time so dangerous. All these Hebrew talents are only means to mislead us, and to make us subservient to the designs of the stranger. It is correct that the Hebrew, regarded from a purely intellectual point of view, appears to display great superiority in a number of respects, the questionable value and unquestionable danger of which are only recognised by the instinct of fine-feeling. We may admire the Jew from an intellectual point of view, but our feelings reject him.

Sombart speaks appositely concerning the "moral mobility" of the Jew; in the pursuit of his purposes "no irksome restrictions of a moral or aesthetic nature are allowed to intervene." His morality is lax and elastic; he is ready, at any minute, to proclaim that odd is even if he sees any advantage in doing so.

"In this respect his poorly developed sense for what one can call personal dignity, is of assistance to him. It is very little exertion to him to deny what he has himself said, when it is a question of accomplishing his purpose."

Thus writes Sombart on page 327. In reality, the Hebrew possesses so little of what we call character, that he is ready at all times to barter his honour and self-respect for material advantage. An old proverb says:

"The Jew will wade through seven puddles, in order to possess one groschen more."

With the help of the Talmudic schooling, the Hebrews are educated to become cunning pettifoggers, for, from youth upwards, the practice of dissimulation is enjoined upon them, practically as a command. There is, accordingly, little cause for surprise when they distinguish themselves later on in life as lawyers, journalists and actors. The art, of being able to transpose one's self quickly into a strange world of ideas, is absolutely essential to speculative dealing; if the Jew did not possess it, how else would he gain respite for himself, entirely dependent as he is on the exploitation of other men, and on the misuse of law and thought? The advantages, possessed by the Jew, mirror his weaknesses; these are shiftiness, evasion, adroitness in escaping from embarrassing situations, all of which he requires in order to conceal his failings from us. There is a well-known contradictory principle in Nature, whereby she endeavours to conceal and compensate for prominent defects by other qualities. She provides weak, defenceless creatures with properties or qualities, which serve as a means of protection against the pursuing enemy. Thus Nature protects the young birds in their nests by their revolting ugliness, other animals by an obnoxious smell or by a disagreeable secretion, the snail, for instance, by a nasty slime. And, in the same way, Nature dispenses properties to a section of mankind, burdened with hereditary weakness, which must serve as a protection. Even the evasive intelligence, craft and cunning are protective qualities of this order, and they are to be found amongst the weak and the criminal. Men of great bodily strength are, for the most part, open and upright, good-natured, patient and obliging. They can put up with a good deal, without losing their tempers, because they know that when the decisive moment arrives, they can rely upon their good, natural strength, which, if required, will sweep every obstacle out of the way. This good-nature and this indulgence, which are sometimes taken for weakness, but which are, in reality, only an expression of self-confidence or assurance, are occasionally displayed also by men of mind and character. On the other hand, it is a matter of common knowledge that weakly and deformed beings display a sharp mental activity, which can even become caustic, and which represents, in their case, a means of defence to protect them against unexpected attacks.

The situation of the Hebrew, when he finds himself in the presence of honest men, is analogous. He, the weakling, who is incapable anywhere of shaping a life for himself by his own exertions, whom political incapacity has condemned to lead a parasitic existence amongst other nations, he, who is wanting in all the higher mental powers necessary to produce an imaginative and creative culture: he, it is, who has been equipped with a cunning intellect, and with boundless impudence and slyness as a means of defence. In reality, the Hebrew is the mental cripple amongst mankind, the type of intellectual deformity. The Jew represents the lower side of human nature. Let those wonder at him who will: we should only feel sorry for him if he did not happen to be, at the same time, a poisonous snake, which endangers the peace and safety of honest humanity everywhere.

But the slyness of mind, and the threadbare morality are still not sufficient to assure him of prosperity; he requires yet another weapon for defence and attack, in order to outwit and overcome honest people. As a substitute for the natural ability, which he does not possess, he has created for himself a principle, in which an almost demoniacal force resides, viz Money-Capital. Money plays so great a part in the existence of the Jew, that the individual sinks into insignificance when compared with material possession. "Whoever does not pay to me my money, deprives me of my honour", wrote old Amschel Mayer Rothschild to the Elector William II. (see page 37), and the socialist leader, Carl Marx, who was himself of Jewish origin, admitted that "money is the real secular deity of Jewdom". From an allegorical point of view it is worthy of note, that the Hebrews erected a golden calf on Mount Sinai, and arranged a dance around it. This is also recognised by Sombart.

"Money, and the increase of money, must always be the centre of interest for Jews, just as it is for capitalism. Not merely because its abstract nature is congenial to the equally abstract nature of the Jew, but, above all, because the appreciation of money is in conformity with another leading trait in the Jewish character viz teleologism. Money is the absolute means: it has but one meaning with regard to the purpose to be realised."

Sombart expresses himself as above in his scientific German, and thereby recognises money as the highest potential in all Jewish endeavour.

Money is, however, an imaginary value, an artificial creation of human speculation. It has nothing to do with nature, nothing to do with organic things; it has no inner relation to the being of mankind. Money does not make a man stronger, wiser or nobler; the capability alone, conferred on it by the human imagination, of possessing, not only buying power, but — in the form of loan capital — power to produce interest, has invested it with an almost supernatural might. And this imaginary might has been recognised by the Hebrew, as the correct means to provide him with a substitute for his deficient powers. Money places the sub-man in the position to pose almost as a super-man, and to force all human affairs under his yoke.

Of what then does the renowned Jewish superiority consist? In reality, of a kind of mental provocation and harassing. It is precisely because the distinctive nature of the Hebrew is averse to Nature, that he is destined to deceive and over-reach the man who thinks naturally. It is because the Jew does not think organically, and consequently does not think naturally, that the unspoilt and unaffected man is unable to keep pace with his speculations. Whilst we are accustomed to think straightforwardly, the Jew thinks, as it were, "round the corner"; his mental process is perverse, warped, subverted. Consequently his conclusions confound all natural logic.

It frequently happens that a man, who has been overreached by a Jew, is unable to restrain a feeling, akin to admiration, for the cunning deceiver. The unnatural sequence of Jewish thoughts confuse a natural brain, so that it loses the power of thinking logically while under the influence of the seductive language of the Hebrew, and falls into a kind of stupor, a condition in which, a weak-willed man, or a man who is unable to think quickly, is inclined to succumb to the influence of an external will. This power of suggestion, which operates by imposing one's own will upon another, is one of the most dangerous means employed by Hebrewdom to infatuate, not only individuals, but whole nations. There is scarcely any other way to explain this extraordinary state of infatuation, in which the civilised nations of to-day find themselves, when confronted with Hebrewdom, than by describing it as the result of a kind of suggestion or mesmerism. Indeed, both states and their populations scarcely know what is really happening to them since the Hebrew, in addition to the demoniacal power of money, has also enlisted that gigantic power to deceive and mislead, which the public press possesses, in order to hypnotise everybody and to paralyse their mental activities.

Perhaps, however, it only requires an unmasking of the hypnotic agent, and a thorough exposure of his dishonest expedients, to break the spell for ever.

F. RODERICH-STOLTHEIM

XV

ORIGIN OF THE JEWISH ENTITY

1. DESCENT OF THE JEWS

Sombart searches around to discover the origin of the Jewish race, and raises the question: whence does it come, and whither is it proceeding? He does not hesitate to describe the Jews as a kind of freak, as a lower order of humanity, of entirely different blood to the nations amongst whom they live. We add to this: difference in blood means also difference in mind and spirit, for, amongst the most important disclosures of the science of race, must be included the fact that certain mental qualities are firmly and inseparably united with a certain kind of blood. In accordance with general acceptation, Sombart believes that Israel, as well as Judah, originated from a mixture of various oriental peoples. This notion is contradicted by the fact, that all Jews regard themselves as the descendants of a common tribal father (Abraham or Jacob), and that already at a very remote period, the Jews were prohibited by strict laws from mixing with other nations. Actually, one can only begin to speak of Jewdom, from the moment when a particular caste arrayed itself in conscious opposition to the rest of humanity, and declined either to mix with the same or to entertain any feelings in common with it. It is precisely the exclusion of their stock from any consanguinity with the remainder of mankind, which makes Jewdom what it is. That Bedouin, that is to say, Semitic tribes have provided the ground-floor of the structure of Hebrewdom, is universally accepted, and Adolf Wahrmund, in his frequently-quoted work: *"The Law of Nomadism and the present-day domination by the Jews"* has provided convincing proof of the spiritual affinity of Hebrewdom with the Semitic desert tribes. Nomadism and changeableness are common to both; the conception of a firmly-founded state is foreign to both, and both seek their salvation in continual wandering and peregrination. They graze the pastures bare, and then move on to where fresh booty beckons to them. Both practise the sudden method of attack, allow no quarter, and exterminate; both are animated by the spirit of the desert, which leaves a train of burnt-out settlements along its track. Amongst the civilised nations, however, our Hebrews have altered the methods of their predatory expeditions. They no longer slay with the blade of the sword, but throttle their adversary with the golden noose of capitalism.[58] The surprise and slaughter of the opponent is accomplished, in its modernised form, on the Stock Exchange. There the dice are cast, which determine victory and dominion; there the economic fortunes and the economic freedom of the nations are gambled with; and as Judah plays with loaded dice, it is assured of victory. There the strangler of nations twines the golden snares, in which he entangles, not only the economic, but also the spiritual and political life of the peoples.

But one must certainly not any longer speak of our Jews of to-day as pure Semites; they have also taken up all manner of foreign national elements; and it is truly remarkable to what a complete extent they have assimilated the same. One is entitled to ask whether the Talmudic spirit alone has rendered this complete adaptation possible, or whether a few drops of Jewish blood have sufficed to give an unvarying stamp or impression — at least mentally — to the entire mass. Externally the Jews of to-day present marked differences in their appearance; Negroid and Turanian (Mongolian) types can be discerned amongst them as well as Semitic. Even amongst the Hebrews, who hail from Russian Poland, one not infrequently comes across blond and watery-eyed examples. It is practically certain that the people, who were formerly called the Chasaren, and who are regarded as belonging to a Finnish-Tartar stock, and who, about 800 years after Christ, formed a separate empire in the South of what is now Russia, went over to Jewdom and were completely absorbed. The Jews themselves are conscious of this racial distinction, for the western Jews, who have come

---

[58] We find here a parallel with the Indian Thags or Thugs (=Robbers), who consider that they can best serve their God by strangling as many victims as possible. Perhaps these Thugs also stand in relation to the old rejected caste of the "Tschandala" (see page 182).

across Spain, call themselves "Sephardim" (if baptised: Marannen), and have North-African blood in their veins, describe the Eastern Jews as "Aschkenasim", and look down on the latter with a certain amount of contempt. In spite of this, the Talmudic law embraces them all, and the Rabbinical despotism welds them into a close caste, absolutely united in its hostility to all non- Jewish peoples.

If, therefore, the Jews of today are not to be regarded as a united race from a physical point of view, all Jewry is inspired, nevertheless, with the uniform racial spirit of Hebrewdom. And — one must not forget this — the spiritual entity is of higher importance to the racial idea than the purely physical, which may well play a part in all manner of chance externals without prejudicing the racial ground-work of blood and soul.

If an explanation is required of what is understood by the expression "Race", it can be formulated on the following lines: Race denotes a community, which, starting from a common ancestor, is based on blood-relationship and exhibits, for that reason, a number of physical and mental characteristics. One must also reckon with the fact that, with the blood, the attributes of the mind and disposition, of the temperament and character, are inherited equally with the bodily properties. The purer and more united the race is, the more stable and constant is this inheritability. Through admixture with other race-elements, racial peculiarities are partly masked, the external ones more so than the internal, but they assert themselves again, often after generations, with astonishing distinctness. One is therefore entitled to say: a race characterises itself by means of a complex of unvarying, transmissible qualities.

The German people of to-day represent a mixture of Germanic, Slavonic and Romanic (Celtic) — or, according to modern methods of indication, of Northern, Alpine and Mediterranean elements, which have melted into a certain sort of homogeneity after the lapse of centuries, at least to the extent, that scarcely any doubt can exist as to the uniformity of German thought and German feeling. It is only comparatively recently, after distinct signs of degeneration have become visible, that it appears as if these racial constants are about to be resolved into their original elements, and, in the course of this process, to release a multitude of mongrel-products (degeneration-forms) which cannot be classified racially.

If the existence of a separate Jewish race is disputed, as Felix von Luschan, amongst others, attempts to do, the contention may, perhaps, have a certain amount of justification, as there was not an origina 1 Jewish race; it appears to me much more likely that the Hebrews arose out of a mixture of the dregs of all kinds of races (compare page 194), a mixture, however, which has been welded by thousands of years of in-breeding into a racial type.

In the meantime, whoever is searching for the anthropological peculiarity of the Jews, will find this rather in the constitution of mind and character than in definite physical relations. It is quite correct that the Sephardim are preponderatingly longheaded, that the Aschkenasim or Chasaren Jews are round- headed, and that the profile of the face passes through a great variety of gradations. Perhaps, shortness of limb can be regarded as the most noticeable physical feature of the Jewish race. Nearly all Jews possess remarkably short arms and legs and a proportionately long trunk. Whilst the normal European, and especially the German fathoms more than the entire length of his body, in the case of the Hebrew it is the reverse. The inferior development of the arms might certainly be accounted for by the fact that the race in question has never occupied itself with honest manual labour, has employed neither weapon nor oar, and, for these reasons, has failed to develop the arms properly. Other unmistakable physical features include the relation and position of the ear to the nose; amongst the pure Aryans the ear and the nose, on an average, are of equal length and are on the same level; in the case of the Jew, variations and startling irregularities in both of these respects are noticeable.

As a matter of fact, however, the Jewish racial constancy is stronger at the present day than is the case in any other human strain, and this is also confirmed by the declaration of Professor Gans, which has been already quoted on page 204. That the peculiar mental tenacity of the Jewish people was already in evidence in the remotest period, is testified to by the excited references of the ancient prophets to this "stiff-necked and stubborn" people.

Jewish peculiarity may also acquire exceptional solidarity from the fact, that this nation, more than any other, possesses a religion entirely suited to its nature, and which occupies itself at the same time, in the most painstaking fashion, with laying down the most detailed precepts for the conduct of ordinary life. Race, religion, nationality, mode of living, and business behaviour are all cast in the same mould as far as the Hebrews are concerned; these are all the uniform expression of the same fundamental nature. The mentality and character of this people, owing to uniform schooling and tense discipline, and owing to the mode of living, which has become strengthened by inbreeding and habitual by the practice of thousands of years, must have established and incorporated itself to an unusual degree so that the Jews are less susceptible to outside influence than any other race of mankind, which is capable of culture and development.

The voluntary segregation of this race, and the consciously fostered aversion to all other peoples, all contributed to maintain Hebrewdom in its singularity. It must be repeated with emphasis: the segregation, so far as the Jews were concerned, was voluntary — just for the preservation of their singularity and their singular rites. Sombart insists that the Jews have not always been "half-citizens" in the strange states, but, on the contrary, in olden times, were frequently actually endowed with peculiar rights and privileges (compare pages 25 and 176). They held themselves aloof, however, of their own free will, from all participation in civic and state affairs; they did not accept their share of the spiritual and political destiny of the nation; they regarded themselves everywhere merely as visitors and foreigners, and were always ready to fasten up their bundle, so that — laden with gold and silver, after the manner of their forefathers — they could slip over the frontier.

Sombart also confirms the fact that Jewish peculiarity did not first develop out of the Diaspora (Dispersion) like biased Jewish historians endeavour to make us believe, but that the Diaspora itself is a production of this peculiarity. Just as invalid is the contention that the Jewish peculiarities are the fruit of the religion, and of the rabbinical doctrines; far rather has the Jewish religion grown out of the fundamental nature of Jewdom, and is the inevitable product of the Jewish mode of thinking. Yes, it is an indispensable expedient for sustaining the Jewish mode of existence. Without this "immoral morality" the Hebrew could not continue. The rabbinical doctrines are merely the undisguised expression of the real thoughts and feelings of the Jew; if these doctrines had been artificially constructed, and had been forced upon the Jews against their inclination, the whole Jewish mass would have revolted against such views of life. But no one has ever heard of anything of the kind. Rather have the Hebrews gladly adopted these senseless doctrines because the latter suit them to a nicety. Sombart is therefore entitled to say that one may, without hesitation, refer back from the peculiarity of the Jewish religion to the national peculiarity of the Jews. Certainly, when he expresses doubt if one is justified in attributing the dishonest behaviour of Isaac, Jacob and Joseph to a fraudulent trait in the Jewish nature, we must leave it to the reader to form his own opinion upon this point.

The legend, which is always cropping up, that the Jews were originally an agricultural people, is to be accounted for by the excusable failure to distinguish between the two tribes, Israel and Judah. The extensively-held opinion — especially amongst theologians — that Israelites and Jews are identical, is an assumption, which must be challenged, for it is refuted by numerous passages in The Old Testament, in which Israel and Judah are mentioned.[59] Ancient Israel was a people, composed of honest husbandmen and graziers, which eventually came under the yoke of the intruding Hebrews. The real Jew made his appearance in Palestine, just as in other countries, as the financial- political usurper; he came with the gold, which he had abstracted from other countries (as in the case of the excursion from Egypt) into the land, and made the honest population tributary to him by money-lending and usury. And thus the honest agricultural Israelites were enslaved by this alien money- bourgeoisie, precisely as many other nations are at the present day. But the detestation of the real Israelites for the new money-lords must have been very pronounced when the Israelitish captain, Abner, answered an unworthy imputation with

---

[59] Amongst other matters, it is worthy of notice that in the apocryphal story of Susanna and Daniel, a sharp distinction is drawn between Canaan's stock and not Judah's on one hand, and the "daughters of Israel" and Susanna as "daughter of Judah", on the other.

the indignant words: "Am I then a scoundrel like a Jew?" (2. Sam. 3. 8.)[60]

2. DEVELOPMENT OF THE JEWS AS A COMMERCIAL NATION

During the subsequent vicissitudes of the people of Judah, there was opportunity and to spare to devote themselves to agricultural occupations; the Hebrews, however, have never availed themselves of the same. They feel little inclination for this burdensome and downright occupation, for it is impossible to make a fool of nature. And already the wisdom of one Talmudic rabbi has said as much in the following words: he who employs one hundred "Sus" in trading, can enjoy meat and wine every day; but, on the contrary, he who expends one hundred "Sus" on tilling the soil, has to be satisfied with salt and cabbage, must sleep on the ground, and endure all manner of hardships. Thus, there is no lack of historians, even amongst the Jews themselves, who openly admit that the Jews are inclined by their very nature to trade, are devoted to it, and are a nation with a very pronounced commercial tendency. Their most ancient scriptures also bear testimony to this fact. The cuneiform documents from Nippur as well, have provided additional evidence that the Hebrews were already wholesale dealers and bankers in ancient Babylon. They cheerfully resigned the dangerous maritime trade to the Phoenicians, for this branch of commerce called for personal courage, and was inseparable from peril to life.

Sombart must credit us with great simplicity when he tries to represent the notorious robbery of gold and silver by the Jews, on their departure from Egypt, as if these were loans of the Egyptians, which the Hebrews were intercepting. This discloses an astounding lack of any understanding for national psychology. Since the Hebrews, in olden times, scarcely ever carried on any other occupation than those of grain-dealer, cattle- dealer, usurer and pawnbroker, it may be taken for granted that they carried on these occupations in Egypt also. I consider it likely that these gold and

---

[60] Harosch keleb anoki ascher l'jehuda?" Kautsch translates: "Am I then a Jewish scoundrel?" — Compare " *Hammer* " No. 259: "The History of the origin of the Old Testament."

silver vessels and costly garments, which the Hebrews took with them on the occasion of their exodus from Egypt, were pledges, which the Egyptians had handed over to the Jewish usurers, into whose clutches they had fallen. (Compare Sombart pages 370—372.) To what an extent the Jewish usurer was in demand in olden times, is testified to by the punitive sermon of Nehemiah, and especially by Amos. 8, 4—7.

It is only part and parcel of the Jewish doctrine and view of the world, that the Rabbis, all their lives, have not disdained to participate most actively in all money transactions. Even Sombart admits, that the Rabbis are, in many cases, the chief money-lenders; there are even passages, which seem to suggest that the Rabbis have a monopoly of usury. Sombart cites an instance out of the Oxford Papyrus, which actually describes a case of Jewish usury on the grand scale, for it is distinctly declared in this document, which is a bond or obligation, that the debt shall be doubled each time that it is not repaid at the appointed term. A true Jewish mode of operation, which we are continually coming across, at all times and in all places. (Compare page 25).

Can it be wondered at that the Hebrews have managed by such practices, throughout the ages, to draw the money of the other nations quickly into their own hands? And thus Sombart remarks, that already in the Hellenic period, and in the time of Imperial Rome, rich Jews were acting as moneylenders to the kings; and much was said in the Roman world concerning Jewish hagglers and usurers. Amongst the Arabs, however, the Hebrew has the reputation of being a born usurer and chafferer. The Jews were likewise the financiers and business-men of the Merovingian kings; and in Spain, where they enjoyed most freedom for their operations, they very soon had the nation in debt to them. Already at the time of the Crusades they were engaged, to an excessive extent, in money transactions, and "bled" the Crusaders mercilessly (compare page 25 et seq.) so that Sombart feels compelled to admit: since we have ascertained something about the Jewish economic life, we see that the loaning of money plays a very prominent part in the same. (Page 375 and following). He adds:

"It is really about time that the fairy-tale disappeared, that the Jews had first been driven into the money-lending business, during the European Middle Ages, because all other occupations were closed to them. The history of a Jewish loan-traffic, extending over a period of two thousand years before the Middle Ages, ought really to be sufficient proof of the erroneousness of this historical fabrication."

And even when the path to other occupations lay open to the Jews, they still turned aside to devote themselves, with preference, to the loaning of money against pledges, like Karl Bücher has pointed out in the case of Frankfurt a. M. Indeed, at certain times, the authorities have even offered premiums to induce the Jews to choose other vocations, but all attempts in this direction proved futile. It is characteristic of the Jewish religion, that the Jewish temples, in olden times, were the centres of the money-traffic, and were, to a certain extent, banking-houses. A large quantity of gold was accumulated in the Temple at Jerusalem. And this alliance between religion and money-traffic is not to be excused on the grounds that other Semitic nations, like the Babylonians, are said to have done the same. At any rate the same reproach cannot be levelled at the Christian Churches. And, although the talents of the usurer are occasionally to be found amongst the other nations, the non-Jewish usurer is, generally speaking, more or less of an amateur; the Hebrews alone have brought usury to an art and a science — have exalted it even to a religion. Sombart also admits, that the Jews have developed the technic of loan-agreements to an uncanny perfection. He says: "If one reads the fourth and fifth chapters of the Baba Mezia, one gets the impression that one is taking part in a usury-inquisition in Hesse, some twenty or thirty years ago, so multitudinous are the tricks and devices, which are introduced into these loan-contracts."

It is, therefore, not without full justification, that both Jewish wealth and the Jewish usurer have become a by-word.

Whilst the priests of other nations have to be the guardians of what is ideal, the Hebrew priests are business-folk to their finger-tips, and even usurers. Sombart says:

"It is remarkable what a number of rich and very rich men there are amongst the Talmudists. It is not at all difficult to draw up a list of several dozen Rabbis, all of whom enjoy the reputation of being extremely wealthy."

But Sombart confesses that all his investigations into the faculty of acquisitiveness, possessed by the Jews, do not satisfactorily account for the phenomenon of Jewish wealth. He has actually forgotten the most important factor, viz that confederation of the Jewish business demeanour, the Chawrusse. The enormous gains of the Jewish capitalists are also only to be accounted for by the existence of the Chawrusse. The characteristic picture in the fourth section (page 47), drawn from the descriptions of the actuary, Thiele, of the criminal court, forms a typical example of the Jewish organisation for acquisition. The Chawrusse continues, at the present moment, on all sides; on the Stock Exchange, amongst the Banks, in the Press, in the "White Slave" traffic, amongst Jewish pickpockets and burglars, and has its ramifications over the whole world. There is only one satisfactory explanation for this phenomenal enrichment of the Jewish people; it is the organisation in bands, of Trade, of Usury, of Fraud, and of Theft; and all these again are federated with one another — however vague and shadowy such connection may appear to be.[61] It is exactly as Herder has already stated: "The Hebrews are a despicable race of cunning dealers, a race that has never desired honour, home and country. That they can ever have been valiant warriors and honest peasants does not appear credible to us, for the disposition of a nation does not alter so quickly."

Sombart makes a last attempt to save the honour of the Jewish nation, and to explain away its peculiarities, by representing the Jews as an oriental people that became mixed up with or dispersed amongst Northern nations, and started a system of culture in conjunction with the latter. Certainly one has every right to refer to the fact, that the penetration of a nation with alien racial-elements

---

[61] There is a particular association in Russia for the purpose of business and exploitation, called Kahal or Kagal, which embraces the whole Jewish community. Important disclosures concerning this are to be found in Dr. Rich. Andree's book: *"Information about the Jewish nation,"* and the *"Handbook of the Jewish Question"* also contains extracts. 26 t h edition page 293—297.

can impart a tremendous cultural impulse. Gobineau,[62] as is well known, has attempted to explain the origin of the ancient cultures, as being the consequence of the penetration of Southern Nations by elements of the Northern race, the blond Aryans, whereby the latter assumed the leadership amongst those, who had been subjugated, and by means of their organising power and heroic mode of thinking, sowed the seeds of future great developments. It is unlikely that anyone will attempt to compare the part, which the Hebrew plays amongst us at the present day, with the above example. Nowhere can the Hebrew be regarded as the bearer of culture and of a new social order; his entire method of working is of too negative a nature. When Sombart continuously talks about "capitalistic culture", he is only using a euphemism all the time. We learnt already at the beginning of our examination of the subject, that although the capitalistic economic method can certainly effect a prodigious release of latent forces, the only result is a rapid wasting-away of the nations concerned, and in no case is a constructive culture ever produced.

Justifiably apprehensive of the above fact, Sombart occasionally speaks of "the strange blossom of capitalistic culture." Far more remarkable is his expressed opinion that this oriental race wastes its best faculties in an environment, which, racially and climatically, is antipathetic to it. On the contrary, it seems to us that it wastes the faculties of others. We can agree with him, however, when he calls the Bedouins itinerant cattle- breeders and nomads, and then continues:

"Such a restless and roving tribe of Bedouins were those Hebrews also, who, about the year 1200 B. C., burst into the land of Canaan, pillaging and murdering, in order to compel the native population to work for them." (Sombart page 405)[63]

He also admits that the land was subdued, less by martial valour than by financial subjugation, and that the Hebrews had

---

[62] Count Gobineau: "*Disquisition on the dissimilarity of the Human Races.*" Stuttgart 1902.
[63] These ideas of Sombart, however, are not original, for they were already expressed in 1886, in the "*Handbook to the Jewish-Question*", which was formerly known as the "*Anti-Semitic Catechism*" of Theodor Fritsch.

known how to make the greater part of the territory tributary to themselves, and thus to achieve the same result by a loan relationship. He allows — as thoughtful Anti-Semites have always represented — that "Considerable numbers of Hebrews resided in the towns, drawing rent and interest, whilst the enslaved population cultivated the soil as if it were a colony or they were free peasants."

All the idle talk about the Hebrews having been formerly an agricultural people, can, as Sombart also admits, be dismissed as a myth; he says:

"But the spirit of nomadism must have remained active in all tribes, for if it had been otherwise, if Israel (should be Judah) had been an agricultural people, even merely in an oriental sense, we would never be able to understand the origin and first formation of the Jewish system of religion."

As a matter of fact, an agricultural people is not wont to invent a religion of usury and deceit, and to choose a God who ordains that the destruction of countries and their populations is a sacred duty. Whatever suggestion there might be of honest agriculture, in the history of the ancient Jewish people, must surely refer to the original and permanent population, the Israelites, and not to the tribe of usurers, called Hebrews, who migrated into the country at a later date.[64] That the Israelitish history has become intermingled with the Jewish, and that, now and again, in the Old Testament, glimpses of a loftier conception of divinity occur side by side with the hate-breathing, revengeful destroyer of nations, Jahwe (Jehovah), is to be ascribed to the influence of the non-Jewish Israelites.[65] Sombart seems to have some hazy notion that such is the case, when he says, that the Pentateuch has been composed to suit the mind of a nomadic people, and when he continues: "The God, who maintained his position victoriously against all other false gods, is a god of the wilderness and of the shepherd. And, in the

---

[64] In number 269 of the "Hammer" W. Scheuermann, in referring to the book of W. Fishberg, an American Jew, traces the legend of agricultural Jews back to the fact, that in olden times, just as at the present day, converts to Judaism from agricultural peoples, were straightway designated Jews.
[65] Compare Th. Fritsch: "Der falsche Gott" (The False God) (evidence against Jahwe] Ninth Edition. "Hammer"-Verlag, Leipzig.

conscious establishment of the cult of Jahwe, all the ancient traditions of nomadism from Esra and Nehemiah are quite distinctly adopted, without any notice having been taken of the intervening agricultural epoch, which, in the case of the Jews themselves perhaps never really happened."

He then cites Jul. Wellhausen, who corroborates as follows: "The priestly records reject every reference to settled life in the land of Canaan; they confine themselves to an exposition of the desert migration, and claim to be, in every sense of the word, desert legislation. Sombart is of the opinion, that if nomadic instincts and inclinations had not prevailed to a preponderating extent amongst the broad masses of the Jewish people, this preponderatingly nomadic religion could never have been permanently imposed upon them. And the destiny of the Jewish nation proves that it has remained a nomad- and desert-race throughout thousands of years.

This is my opinion as well. But all this again is nothing more than what discerning Anti-Semites, who, so far as ethnological matters are concerned, are far in advance of their times, have been insisting upon for decades. But, in order to avoid all points of contact with these intelligent racial-psychologists, Sombart finds it necessary to speak about "anti-Semitic pamphleteers", who have drawn upon these facts, in a most odious fashion, in order to obtain material to carry on their "campaign of abuse". He can know very little about those concerned, when he includes Eugen D•hring and Adolph Wahrmund amongst writers of this class, for both of these, and more especially the latter, have only written in a most refined and scholarly manner concerning the Jewish problem. Sombart regards all anti-Semitic utterances as "silly and odious"; but what he has to offer us, although presented in another form, does not differ essentially from the conclusions of those far- sighted men, who had comprehended the racial problem long before certain loquacious sciolists had formed even an idea on the subject.

He is justified, however, in his derision of our incorporated professional wisdom, which proceeds crablike, with logical considerations of the following kind: "In olden times agriculture was carried on in Palestine; at that time the Jews inhabited Palestine;

consequently the Jews have been agriculturists." Really, one might just as well argue: at the present day the Jews hold a dominating position in Germany, and since the German Nation, which maintains itself for the greater part by agriculture, has reached a high stage of culture, these Jews must be agriculturists, and the creators of the German culture!

3. DISPERSION OF THE JEWS OVER THE EARTH

Sombart has only irony for the Diaspora, which provides a most acceptable motive for evoking howls of lamentation from the children of Judah, and a whine of sympathy from many other sentimental people.[66] He is of opinion that if we wish to be honest with ourselves, we are quite unable to form any correct impression of the exile, whether of the departure or of the return. The Jewish account states: "And Nebucadnezzar led away all the captains and all the soldiers; ten thousand were led away, and all smiths and metal-workers; no one was left except the common people of the country." And when it proceeds to state: "He led away all the nobility of the land from Jerusalem into captivity at Babel", the thought occurs to us, that perhaps only the parasitic upper classes were transported, whilst the honest, agricultural population was allowed to remain undisturbed (2 Kings 24, 14—15 ; 25, 11 — 12). There is obviously a mistake in Luther's translation of the latter passage. This reads: "But the rest of the people, who remained in the town, and who sided with the King of Babel, and that other poverty-stricken section of the populace, were led away by Nebusur Adan, the Governor." This must manifestly mean: — "not away"; — for, later on it reads: "and the Governor called for peasants and vine-dressers from amongst the lowest in the land;" and again, later on, in verse 22, that the king had placed "the remainder of the people" under the order of Gedalja.

---

[66] Amongst other things it is interesting to know that Alexander Dumas, in his play: "The wife of Claudius", which glorifies the Jews, makes his hero, Daniel say: "the Diaspora has not scattered us; on the contrary, it has extended us in all directions. In consequence, we enmesh the whole world in a net so to speak".

To the Governor, Nebusur Adan, Sombart gives the title "Chief of the executioners". — What is then the object of this objectionable translation? Does it not disclose the ancient Jewish hatred for the enemies of Judah? — But Sombart himself, referring to the exiles, speaks in confirmation of the above:

"The real country-people were not to be found amongst them. Thus the wisdom of the Assyrian kings obviously recognised the kind of plague, which was afflicting the fruitful land of Canaan, and endeavoured to purify the new province by deporting the parasitic class — the plutocracy — and leaving the honest peasant and working-class undisturbed in the country."

Excellent! This is exactly the reading which the Anti-Semites adopted 30 years ago. And we are in agreement with Sombart, that these honest people were the remainder of the original native tribes. Thus our author, (Sombart) has adopted the perception of the despised Anti-Semites, in its entirety, when he characterises the dominion of the Jewish nation in Palestine, and the conditions, which they took along with them to Babylon, in the following words:

"Town-bred masters, who are, at the same time, money-lenders, have their land cultivated by non-Jews, who act as tenant-peasants; that, at any rate, is the typical picture, which we obtain from the Babylonian Talmud."

Sombart allows it to appear, that the exile of the Hebrews in Babylon, was by no means enforced by compulsion, and that the Hebrews, on the contrary, had gone there voluntarily so that they would be able to practise their usury to greater advantage in the centres of culture.

"For", he says, "we never learn that those self-banished Jews ever returned to their native soil, after they had acquired a small fortune, like emigrant Swiss, Hungarians or Italians do, at the present day. They remained, on the contrary, in the foreign cities, and maintained merely spiritual-religious relations with their native land. At the most — like genuine nomads — they undertook their annual pilgrimage to Jerusalem at the Feast of the Passover."

The diffusion of Hebrewdom over all lands, open to commercial intercourse, must already at that time have been considerable, for, referring to Strabo (B. C. 63 to A. D. 24) Josephus writes, that it was not easy to find a single place on the inhabited earth, which was not occupied and dominated by this race. Philo (about 20 B. C to 40 A. D) also reports that the Jews resided in numerous maritime and inland cities of Europe, Asia and Libya. We do not hear, however, of any brutal act of violence, which caused them to be dragged thither against their will; for this reason, the dispersion of the Jews throughout all lands of culture has been manifestly voluntary. How closely packed they were, for example, in Rome, during the early period of the Empire, is testified to by various authorities. An embassy from the Jewish King Herod to Augustus, were accompanied by about 8,000 members of their faith, who were domiciled in Rome, and in the year 19 A. D. 4,000 men of military age, who had been released, and were "infected with Egyptian and Jewish superstition," were sentenced to be deported to Sardinia (Page 430; according to Tacitus, Suetonius and Josephus; the last-named is said to have been a favourite of Vespasian).

Sombart goes on to speak about the very considerable immigration into the German Empire, and shows, by means of figures, how the Hebrews are streaming from the East of the Empire to the West, and especially to Berlin. It certainly sounds more than strange when he speaks of "a people hunted from place to place." We, for our part, are of the opinion, that if the Jews move from Birnbaum and Meseritz to Berlin, they do so because they can do better business and procure more pleasure in the metropolis, and not because someone has hunted them thither. At the present moment, actually more than half of the Jews in Germany reside in the large cities, feeling more in their element there, because the brisker business-life, as well as the pleasures and noise of a large city, are more in accordance with their taste. It is also apposite, when Sombart, in another passage, compares the great modern cities to the desert, indicating thereby, that the spirit of the nomad and of the desert has a close affinity to that of the modern cities, and that the great modern city acts devastatingly on the national life. "Desert and Forest," says he, "are the great contrasts, around which the distinctive natures of countries and of mankind group themselves."

The forest is actually the real birth-place and home of the German, and it was on this account that Germania or ancient Germany appeared so gloomy and abhorrent to the Romans, who disliked forests. At the present day, the real German can prosper only in the field, and in the forest; and, as forest and desert are contrasts, so also are the two extreme contrasts of mankind to be found in all that pertains to the German, on one hand, and to the Hebrew, on the other. It is a firmly established fact, that agriculture has, at all times, been the most important institution of the Germanic races, and was never entirely unknown at any epoch of early Indo- Germanic history. By living and working continually in the presence of Nature, as peasantry must of necessity do, the essential and true nature of the German is formed, as indeed is that of all really-constructive, cultural peoples. The estranged attitude towards Nature is the hall-mark of the Semitic race, concerning whose tribal father, Cain, the murderer of the gentle and peaceful husbandman, Abel, it stands written: "A fugitive and vagabond shalt thou be upon earth! Let thy hand be against everyone, and everyone's hand against thee!"

Sombart betrays his prepossession for Jewdom, by commending what a 16th century Jewish physician in Spain has excogitated, to account for the "high-spiritual" nature of the Jew. He — the physician — is of opinion that the dry, pure air of the desert, the "clear water", and the "delicate food of Manna" have produced a marvellous spiritual refinement in the Jew. The ridiculousness of this perception is obvious. Must not correspondingly all Bedouins also have refined spiritual natures? And how will Sombart explain away the fact, that the Arab, strangely enough, who must certainly be regarded as a true son of the desert, feels himself separated by a yawning chasm from the Jew? There is scarcely any other nation, which fosters such abhorrence for the Jews, as the Arab. Arabian authors have expressed their contempt for the Hebrew in the most biting terms. Already in the year 545 A. D. Abd al Oâdir a-Ilani wrote as follows:

"The Jews, who live scattered throughout the entire world and, in spite of this, hold firmly together, are cunning, misanthropic and dangerous beings, and must be treated just as one treats a poisonous snake, namely, by stamping on its head immediately it approaches; for, if one allows it to raise the head for one moment, it will infallibly bite, and the bite is fatal."

And when Sombart makes a further attempt to account for the peculiar disposition of the Hebrew, by ascribing it to his former life in the desert, one is entitled to meet him with the question: why then have not the Arabs become Jews? — why have they preserved a disposition, which can be regarded as aristocratic and heroic in comparison with that of the Jew? Sombart attempts to explain away the malevolent attitude, assumed by the Jews towards the Northern nations, by attributing it to the "wet-cold" manner of the natives of the North.[67] But this attempt at defence is also doomed to failure, for we see how the Hebrew, in southern countries such as Egypt and Morocco, behaves in exactly the same way and becomes usurer, just as he does in the North. And when it is finally brought forward in excuse of the Jew, that his bad character must be attributed wholly to the circumstance that, for thousands of years, he has been the appointed custodian of the monies of the various nations, we then ask: who appointed him? Did he not choose this rôle himself? — With regard to this particular aspect of the Jewish question, there is a favourite perversion or distortion of facts, which is repeated to satiety, and which is in conflict with all history, especially with the spirit of the Old Testament. It must be included amongst the clumsiest subterfuges, employed by Jewry, but unfortunately belongs also to those, which impose most easily on the idealists amongst our fellow-countrymen. The Jew is always represented as having had his particular rôle forced upon him, against his will, while, in reality, he has chosen this rôle of his own free will, in order to create conditions around him, which are congenial to his nature. When Sombart says: "They became the lords of money, and by means of money, which they made subject to themselves, lords of the world",

---

[67] In former times, the attitude of the Germans towards the Jews, as such, was by no means hostile (compare page 25). But the Jews have abused the great patience of the Germans, beyond endurance, and have thereby incurred the lasting hatred of their hosts.

these words amount to a confession that the Hebrews made themselves masters of money in order to dominate.

To anyone, who looks more deeply into the matter, the question certainly occurs as to whether the actual existence of money does not introduce such a dangerously deceptive and unnatural factor of power into human life, that the deceitful spirit of the Hebrew is thereby accorded the utmost license to develop its sinister activity. It is quite possible that the nations will not be freed from the Jewish plague, until they can get rid of the ban of money — that kind of money, the value of which rests on a fiction, and which introduces a demoniacal element into culture, or, until — according to Lagarde's plan — the State takes the entire money-business into its own hands. The Hebrews did not invent money, nor have they dug the glittering gold out of the bowels of the earth; but they may well have devised that misuse of money, which, in the shape of loan-capital, loads the honest, productive nations with fetters of interest to all eternity. For, the strange mystery connected with money, lies not so much in the money itself as in the notion or conception of capital, which is derived from money, and in the further notion or conception, which is inseparably connected with the former, of unnatural, "everlasting interest." It is unnatural to demand for a loan of money, so long as it is not repaid, a continuous, unchanging rate of interest for hundreds and thousands of years. It is here where the source of the distress of the honest, productive nations lies; here we find the cause of the unlimited growth of Jewish capital and Jewish dominion.[68] Sombart is therefore right when he says: "money places in the hands of the Jew the means to exercise power without being strong." In very truth, the feeblest and most cowardly nation in the world, by a misuse of the glittering gold, have arrogated to themselves, the demeanour and position of lords and rulers.

It is amusing to read Sombart's account of how hateful the German-Polish Jews, the so-called Aschkenasim, are to the

---

[68] Theodor Fritsch has already proposed in 1892, that it should be made obligatory and legal, to include, in every loan-contract, provision for the reduction of the debt (so-called sinking-fund) so that the debt could be paid off within a conceivable time. — Compare "*Land-usury and Stock Exchange*", Leipzig 1892.

Sephardim, their western brethren-in-faith from Spain and Portugal (compare page 221). At Bordeaux, in the year 1761, the Portuguese Jews brought about a drastic order, that all foreign Jews should leave Bordeaux within 14 days. They called the eastern Jews "vagabonds", and took the utmost pains to get rid of them as soon as possible. Now if the more "aristocratic" Jews themselves harboured a detestation for the lower-class Hebrews, the Aschkenasim, how can anyone take it amiss when we feel this aversion in an enhanced degree? For the Sephardim and Aschkenasim are, to say the least of it, closely united by the ties of religion, morals, and their conjoint view of life; how then, shall these abhorrent beings not be doubly repulsive and hateful to us, to whom their feelings, mode of thinking, and entire nature are completely alien? The spiritual and spiritual-moral difference between these two sections of Jews cannot well be great; for they are both steeped in the atmosphere of the Talmud. And even Sombart admits, that the habits of those of Jewish blood, however low in the social scale they may be, acquire a remarkable fixity: for instance, inclination for petty deception, obtrusiveness, lack of self-respect, lack of tact etc.

* * * * *

These selections from Sombart's writings should suffice to convince anyone who is visibly anxious to regard the Hebrew in as favourable a light as possible, but who is, at the same time, unable to close his eyes to a number of serious faults and failings in the Jewish disposition, in themselves of sufficient warranty for regarding the Jews, in the midst of the cultured nations, as a highly undesirable, and entirely alien element, that the aversion and dislike, felt by the moral nations for the Jews, has been thoroughly deserved by the latter.

It is most valuable, when a man, who repudiates the slightest tendency to anti-Semitism, and who collects carefully every word said in praise of the Jews, makes such important admissions. It is for this reason, that so many passages from Sombart have been quoted and criticised, although the same contain little that is new for anyone, versed in the Jewish question. It is evident that Sombart has learnt much from the Anti-Semites, but he employs the tactic, which, though it may be ingenious, is certainly not noble, of repudiating the source of his instruction. It is to be hoped that our German countrymen will be ready to believe certain facts when stated by a person, who refuses to be regarded as an Anti-Semite, although they would flatly decline to accept these same statements when made by a declared Anti-Semite.

XVI

THE INFLUENCE OF THE JEW

UPON WOMANKIND

Women exert an important influence upon the development of retail trade. It is they, who superintend, for the most part, the purchase of necessaries for the household; it is through their hands that the greater portion of the income, earned by the man, is returned into business life, and it is for this reason surely, not a matter of indifference to whom women entrust their custom.

It is now a generally recognised fact, that most women and girls give Jewish shops the preference. The apparent cheapness of Jewish goods might be brought forward as an explanation of this. Women — and even those women, who are by no means entitled to include thrift, in its true sense, amongst their other virtues — seem to find a peculiar pleasure in the mere idea that they have been successful in purchasing some article at a cheaper price than it is usually sold for — even when this supposed cheapness exists only in the imagination of the purchaser. Such women regard this result as being directly due to their own cleverness — in some cases, perhaps, even as a triumph of their own personal charm. For this reason, the shopkeeper, who, by exposing his wares in calculated disorder to be pulled about and hunted through, advances half-way to meet this fancied feminine capacity for ferreting-out and overreaching, will stand a far better chance of doing business than a rival tradesman, who prefers a conventional and orderly method. Women often require "chance goods", and, for that reason, visit by choice those shops or stores, where everything lies jumbled up together, and where they imagine that they will be able to pick up something cheaply: they pass by the well-ordered shops, so, at least, is the admission of a domesticated woman, who knows her own sex. By the cunning utilisation of this feminine weakness, the salesman is enabled to kill two birds with one stone; he confers a special favour upon his female customers, and saves himself the trouble of sorting out and arranging his rubbish, of which task his customers obligingly relieve him.

If, in addition to this, the same salesman knows how to create the impression that, overcome, as it were, by the personal charm of a female customer — and of her alone, he is prepared to part with some article under its proper price, he will infallibly secure her goodwill. And if, moreover, he is expert and nimble enough to flatter all of his customers in like manner, and to lead each individual on to believe that she has been especially favoured before all other customers, he will have no cause to complain of bad trade.

Our women are extraordinarily simple when confronted with any economic question, although they surpass men in many other matters, where cleverness and intuition are required. They allow themselves to be perverted by the dazzling exterior of an object, and to be guided by the prospect of a momentary advantage, without taking any account of the further consequences of their conduct or action. They do not stop to ask whether they are supporting, with their custom, principles, which are unsound, and business practices, which are harmful, and are thereby depriving genuine and deserving tradesmen of their custom, perhaps forcing entire branches of industry into difficulties, promoting inferior manufacture, and, briefly expressed, imparting an ominous tendency to all business-life. All such considerations are foreign to them.

Possessing these particular failings, they come face to face with the natural disposition of the Jew, who is likewise the man who believes in and upholds the dazzling exterior and the momentary advantage. The Hebrew, who takes more pains to study the psychology of his customers than the trader of Aryan descent — because he looks for his return less in the quality of his goods than in the exploitation of human vanities and weaknesses — has always been able to detect these peculiarities in the feminine disposition, and has known how to take the fullest advantage of the weak side of woman. As it is, his shop-window acts confusingly and disturbingly on the feminine mind. It is difficult to define exactly what the particular art may be, which the Jew makes use of in displaying his goods, so that the same have a more attractive effect upon the glances of the passers-by than the wares in the window of a tradesman, who is not a Jew. There must be some kind of affinity or connection between the capricious and abstracted nature of the average feminine mind, and the Jewish manner and touch when they exhibit or display anything; for the Jews most certainly do not show superior taste in the arrangement of their wares, and it is rather a bewildering jumble or an obtrusive thrusting-in-the-face of certain articles, which seem to excite and lure the female spectator. The Jew also tries to puzzle and confuse by marking up unusual prices. An article in the shop of a tradesman, who is not a Jew, which remains comparatively unnoticed at the price of 75 Pfennigs, can be prominently displayed in a Jewish shop at the price of 97 Pfennigs, and here it seems, all of a sudden, to create the impression as if it were in reality several Pfennigs cheaper than elsewhere.

At any rate, it is a matter of fact that the Jewish show-windows exert an almost mesmeric influence over the great masses of curious and inquisitive people. But for all that, the Hebrew despises no other means whatever, by which he may achieve the same result. Calculating upon the herd instinct of the public, many of the larger Jewish businesses engage and pay people, solely for the purpose of walking to and fro on the pavement in front of their establishments, at such times as the traffic is at its height, and of occasionally stopping before the show-windows as if curious and interested. Their example prompts others to imitate them, and businesses of this kind are always besieged by people. As soon as one of the hirelings separates himself from the throng, and enters the shop, the movement seems to become contagious, and others follow.

An unceasing and striking series of advertisements in the newspapers by the Jewish business-houses, also contributes to attract custom to their shops, and in this particular sphere of activity, the Jewish trader gives full rein to the obtrusiveness and heedlessness of his race. Doubtless such artifices ensure that Jewish shops are more extensively patronised than other establishments, but still they are not sufficient, to account for certain, almost unaccountable phenomena. It is rather the personality of the Jew himself, which acts upon so many women with absolutely forcible suggestiveness.

Without doubt, the well-known susceptibility of our women for everything "foreign", has prepared the soil for this astounding Jewish influence. It is an absolutely incomprehensible fact to people from other countries, that representatives of our womanhood — from school-girls up to women in the forties — are to be found in large numbers, who comport themselves towards negroes as if the latter were of their own race and standing, and who behave in a downright shameless manner towards the various men of colour, connected with exhibitions etc.; and others again, in the colonies, whose conduct with respect to the natives discloses an unbelievable intimacy. A state of things, which, quite apart from the unrestrained sensuality involved, is a melancholy indication of a steady decline in national and racial self-respect. All this has reference to the relations, which — unfortunately — subsist between a large section of our womankind and the Jews.

And now it becomes necessary to step aside into a dark territory, which the majority of our contemporaries pass unsuspectingly, but which must be explored and opened-up in order to help to account for the unholy influence, which the Jews have acquired amongst us. Certainly it is a region, which a clean-living and conscientious man enters with reluctance, and it was long before I could make up my mind to lay it open to the public view. But as this book, by reason of the serious and economic matter which it contains, runs but little risk of falling into the hands of the young, the idle, and the pruriently- inclined, it will not be dangerous, in the presence of mature readers, to treat with candour a subject, which, as a rule, is wont to shun all publicity. As it is a question of the secret undermining of the moral and physical strength of our nation by the machinations of the Hebrews, undue sensitiveness in this respect may well be laid aside for once. Moreover, the discussion of this question cannot be avoided here, because it is necessary to a proper characterisation of the racial and ethical domain in which the Hebrew lives, and out of which sphere he moulds his life and carries on his business. In order that the chief features may be recognised, it will be best to cite some instances, selected from the experiences of daily life. As an introduction the following remarks are not out of place. The many thousands of single and married Jewish sensualists are causing such devastation amongst our young women, that from this quarter alone the ruin of our nation is assured, without taking into consideration all the other closely- connected economic and social evils. So much can be learnt from a thoughtful perusal of the following pages. But, from my own personal observation there are many, in other respects experienced men, who are ignorant of these facts, or, who are ignorant at any rate of the extent and depth of the injury, which is being inflicted upon our nation; they simply proceed blindly on their way.

There is no doubt whatever, that the real nature of the Jew is completely unknown and incomprehensible to the great majority of the most educated people of to-day. They have had no opportunity to gain an insight into the more secret machinations of the Jew. Their acquaintanceship with Jews is confined, for the most part, to occasional and brief contact in social and business circles, and, since in this respect the Hebrew is wont to show his most harmless and agreeable side, there is little cause for wonder when one repeatedly hears, that the Jews are really nice, decent, amiable people. Others again, only know the Jew from flattering literary presentations of him, like "Nathan der Weise", or Sir Walter Scott's "*Ivanhoe*", and are inclined also, to transfer their instilled and unquestioning reverence for the Biblical Patriarchs to the Jews of to-day. And has not our light literature always been utilised in a most subtle manner, by Jewish authors, to convey an entirely misleading portrait of the Jew? With a cunningly calculated appeal to German susceptibility, Jews and Jewesses have been portrayed invariably as high-minded, innocent beings - as patient creatures, bearing their burden of "eternal pain", because they have to suffer severely under the prejudice and unfounded hatred of the malicious Christians. Moreover, as our daily press and our literature are completely under Jewish influence, all personalities, who come into publicity, are appraised and judged accordingly as they show themselves well-disposed, or the contrary, towards Jewdom. This circumstance has always formed the standard of criticism for Jewish authors, and is more the case to-day than ever. The consequence is, that from youth upwards, our dispositions are made susceptible to a false philanthropy, and become especially sympathetic to the "poor, innocent, persecuted Jews." And, in riper years, "refinement" and "tolerance" both play a part in shielding the Hebrew of to-day from any unpleasantness, which he might experience on account of the mediaeval prejudice. Yes, we actually give ourselves trouble, not only to make all manner of excuses for the Jews, because of the illusory state of suffering, in which they are supposed to live, but even to assist them, and to further their interests whenever we can, just as if we had to make restitution for an ancient wrong, which our ancestors are supposed to have inflicted on them.

Such a sentiment does credit to our hearts — but what about our intelligence? All people, who are acquainted with history, and the actual facts of life, know perfectly well that the Jews have never emerged guiltless from the occasional disasters, which they have encountered, (compare page 25 and following) and that the tales of cruelties, said to have been perpetrated against the Hebrews, proceed, in many cases, from the imagination, and in others, from gross exaggeration. Thus, the so-called "Jew battles" of the Middle Ages were confined, for the most part, to an expulsion of the Jews, who had become far too numerous, from the towns and districts in which the economic pressure, directly due to their usurious practices and manoeuvres, had become unbearable. As a tremendous clamour arises from the whole of Jewry, at the present day, whenever one of their race loses his life, or has even one hair of his head touched, one can easily understand how it is, that all incidents, in which Jews have figured as the injured party, have been so extravagantly described in history.

* * * * *

The only person, who really understands what the Jew of to-day is, must have had the opportunity to associate with him on intimate terms for years; but an opportunity of this kind does not offer itself to many. For the Hebrew is just as cautious on his side in the selection of his intimate friends as any intelligent German might be; and the latter knows instinctively, in spite of all conventional toleration, how to preserve a certain distance between himself and the Jew. Of all the greater importance then, are the experiences of Jewish companionship, which we will now let our correspondent relate in his own words.

"I came, as a guileless youth of twenty, from a small provincial town to Berlin. Chance brought me into the company of Jews of the same age as myself. I was introduced by them into their family circles, and both saw and heard there much that came as a surprise to me. As the acquaintanceship with my Jewish friends became more intimate, opinions and sentiments were occasionally expressed in my presence, which secretly horrified and angered me. But whenever I attempted to remonstrate, I was met with such universal laughter that I began to be ashamed of whatever delicacy of feeling I still possessed.

In the circle of my more intimate Jewish friends, the conversation turned almost exclusively upon women and sexual matters; they preferred to boast about the various tricks and artifices, which they had employed, in order to seduce innocent girls; and, in no case, did any one of them display the slightest trace of being conscience-smitten. It was regarded as a matter of course, that the female servants must be at the disposal of the men in the Jewish household. 'We have just got a new servant', announced one. — 'Is she pretty?' asked another. 'Well, it is scarcely likely that my father would select anything bad for me', was the answer. — One related with considerable ill-temper, that a servant-girl, who had only been a short time in his family, had rejected his advances; that his father, however, had very soon brought the girl to reason by saying: 'Have I not engaged you as "general servant"? Very well, then! this is included in your duties!" — And the universal assent of his listeners, proved that they all regarded the incident from the speaker's point of view, and approved of the way it had been dealt with.

Many years later, after other events had combined to make me a convinced opponent of the Jews, these first and lasting impressions of my early manhood came vividly into my mind.

I had, without success, repeatedly endeavoured to convince a well-known educational reformer of the injuriousness of the Jews. He was too much of an idealist, and was too remote from practical, every-day life, to be susceptible to the influence of commercial, economic and political facts. According to his opinion, all hostility to the Jews arose from the incapability and envy of the "Christian" business-people, who did not feel able to compete with the "superior" Jew. In order to bring him down from his Utopia into a sphere, in which every man, who had any regard for morality and decency, would find it difficult to control his anger, I related to him some of my past and recent experiences as set down in the chapter on "Jews and Women." Still, even these made no impression upon him; he regarded them either as incredible, or, at least, as grossly exaggerated.

After the lapse of considerable time, he called on me again, and made the following admission:

"I must confess that I have become convinced, that the descriptions, which you gave me, of the relations between Jews and women are believable. At Munich recently, a passenger got into my compartment, and I soon recognised, in the course of conversation, that my companion was an educated Jew in very comfortable circumstances. He might have been either a merchant or a banker. The conversation happened to turn upon the servant question, and he exclaimed: 'At last, thank God, we have again found a nice and proper kind of servant- girl.' When I asked him if it was difficult to get servants in Munich, he replied: 'There are servant-girls enough to be had, but when I engage a girl I have my own particular conditions. I have a son, who is fifteen years of age, and one of my conditions is, that he shall have free access to the girl.' "

The relater continued:

"I could scarcely believe my ears; my heart almost choked me, but I managed, with an effort, to assume an appearance of indifference, and asked: 'What does your wife say to this?' The reply was: 'What should she say? my wife is a sensible woman. Is it likely that she would wish the boy to have intercourse with unclean, street prostitutes? It can only be a source of satisfaction to her, that her son should have access to a clean and healthy girl in his own home!"

Our educational reformer was still more shocked at this answer than he had been at the first; but it had at last dawned upon him what a world-wide gulf lay between Jewish thought and Jewish perception, and ours.

But how few of those sentimentalists amongst us, who are always disputing and denying everything, of which they have not had any personal experience, have such a drastic opportunity of refuting their Nathan-like views of the Jewish character? One recognises one fact: the education of the Jewish youth is a very different process from that of the German. Is there any cause for wonder, when boys, growing up into manhood, continue to extend the experiences, which they have gained in the manner described above, so ruthlessly in every direction, that they become accustomed to regard every female, who, according to their view, is socially inferior, or who may be dependent upon them for a living, as an instrument for the gratification of their lust? Anyone, who does not shrink from the only conclusions, which this summing-up of the situation will admit, cannot be astonished at the racial degeneration, which is making itself only too visible by the countless thousands of illegitimate and falsely-legitimate children, resulting from this Jewish-German sexual intercourse; and the easily-recognisable mixed-type, to be found amongst the populations of Berlin, Frankfort, and other cities and districts, which teem with Jews, will not come as a surprise and shock to the honest observer. And, keeping pace with this, is the appalling decay of the national character, which is the inevitable consequence of mongrelising the race, and which invariably means national ruin. A nation can save itself from moral lapses and relaxation; but never from racial decay. Ancient Rome is a historical instance of the former case, France of the latter.

The lascivious impudence, displayed by the Jewish youth especially towards female employees in business-houses, in dancing-establishments, and in restaurants, and generally towards females of no social pretensions or devoid of all worldly experience, is only too well known. Neither married women, nor girls, scarcely emerged from childhood, are safe from the importunities of the most conscienceless of these fellows, and an unending succession of cases of this nature occupy the police-courts, and would soon attract the attention, even of the most stupid, if the names, nationality, etc. of the criminals were not intentionally and systematically suppressed in all the newspapers. It is a fact, confirmed by many police-court cases, that Jews violate, for preference, maidens, who are so young that they are only to be regarded as girls, and even children. For these unnatural offences a kind of authority is actually to be found in Talmudic literature; for a Talmudist Rabbi endeavours to prove, by going into details, why a girl of three years of age is fit for sexual intercourse.[69] Berlin, at the end of the "seventies" in the past century, was the real field for conducting observations of a very convincing nature. The advance of Jewry was at that time extraordinarily in evidence. The fraudulent manoeuvres on the Stock Exchange, during the so-called "promotion years," had brought enormous wealth to the Hebrews, who forced themselves to the front in all directions, in society as well as in public life. Even then, one could not avoid seeing what was a deeply humiliating sight for every honourable German, namely, splendid specimens of German womanhood hanging on the arms of Jews — and even then not enjoying, at least, the respected position of a married woman. Dazzled by the flash appearance and behaviour of Hebrews, who have amassed wealth in every conceivable manner, and allured by the most cunning methods of seduction, countless women, well qualified to be the mothers of the nation, fall victims, year after year, to the Jews, and descend to the level of purchasable commodities. Prostitution always flourishes luxuriantly wherever the Jews live and have lived; it is a matter of common knowledge, that a notorious law-suit scarcely ever runs its course without implicating one or more Jews, either as "friend," seducer, usurer, cheat, or receiver of stolen goods. The Leyden Papyrus, which dates from Egyptian antiquity, as well as the Old Testament, refer frequently to Jewish sexual excesses.[70] The Jew, as Oriental, is a supporter of polygamy, or, as the well-known Jewish author, Max Nordau, (Südfeld)

[69] Compare Fritsch: "Der falsche Gott", (*Evidence against Jehovah or Jahwe.*) 5 Edition (1919) page 77.
[70] Compare: "Handbuch der Judenfrage" (*Handbook of the Jewish Question*) 26 t h Edition. Page 240.

expresses himself, "is not a monogamous animal." If he happens to live in countries, where monogamy alone is legal, and conforms outwardly to this law, he can always find plenty of ways of evading it in order to indulge his oriental proclivities. Jewish married women place no obstacles in the way of their husbands in this respect, whether it is because the idea of polygamy is something innate in them, or because they derive a secret satisfaction from seeing the women of a foreign race — rivals in a double sense — in a state of complete subjection to their husbands. With regard to the phenomenon, it is interesting to establish how occurrences of this kind are judged by Jewesses.

In the *"Lit. Echo"* (1912. Number 3) the Hebrew woman, Anselma Heine, deities her racial companion, the author Jacobowski. In the course of her article, she treats of his love affairs, and expresses herself in connection therewith as follows: "Suddenly I discovered in him the ancient typical trait of pain, peculiar to his race. He experienced a vindictive rapture in displaying his power over women, and never indicated the plebeian with more scorn than when he boasted, how he had subjugated the elegant wives of the blonde nobility by brutal force."

- Only let anyone try to imagine to himself, if it could be possible, that a Christian authoress would announce to the whole world, with such a voluptuous thrill of veneration, confessions, like those above, of the sexual triumphs of a fellow-countryman over Jewesses.

And still one more instance of this kind. — The publishing house, Velhagen and Klasing, of Bielefeld and Leipzig, which has gradually built up a sound literary reputation by the loyal and strictly evangelical inclination of all their publications, and especially as publishers of the family paper, "Daheim", has been issuing for about the last twenty-five years, the "Monatshefte" (*Monthly Numbers*) which form a periodical of interesting contents, edited by H. v. Zobeltitz and P. O. Höcker, and which of late has been giving preference to novels from the Jewish pen. The following noteworthy passage, concerning the Jewish hero of the story, is to be found in the novel, *"Der Tunnel"*, by the Jewish author, Bernard Kellermann (Fürth), published in the periodical.

"S. Woolf was a perfect specimen of a gentleman. He had only (!) one vice, and he concealed it carefully from the outside world. It was his extraordinary sensuality. The blood began to sing in his ears as soon as he caught sight of a young and pretty girl. He travelled at least once every year to Paris and London, and had his "friends" in both cities. From these expeditions he occasionally brought back "nieces", whom he transplanted to New York. The girls had to be young, pretty, and blonde! S. Woolf avenged (!) in this way, poor Samuel Woolfsohn (his father) who, years before, had been hopelessly driven out of the field, so far as all good-looking women were concerned, by the competition of stalwart tennis-players and large monthly cheques(!) He took his revenge on that blonde race, who had formerly spurned him with their feet. And, above all, he recompensed himself for the privations of his youth."

Thus, the cynical debauchee, who comports himself with "blonde girls" as if they were nothing more than so much "human flesh", captures them, enjoys them, and then flings them on one side, is, according to Jewish notions, the "pattern of a gentleman"! And then this foolish idea of revenge: because old Woolfsohn could find no favour in the eyes of German women, is that any reason why his son should revenge himself on other women of the blonde race? Has not the Jewish author here, by mistake, revealed too much? — Accordingly it is not inclination, or mere sensual desire, which attract the Hebrew to the blonde women, but rather — Hate and Revenge! He desires to ruin and dishonour as many of these females as possible, whether they stand in any sort of relation to his scheme of "revenge" or not, and thus procure retribution — for what? — for a wrong existing only in the Jewish imagination, which is clouded with conceit and hatred. Verily, logic of this order can only flourish in the swampy carnal-mindedness of a people, who celebrate today, just as they celebrated more than 2000 years ago, with songs of triumph, the remembrance of the massacre of those 75000 Persians, who fell victims to the lust for revenge of the strumpet Esther and her cousin Mordecai.

But — without doubt — the real motive for the feeling of revenge lay, as far as the Jewish "gentleman" was concerned, in the concluding sentence: "he compensated himself for the deprivations of his youth," by dishonouring, with the help of his money and all the tricks of the professional seducer, as many women of the blonde race as possible: and the incarnate hatred sweetened his triumphs.

And what about the "ancient, typical trait of pain in the Jewish race" — "the eternal pain of the Jews" of Heine, Jakobowski and company? It is nothing but the mortification of Mephistopheles that he is not left at liberty to do exactly as he likes; the mortification of Shylock when he is prohibited from mutilating his business rival in order to gratify his demoniacal hatred. This pain, born of hatred and insolent pride towards everything that is not Jewish, is certainly an ancient inheritance of the race, and one of its fundamental and lasting characteristics. The Jew disguises or conceals it under the appearance of melancholy, whereby he deceives simple- minded people so long as he has not the opportunity to, or dares not exhibit his real nature; it discloses itself as insolent sensuality or ruthless rapacity, when it feels that it is safe enough to step, unveiled, into broad daylight. Woe to those, who allow themselves to be deluded by the harmless exterior; and may shame and disgrace descend on all who assist the Jew in deceiving the rest of humanity as to the true nature of his "pain" and "revenge".

What kind of spiritual offspring this "typical, ancient pain" of the People of God is, is disclosed in a poem, published in the Jewish periodical, "*Die Aktion*" (February 1913), from the pen of a certain Paul Meyer. Perhaps it may open the eyes of a few, here and there, as to the thinly-veiled "ultimate aims" of Jewdom.

* * * * *

THE MERRY SONG OF THE VAGRANT AHASVER

Behold! I am a man rooted to no spot,
A man unwedded to any environment:
The narcosis of home-sickness

Does not drive my heart into my breeches,
For I am proof against grief.

If you drive me from your thresholds,
I still remain more sought-after than anybody else,
Your cries of envy resound,
For I drink at your fountains,
And I weigh up your values.

The sleek skin of my soul
Conceals what I have expiated as a beggar,
Still, my booty mounts up
And, your brides call joyfully to me
— me, the refuse of a foreign desert.

Yawningly you exhale your tobacco-smoke
As you honourably digest your meal,
But I am a clever juggler,
And I know how to excite your vices
So that they develop to the utmost.

Thus I continue to play the game
Of my mature insolence,
The strange, very subtle, final aims
Of my Asiatic blood,
Which are hidden from you!

It is a fact, that the Rabbinical doctrines of the Talmud deny the right of the Jewish wife to raise any objection to the intercourse of her husband with women, who are not Jewish, even though the latter may be married. The circumstance, that the marriage of those who are not Jews is, according to Rabbinical perception, not to be regarded as marriage but "as no better than the living-together of beasts", is confirmatory of the above. According to Talmudic doctrine those, who are not Jews, are not even to be regarded as human beings, but only as "animals in human shape." (compare page 57).

A perception of this kind accounts for a whole series of Jewish views, which would otherwise be enigmatical to us. An animal has no moral rights, and consequently Rabbinism does not recognise any moral duties on the part of the Jew towards those who are not Jews. A beautiful woman, who is not Jewish, is nothing more than a beautiful animal in the eyes of the Jews, and therefore the individual Jew is at liberty to do with her as he likes. In any case there is no necessity for him to trouble his conscience with what becomes of her.

Now and again, one hears the voice of a superior type of Hebrew, frankly admitting and disapproving of this shameful behaviour on the part of their racial companions towards women, who are not Jews. Conrad Alberti, (Sittenfeld) for instance, writes as follows, in M. G. Conrad's "Society" 1889 No. 2, after he had spoken of Jewish intolerance towards those who are not Jews:

"The only exception is the sexual intercourse, and especially the behaviour of rich, young Jews towards girls of the poorer class, seamstresses etc. This reaches an incredibly low level of cynical brutality, and one to which I have never seen young men sink, who belong to the Christian faith. The latter, for the most part, still preserve some lingering traces of shame in the presence of the opposite sex, but, in the case of our young "jobbers" of the Stock Exchange, not a spark is to be found."

The thousands of girls who, year in and year out, come to their ruin in Jewish business-houses and in Jewish families, could provide terrible evidence that the honest admission, quoted above, is founded upon fact. Certainly the objection is justified, that employers and people in positions of authority, who are not Jews, frequently abuse their position in the same shameful manner; but in all cases of this nature a characteristic difference always distinguishes those cases, where the culprit is a Jew, from those where he is not. And this difference lies in the attitude, which Jewish women take up towards such conduct on the part of their men-folk. When confronted with the complaint of a servant-girl, that the "master" or "young master", is annoying her with his attentions, a German married-woman will, in ninety-nine cases out of a hundred, prepare a very bad time indeed for the men of her household, and will replace the girl by one less dangerous. It is far otherwise with the Jewish wife or mother. She not only shows herself "tolerant" to her growing-up son, but overlooks as well the weaknesses of her husband, and actually assists him to attain his object — thus following the example of Sarah — by advising the girl, in her own interests, to yield to the desire of her pursuer. In one particular instance, the words were repeated to me, with which a rich married Jewish woman received and disposed of the complaint of her pretty housemaid, that the master of the house was persecuting her with his attentions. Smiling almost sympathetically, and with a goodwill, which had something motherly about it, the mistress of the house spoke to the girl: "What a foolish child you are! You are young, and you are pretty; if you leave and go into another house, there will be men there also, and they will also pursue you with the same object. And if you again leave your place and go to another, it will be the same there as well. Men are like that; a pretty girl is never free from pursuit. And at last you will yield. — Be sensible, and remain here; my husband is rich and can pay you well!"[71]

In the case mentioned above, the girl possessed character enough to at once take her departure, but how few others would be strong enough to resist such plausible argument and insidious temptation? They fall victims to the Jews, and preserve silence concerning their shame. Moreover, the Jew is astute enough to flatter the vanity of the girl by timely presents and liberal treatment, so that those who have fallen, after they have once lost the first sense of disgrace, find little difficulty in speaking in glowing terms of their Jewish employers.

This story may surprise some readers on account of the peculiar attitude assumed by the Jewish married-woman, but this fact is nothing new to anyone acquainted with the circumstances; and, quite apart from the Talmudic perception, to which attention has already been called above, this behaviour arises out of another and absolutely materialistic frame of mind. The Jewess knows only

---

[71] It is well known to the inhabitants in Berlin, that, in consideration of a special payment, many registry offices for servants dispatch all good-looking country-girls, who apply to them for situations, exclusively to Jewish households.

too well, that her lascivious husband will not be satisfied with intercourse with only one woman. Accordingly he will seek opportunities away from home. This, however, is generally expensive, and carries, moreover, dangers in its train — not the least of which are those affecting health. The astute, saving Jewess reasons thus with herself: a healthy servant-girl, who is paid a few thalers more than the usual wages, and who receives an occasional present in addition, is the cheapest expedient for appeasing the lewdness of the husband: and, of course, danger of infection is greatly reduced.

* * * * *

It has already been intimated above, that the personality of the Jew exercises a remarkable, even a puzzling influence over many women, which can be described as suggestive and will- destroying. When, during the past nineties, this subject was, for once in a way, treated to a public discussion in the periodical "*Deutsch-sozialen Blättern*", personal experiences and observations, confirming this influence, poured in from all sides. Powers are seen to be at work in the background, which one is tempted to call demoniacal, and there is an unnatural sensual stimulation, which apparently robs the victim of her reason. The rôle of "enchanter", which one otherwise assigns to the female, seems in this case, by some inexplicable means, to be transferred to the opposite sex. And this power must be described as unnatural and disquieting, because the woman, who is accessible to its influence, appears to succumb literally without showing the slightest trace of resistance.

Amongst the communications already mentioned are the following, which have been selected as particularly characteristic. A lady describes what was actually observed on several occasions:

"A somewhat shabby-looking Jew met a respectable middle-class woman. He glances at her, she stops, remains standing as if rooted to the spot, looks round after him and finally follows him. — Much the same thing happened in another street, where a red-haired Jewish clothes-dealer was standing at the door of his shop. A respectable young female, in fact scarcely more than a school-girl, passes by, and the Jew catches her eye or whispers something to her; she stops suddenly as if shot, and remains before the next shop-window, her gaze fixed on the Jew. It is not long before she follows him into his shop. An old and ugly Jew called, ostensibly on business, at the house of the young widow of a merchant, who had but recently died. She admitted him again the same evening, and allowed him to spend the night with her. She came from a good family, and was educated and refined; he was a repulsive old fellow, devoid of refinement." — The lady continues:

"The question arises: are, perhaps, secret Talmudic arts at the bottom of all this? — It is said that many Jews have brought their art to such a pitch that they can, with one glance, cause a female to quiver and tremble just as if she had received an electric shock. — A lady, who had allowed herself to be implicated with a Jew, gave the following account to her family as soon as she had regained her senses: the first time when the man spoke to her, and gazed at her with his penetrating dark eyes, she felt stricken to the core, and from that hour she had been drawn as if by an irresistible force to him; that he had appeared to her in dreams, etc...

Who is going to solve this riddle? Is it the look (perhaps that which the Italians call "jettatura") or is, perhaps, the extraordinary Talmudic knowledge and experience of life acquainted with secret alterations in relations — with certain mysterious, sympathetic forces? Or must we, in these cases also, take into consideration Jewish energy, whereby the Jews have perhaps learnt how to dominate the mind of the female?"

As a matter of fact, in such cases as these, one is confronted with something obscure and mysterious, which must be made clear at all costs. The great majority of the countless girls and women, who have fallen victims to Jewish seducers, relate afterwards that they were driven towards them, as it were, by some unknown evil power.

Unquestionably many Hebrews utilise hypnotic powers in order to render women submissive to their will. A correspondent, writing from Triest, on the 16th of July 1913, announces:

"The authorities here have just succeeded in arresting a certain Ziffer, who had abducted a 19 year-old girl of noble descent, and daughter of a great silk manufacturer, after he had previously hypnotised her. It is said that, two years before, Ziffer had abducted the wife of a Breslau sugar-refiner by employing similar methods."

Further, one read in the Berlin papers of July 20th 1913: "The tragic fate of a young girl, who had been robbed by a marriage-swindler of all her savings, and who had committed suicide in her despair, was revealed yesterday in the course of a case, which came up for hearing before the 2 n d Vacational Criminal Chamber of the Provincial Court of Justice. As the result of the enquiry, the fitter Frederick Ziffer was brought up on a charge of fraud. In April of the same year, the accused had made the acquaintance of the single woman, Johanna Simon, who had arrived in Berlin from her home a few days before, in order to take a situation as companion. Ziffer represented himself to the girl as an engineer, and promised, after a short acquaintanceship, to take her to South America and to marry her there, describing to her at the same time in glowing colours, the delightful life which would be their lot. As the girl, who was a strict Catholic, had once stated, that she would not marry out of her faith, the accused, who was a Jew, pretended to be a Catholic also, and carried his hypocrisy so far, that he raised his hat ostentatiously every time when he passed a Catholic place of worship in the company of the girl. By all kinds of pretexts, he succeeded in inducing the inexperienced girl to part, by degrees, with her entire savings. When he had extorted the last farthing from her, and had, in addition, brought her to physical ruin, he let fall his mask, and became brutal and callous. After the victim had given notice to the police, it came out that the accused had already deceived and robbed another girl in a similar way. — The Court, with regard to the proved bad character of the accused, sentenced him to ten months' imprisonment. — The next day, the girl, who had gone to Hamburg, committed suicide in despair at her ruined life. On appealing against his sentence, the accused had the incredible impudence to maintain that it was grief at his punishment, which had driven the girl to take her life. In spite of this, the Court actually reduced the sentence! The final judgment was six months and two weeks imprisonment."

This is one example of thousands. — It was the custom, in the "dark Middle-Ages", to safeguard the community against the repetition of a similar crime, by hanging the scoundrel out of hand. The occasional outbursts of outraged national feeling at Jewish misdeeds have been most erroneously described in our falsified historical records as "Jew-baitings". For his "servitude" under German law, Ehren-Ziffer will know full well how to satisfy his "typical, primitive Jewish pain" by taking further revenge on the female section of the blonde race as soon as his mild punishment is completed. — And the men of the "blonde race?" Are they too "tolerant" and too "refined" to be any longer aware that the honour of the blonde women is also their own honour?" — Just as in the case of Ziffer, one is also inclined to assume the presence of some hypnotic power, when one observes how even old and ugly Jews render young females docile and submissive to their desires. Many a story could be told, in this respect, by the small rooms behind the actual shops, into which Jewish dealers know how to entice pretty customers during the slack business hours, usually under the pretext of showing them some exceptionally attractive patterns or garments. Feminine curiosity can seldom resist an invitation of this kind, and the Jew then has it in his power to create such compromising situations — for instance, by a further invitation to try the garments on — that the feminine nature proves too weak to resist any familiarity.

'A respectable young woman, who had been enticed, in the way described above, into a small room leading out of the shop, became absorbed in the examination of some particularly beautiful patterns: hearing a peculiar rustling sound behind her, she turned sharply round and saw — the Jewish shop-keeper standing completely naked before her. With a cry of horror, she rushed out of the shop.'

But even if one is not willing to accept the theory of hypnotic influence, the weakness of women, when confronted with Jews, can be reasonably accounted for by other facts. Already in their own ancient writings, in The Old Testament and in The Talmud, the Israelites are described as a voluptuous and lewd people, who were addicted to the grossest sensual excesses. Lust and desire stand written on the faces of the Hebrews, and this is not without effect upon weak people of the opposite sex. But, above all, it is the complete absence of the sense of shame, which makes the Jew so dangerous to women, and which makes the game so much easier for him to play. The Rabbinical writings bear ample testimony as to the complete absence of all sexual shame amongst the Hebrews, by relating, unabashed, the most intimate affairs, and always in a manner as if the most harmless and ordinary topics were being discussed.

A particularly significant example, taken from the book of Benakhot 61a relates as follows:

"Kohana, as a youth, was the pupil of the wise Rabbi Rabhs. Observing one day that his master was engaged with a young and strange girl, he concealed himself under his — the Rabbi's — bed. The Rabbi and his female companion came in, and laid themselves down, chatting and laughing... When the woman began to utter cries of pain, Kohana called out from under the bed, making use of a Talmudic phrase: "It looks as it the mouth of Abbas had never yet tasted food." He intimated, of course, that the woman was still a virgin. The Rabbi answered: "Are you here, Kohana? Go away, it is not proper." But Kohana replied: "It is only for the purpose of acquiring knowledge, Master; I want to learn from you in all particulars."

That the pious books of the Jews consider such muck as this as fit for narration, is sufficient comment on the Jewish perception of morality and decency.

Hampered in no way whatever by ethical considerations, the Hebrew carries his lustfulness openly for all to see, and thus discovers and arouses latent, kindred feelings in the opposite sex. The nature of woman is adaptable; it acquiesces involuntarily and unconsciously in the actual feeling and way of thinking of the man, with whom she comes into immediate contact, and for whom she feels sympathy. In proximity, to a noble-natured man, a woman will also preserve and uphold all her innate dignity and distinction; but, brought into close contact with a low voluptuary, she is just as much in danger of sinking to his level. Now the Jew has a peculiar knack of speaking of sexual matters, as if these were perfectly harmless and ordinary topics of conversation, and in this way he contrives to lull, or even deaden a woman's natural sense of shame. In the vicinity of the Jew, feminine sensibility sinks to the lowest plane; one may even go so far as to say that each Jew transforms the women around him into prostitutes. As he regards them merely as instruments for gratifying his lust, they, for their part, accept his appraisement of them, and no longer feel acutely that this appeal to their animal instincts is a gross affront, or, at any rate, do not resent it to anything like the same extent, which they would, if it were made by other men.

The late Professor of Natural Philosophy at Leipzig — J. K. F. Zöllner, who died in 1882, has preserved for us in a small brochure, the various tricks and frauds of the Jewish swindler, Glattstern. Some of these are worth repeating in the form of a contribution to this chapter.

Glattstern, an indigent Polish-Jew student, who, in addition was half- blind, had somehow managed to gain a footing in the best Leipzig families, and to associate on the most intimate terms with the daughters of the same. He represented himself everywhere as a well-to-do man, and procured the means for playing the part, on the one hand by patent-swindles, on the other by instituting collections at the best social functions, ostensibly for charitable purposes, but in reality for his own pocket. He employed a trick, the main feature of which was to start a subscription by laying a bank-note for a large amount on the collecting salver, an example which prompted others to give lavishly; he then embezzled the proceeds. When he was sentenced by the General Court of Justice at Leipzig to six years imprisonment, he left the daughters of several wealthy families with the best prospects of becoming mothers. Influential people must indeed have interceded on his behalf for, strange to say, he was pardoned after the expiration of two and a half years.

Amongst the especial exploits of this dissolute rogue must be included the following: he had provided a poor woman, whose husband acted at the same time as his private secretary, with the means to fit up and stock a small shop, in order to carry on a business in selling and repairing washing-garments. The main responsibility of the woman, however, was the engaging and employing of a number of young seamstresses and female apprentices, who worked in a small room, which was lighted by a sky-light, and which le d out of the shop. Glattstern was accustomed to come, whenever he liked, whether in the daytime or in the evening, to send away the owner of the business on some pretext, and then to lie down with one of the girls on the sofa — in the presence of the others. After this had been witnessed several times through the glass roof by the neighbours, notice was given to the police, who then interfered.

This is not the only case, of which I have been personally informed, where Jews have satisfied their lust in the presence of other women and girls. And, strange as it may sound — each of those present, standing under the ban of this shamelessness, had accepted the occurrence as inevitable, and kept silent also concerning it, so long as particular circumstances did not lead to a discovery. Just as the mere glance of the snake is said to have the power of paralysing a bird with horror, so does the behaviour of the Jew appear to effect a complete paralysis of the senses in the case of the weaker- minded females, and to blast them as it were with a curse, from which there is no escape.

Women of character and noble-mindedness, on the contrary, feel an unconquerable aversion towards the Jews and all that is Jewish, and, thanks to their fine instinct, they are conscious of the repulsiveness of the Jewish nature even when it escapes the eye of an observant man. On the other hand, weak and vain women succumb to the influence of the Jew as if bereft of will-power. In this case, it looks as if the conditions, governing the mixing of races, were playing a part. A being, who is racially clean and true to type, is keenly alive to the alienism and enmity of the Jewish nature, and avoids the destroyer either consciously or instinctively. In the case of the mongrel or mixed breed, however, all these fine instincts, as far as one can see, are extinguished, and, incapable of resistance, it becomes the victim of the enticer.

One can, if one chooses, discover a higher purpose at the back of these events. And that is, that the Jew has been sent, as it were, amongst mankind, in order to help to destroy and obliterate all who are feeble in their vital instincts, that is to say, all who are degenerate and of little value. An explanation on these lines might afford some consolation, if it were not a fact that it is precisely the most pronounced Germanic type of woman, which is most eagerly pursued by the Jew, and which eventually succumbs. As the Jew represents, in all respects, the exact opposite of the Germanic man or woman, he does so in this particular respect as well, and it is just the sexual contrast of both races, which seems to operate bafflingly and fatally.

At any rate, one can derive from the above considerations the firm conviction that if the Germanic and Jewish races are to live lastingly in close contact with one another, it spells doom for the former, and must lead inevitably to the decay and disappearance of Germanic ethics and racial characteristics.

* * * * *

Amongst the various methods of seduction, which the Jewish girl-hunter is wont to employ, preferably as a last resource, when he sees that he will not otherwise attain his object, is that of "betrothal" or "engagement". It is simply incredible how infatuatingly the prospect of the "ring on the finger" operates on the disposition of simple and innocent women. But what power this method can exert, is known only too well to the Jewish snarer.

Two commercial travellers — a German and a Jew — were gossiping in an inn about another hotel in G... and doubtless considered that no one overheard them.

"I recollect", remarked the Jew, "that I once went there years ago. Quite an interesting incident was the cause of this. I had "picked up" an extremely pretty girl in the course of my railway journey. She was scarcely more than a school-girl. After a time she became very confiding in me, and we became engaged..." "Engaged?" asked the other astounded. "Well, yes, what one calls engaged", continued the Jew, in a tone of amused indifference. "I gave her a ring — I always carry several cheap little rings with me for this purpose. I then persuaded her to get out with me at the station at G... by telling her that we must solemnise our betrothal!" concluded the Jew, laughing, "and we then spent the night together in the hotel we have just been speaking of." "And what was the end of it all?" asked the other. "God only knows," replied the Jew, in his nasal, indifferent tone of voice, "she continued her journey the next morning. It is a pity, for she was a nice, little thing... "

The Jew also does not hesitate to promise marriage, if it is necessary to make a formal promise in order to gain his purpose; he knows that, in any case, the matter cannot affect him seriously. As soon as he wishes to get rid of the girl, all that he has to do, is to acknowledge himself a Jew, and to declare with feigned distress, that all his relations are bitterly opposed to his marriage with a Christian. Under the supposition that the relations of the girl also, would refuse, in all probability, to hear of her union with a Jew, he plays the rôle of a man, afflicted with misfortune, and parts from the woman, whom he has deceived, assuring her that he will never forget, for the rest of his life, his one true love affair— only to begin the same game with another woman the next day. German girls, for the most part, are confiding and naive enough to accept such miserable subterfuge as something genuine, frequently even to defend the impostor against the accusations of others, and actually to bear in their minds an affectionate remembrance of him.

That section of the German Press, which occupies itself especially with social matters, remarked, after describing a number of cases of this kind:

"Is any law-suit of a disgraceful nature ever heard of in any law-court throughout the whole, wide world, without Jews being either directly or indirectly involved in the same, whether as seducer, keeper, inciter or in some such unsavoury capacity? Wherever it may be — we always find that it is the Jew, who is the most daring seducer, and to whom no one's virtue, no one's beauty, no one's honour is sacred, when it is a question of the gratification of his lust. One is even inclined to believe that it is not merely sensuality, which impels him to this, but that he experiences a devilish and malignant joy in undermining moral feminality, and in dishonouring those, who would otherwise have been the respected wives of German men. Shameless as he is by nature, he makes use of the circumstance that desire awakens desire, especially when it is displayed, brazenfacedly — without the slightest trace of shame — for all to see. In sexual life, the animal appeals to the animal; and it is precisely in this respect where the lowest and most animal nature finds the best opportunity to display its power. Therefore, there is nothing to be astonished at in the fact that an animal-desire, proclaimed without the slightest restraint, must make an irresistible impression upon a weak and impressionable nature.

And there is still another psychological factor, which cannot be left out of account; an absolute lack of shame, which is openly advertised, deadens the sense of shame in others, and arouses shamelessness. One thing is quite certain, and that is, that one feels far less shame in the presence of the Jew, than in the presence of any other man. Why do the peasant, the mechanic, yes, even the land-owner, the officer, and — the clergyman, when they get into money difficulties, apply to a Jew rather than to a friend, a bank or a loan-office? — "One does not feel ashamed in the presence of a Jew!" This frequently-heard phrase solves many riddles. And, as a matter of fact, one has many a transaction with the Jew, which one would anxiously conceal from the eyes and ears of other men; one does not feel ashamed in the presence of the Jew because the Jew does not know what shame is.

And to this cause also must be attributed the extraordinary faculty for bribery, possessed by the Jews. "Moral Nihilism", i. e. the renunciation of any higher standards than those of money and enjoyment, is proclaimed with such imperturbable assurance by the Jew, that he is able — at any rate for the time being — to degrade the sentiments of others to his own low level.

This forms the base for the fearfully corruptive force exerted by the Jew, also with respect to feminality. The Jew allows no other feeling to come to the surface in his vicinity than a lust for enjoyment and profit. Is it then essential that he should possess any particular or especial power for this purpose? By no means! Wherever the lowest and crudest instincts appear unrestrained, it is impossible for anything, higher and more refined, to hold its own. The erroneous doctrine of the victory of what is better, in the "free interplay of forces", leads in reality, step by step, to an absurdity.

Furthermore, it is extremely useful to the Jews that the superstition concerning the particularity and preferableness of the "People of God" is inculcated into us from childhood upwards, and it is precisely the female disposition, which clings more tenaciously to all superstition than the sober sensibility of the man. And, in addition to this, our women are given an entirely wrong idea of what constitutes the ideal man. On the stage, the role of the lover is played, for the most part, by Jewish youths; in our romantic literature, which is now completely Judaized, the hero of the story is almost always a Jew, while the rule of the duffer, the dupe, of the altruistic seeker for the ideal is assigned to the German. Is it to be wondered at then, it the misguided taste and bewildered fancy of our young girls see, in every half-grown black-headed Jew-boy, the hero of a romance, and are "enchanted" by his appearance? The general German folly, which makes a special point of admiring everything which is un-German and alien, also plays its part. We have, as a matter of fact, for decades encouraged a culture of what is oriental in the higher branches of literature, in the ladies' journals and fashion-papers, in Art . . ."

It is, however, not only the honour and moral purity of German women, which are at stake; their physical health is likewise endangered. Whether it is that the peculiar nature of the Jew exhausts the female body to an unusual degree, or whether it is that physiological circumstances, connected with the act of circumcision, play some part — it is sufficient to state the fact, that women, who have been accustomed to have sexual intercourse with Jews, suffer from a variety of uterine disorders, and remain barren. Yes, one can go so far as to say: women, who have been accustomed to sexual intercourse with Jews, are lost to the other race. And, if enquiry is being made at the present moment to find out the causes of the decline in the birth-rate, there ought to be no delay in directing attention to the influence of this racial alien in our midst, who ruins the women, not only morally but physically, and who threatens, together with the widely-spread efforts to check conception, to become always more and more injurious to the community.

And it is not difficult to conclude from all this, that the Jewish race is the principal carrier of sexual disease amongst the other nations, which could not very well be otherwise, considering how unbridled their sensuality is. And even when he is afflicted with an infectious disorder, the Jew will still not place any restraint on his lust. One recalls the disclosures of young Jews, according to which, a fiendish kind of rapture is experienced by them in seducing — in spite of their diseased condition — what is, in all probability, still an innocent girl.

A terrible picture of such devilish cynicism was revealed in the course of a judicial proceeding in February 1904.

The trader, Julius Klippstein, married man and proprietor of a money-lending business, which he carried on under the name of Jacob Weg. was brought up before a jury in the Law Courts at Munich. He was charged with perjury, and with incitement to perjury. Klippstein had attempted to induce the wife of a postman, who was under examination, on account of some other misdemeanour, and was one of his customers, to deny on oath the fact that Klippstein was, in the course of his business, in the habit of having immoral relations with her. Klippstein denied the fact. The woman, however, confessed eventually, in spite of the present of money, which had been promised to her. The examination of Klippstein now brought to light, that it was a regular part of the daily proceedings for him to make immodest proposals to the female customers. The State Attorney had found out no less than 35 women and girls, who had come to their ruin through Klippstein. They all appeared in court as witnesses. Their joint evidence furnished the material for a terrible history; some cases were little removed from rape. Klippstein proceeded to sell up the goods and chattels of certain women who resisted his advances. He only postponed execution, and granted a longer period for payment, when the women yielded to his wishes. These unfortunate beings consisted, for the most part, of the wives and daughters of workmen and small officials. As a consequence of his licentious mode of living, Klippstein suffered continuously from a revolting disorder, which he communicated, moreover, to the victims of his lust. His wife had been infected by him, and had had to undergo a severe operation; the cook in his own household, with whom he also had relations, suffered from the same disorder — and the same was the case with his seventeen year-old son, who had taken his father as a pattern. — Klippstein was sentenced to 1-1/3 years (!) imprisonment.

The social democratic *"Münchener Post"*, one of the few papers, which published this unheard-of history, as a public warning, stated also: "During the retirement of the jury, the accused was busily muttering Hebrew prayers in his cell. Various divorce proceedings are the further consequence of this case." — The *"Deutsche Handels-Wacht"* had also something to report concerning the personality of the accused:

"Julius Klippstein had already been arrested and detained on a charge of rape, in his former domicile, Giessen, but had managed to secure an acquittal. After moving to Munich, he had carried on his business, scarcely for a year, when he entered into an "arrangement" with his creditors, whereby the latter incurred a loss of 25,000 marks, and he then embarked on a fresh career of debauchery, which simply beggared description. "If you are nice to me", he was wont to say to his female employees, "you will have a good time; but if not, I will make your life a hell." A girl, employed at the counter, who had energetically resisted his advances, and had, on that account, been disgracefully abused by Klippstein, complained to the book-keeper of the business, who told him, straight to his face, that he ought to be locked up. This, however, did not trouble that man of honour in the least. His customers, both girls and women, were assailed in the same way as the servants of his household and the employees in his business, and he compelled many of them, as mentioned above, to yield to his wishes, by threatening to seize and sell up the last of their belongings. Some things, which happened, cannot even be hinted at."

The paper adds:

"Naturally we shall at once be accused of unfairly suggesting that what is an isolated incident, is of general occurrence, but we feel ourselves compelled to say that the case of Klippstein is more or less typical of certain kinds of business."

At the same time the " *Hammer* " made the following remarks: "It would be mock modesty to forbid the public examination and discussion of such disquieting excrescences as these. A danger lurks in the gloom of concealment, the effects of which are inconceivable as regards their range and extent. Anyone, who has affection for his nation, must open his nation's eyes to such horrors. The great, public press has taken no notice whatever of these unheard-of occurrences — not even that section, which is fond of stepping to the front as the special guardian of the national morality and rights, and which otherwise makes a huge fuss over every trifling scandal. A remarkable confusion of moral conceptions dominates our dear public. When some rough words are spoken to a few recruits, and an exceptional blockhead amongst them happens to get a smack on the head, all the newspapers work themselves up into a state of fury, and inflame public opinion for weeks with the "incident", and the Reichstag occupies session after session with the discussion of like occurrences. But when it is a question of criminal acts of the basest description, and the honour and health of numerous women and girls are at stake, everything is enveloped in silence. Why did not Herr Bebel, who is so ready to play the part of a censor of morality in his book *"The Woman"*, discharge some of his moral wrath in this particular direction? — Are not the majority of the victims the wives and daughters of workmen and minor officials? — We should much like to have an answer to these questions."

* * * * *

THE TRAFFIC IN GIRLS

The Hebrew has made almost a principle of degrading woman, both in illustration and text, as well as in speech and in action. He dominates the stage — and now the cinema as well — with his insolent lasciviousness; the shops, where the most shameless books and pictures are sold, are kept by Jews (mostly under a Christian pseudonym), who are also purveyors of the worst kind of appliances for preventing conception and procuring abortion. So it is scarcely to be wondered at that the profoundest disregard for mankind in general, and more especially for young unmarried women, as well as the degradation of commerce to its lowest conceivable plane, should proceed from the Jew. We refer to what is known as the "White Slave Traffic", and in particular to the traffic in young girls. It denotes the most infamous degeneration of the business instinct: trade in living human flesh, sale of souls for the sake of foul profit. It was reserved for Hebrewdom to develop this vile business, systematically and on a grand scale, until it grew into a vast organisation, which embraces half the world.

In olden times the slave trade was already a Jewish speciality. Not without good reason did the eminent Polish painter Henryk Siemiradzki depict the two slave-dealers, in his celebrated picture of ancient Roman life: *"The Vase or the Woman"*, with unmistakably Hebraic features. Even in the Carlovingian time, the slave trade was preponderantly in the hands of the Jews.[72] Thus, in conformity with the original state of affairs, the dealers in girls of the present day are, almost without exception, Jews: and this is admitted by the Jews themselves. On the occasion of a conference, which was held in London, during March 1910, protesting against the traffic in women, *"The Jewish Chronicle"* of April 2nd 1910, acknowledged that "the Jews in this particular sphere of activity far outnumbered all the other 'dealers' ", and added; "the Jewish trafficker in women is the most terrible of all profiteers out of human vice; if the Jew could only be eliminated, the traffic in women would shrink, and would become comparatively insignificant."

If avarice and greed for profit occasionally tempt the man of Aryan race to engage in businesses of a doubtful nature, and if his sensuality also calls for many a victim, it is improbable that a man of genuine Aryan race has ever descended to such cold-blooded commercialism and malicious subtlety as is required to carry on the "White Slave Traffic"; if such has been the case, it is an instance of

---

[72] See Dürr and Klett "Weltgeschichte" (*History of the World II,* page 56).

moral abortion.[73] Only by means of the Talmudic perception, which regards all who are not Jews, as beasts (see page 57), and more particularly so the women who are not Jewish, is it possible to find an explanation for the cold-blooded behaviour of the Hebrews towards women, whom they treat as if the latter were articles of merchandise. And, one is justified in asserting that the extent to which the Jew avails himself of cold calculation and cunning dissimulation, in order to entice young and unsuspecting girls into his trap, for the most part either by betrothing himself to them, or by promising them marriage or a good situation in order to induce them to run away from their parents' home, and then, after "his passion has lost its novel force", handing them over like ordinary merchandise to another, and surrendering them, beyond redemption, to ruin — would be practically impossible to parallel in the case of any man of Aryan descent (Compare the case of Ziffer on page 260).

As a Jew is always ready for the purpose, when it is a question of screening the pernicious activity of the Jew, so it is in this particular case also. All the exertions of "charitable women" and "social workers" on behalf of the miserable victims of the "White Slave Traffic" are rendered, for all practical purposes, null and void from the beginning, by the fact that Jews place themselves at the head of these organisations. In this way, every genuine investigation is held up.[74] For it is the aim and object of the Jews, always and

---

[73] One does not allow one's self to be misled into regarding an unmitigated Hebrew as not being a Jew, merely because his name has a very genuine German sound. In the publication of the names of malefactors also, the Press is deceit itself. Every day it succeeds in "misprinting" an unmistakably jewish name so that it assumes the shape of a genuine German one.

[74] Here is an instance, which is worth mentioning as significant of women's work in this direction. There is an association in Munich, presided over by Princess Sulkowska, and called "The German League for combating the traffic in women." The committee includes, in addition to several other titled ladies, three men as well, the publisher of the society's organ — "The Human Market", and two Jews — the General- Superintendent, D. Possart, and Oscar Tietz, proprietor of a great shop or "stores". The secretary, who acts also as editor, signs himself Robert Heymann, and makes the third Jew. A printed slip had already been attached to the first number, intimating in a significant manner, that a change in the editorial had become necessary, because the contents of the first number 'had not been all that was desired.' Whoever reads the same, will find it incomprehensible, generally speaking, that wishes have been met: it is piquantly dished-up pot-pourri, in which the experienced reader can at once detect the purpose to prevent, at all hazards, any exposure of Jews.

everywhere, to weaken, emasculate, or to divert against those who are not Jews, any accusation, which might prejudice a Jew, until the gravest affair fades away into insignificance or is transformed into a comedy.

The literature upon this subject is copious enough to preclude any necessity here, of going into the more intimate details of this sorrowful business. One account alone, taken from actual life, is sufficiently eloquent to reveal all the ignominy of the conditions, and to provide testimony as to the long period throughout which this shameful trade has been carried on.

Otto Glogau's "Kulturkämpfer" (*Combatant for Culture*) No. 3 of 1880, contains the following description of Rio de Janeiro (from the pen of a former German Consul):

"Could anything well cause us deeper shame, when we visit the wonderful capital of Brazil, than to observe that German and Austrian girls compose one of the largest sections of the local prostitutes? Whole streets are occupied by them, and from open windows, in the most shameless fashion, they endeavour, in their native tongue, to entice passing men to visit them, and even in the numerous pleasure-resorts of the same city, one is pestered with their importunities.

"The majority of them are very young, and it can be proved that they have not emigrated of their own accord, in order to earn money in a foreign country, in this unclean fashion, but are the unfortunate victims of Jewish procurers and procuresses, who have carried on an undisguised traffic in German girls to Rio for several years.[75] At last this assumed such dimensions, and operated so alarmingly upon the already very feeble morality of the Brasilian capital, that the local government was forced finally to interfere, and to order the deportation of the Jewish procurers, who posed, for the

---

[75] To such an extent is this traffic a Jewish speciality, that the brothel-keepers are officially and openly spoken of as "os caftens", (Andree: *"National History of the Jews"*, "Volkskunde der Juden" page 253.) In New York matters have reached such a pitch that the brothel-business has been converted into a Trust! At the head of this "Trust" is a Jew called Goldberg (still another "Dutchman"). See *"The Hammer"* No. 267 (August 1913).

most part, as dealers in jewelry and precious metals, but whose principal source of income was the traffic in women.

In Rio de Janeiro, in the month of December, the following persons were "moved on." Markus Shomer. Moritz Silbermann, Markus Weinbach, Tebel Silbermann, Moses Silberstein, Moritz Eisenberg, Johann Freund, Adolf Bernstein, Tobias Saphir, Hermann Ficheler, Gerson Baum, Markus Schwarz, Hermann Beitel, Markus Freeman, Samuel Auster, Karl Bukowitz and Abraham Robins. — They drove in carriages to the place of embarkation, and engaged first-class cabins on the steamer "Equator", which was to take them to Buenos Ayres; they were enabled to travel in this style out of the iniquitous profits which they had pocketed in Rio. However, on arrival in Buenos Aires, the unclean company were disagreeably surprised to find that the police had boarded the vessel, and had protested against their landing, in consequence of which action these "uncles" will again make old Europe joyous with their presence.

According to the newspapers of Rio de Janeiro later on, twenty-three Jews, who had been convicted of traffic in girls, were again ordered to leave the country, and simultaneously their unfortunate victims were relieved by the authorities of any obligation with regard to repayment of any pecuniary advances, which had been made to them by the Jews, for the purpose of paying their passages and other inevitable expenses, a measure, which enabled the women to withdraw themselves from the dens of vice, if — which, however, is much to be doubted — public compassion would smooth their future path, and charitable souls would interest themselves in the fallen. — But, praiseworthy as the measures taken by the Brasilian Government undoubtedly are, the evil is far from being extirpated, and will soon break out again in a new form. Complete suppression is only possible, if the procurers are attacked here in Germany and Austria, where they obtain their supplies. In order to ascertain their names, it would be necessary for the German police to communicate with the authorities at Rio de Janeiro, so that the latter could institute an official examination of the unfortunate creatures, who have become the prey of the vilest form of greed. — But, enough of this miserable business, which compels many of our countrymen in Brasil to blush with shame, and makes it the bounden duty of the German press to call upon the proper authorities to intervene."

The following notice, taken from the *"Tägliche Rundschau"* of the 24th July 1913, will serve as proof that these conditions, in still more recent times, have not altered but have, if anything, grown worse.

"Abduction of 4,000 girls. The Russian (i.e. Jewish: author) "White Slave" trafficker, Jakubowitsch, who was arrested the day before yesterday in Hamburg, is regarded as the business-principal of the entire trade in women, which is carried on in the east of Europe. Several thousand cases alone have been brought home to him. According to reliable statistics, more than 4000 girls have been passed through German ports, for this purpose, during several years."

Although a "League for combating the "White Slave traffic" has been instituted, although severer measures have been ordained by the Government, although every year a few procurers and procuresses are arrested — who are always and exclusively Jews — the hateful business still flourishes, to the shame of "moral" Europe, and as an infamous reminder of the feebleness of will, sickly tolerance, and last, but not least, of the uncontrolled dread of the Jews, which possess the majority of our "cultured" men and women, up to the highest circles, and which sap any collective effort at its inception.[76] The power of infatuating the female mind, possessed and exerted by the Jewish commercial competitor, appears, indeed, to verge on the supernatural, and this much must have become clear to the readers of this chapter. It is all the more necessary then, to expose this power, and to warn all people of its dangerous nature.

---

[76] "Our consideration for the Jew is carried to an incomprehensible extreme. To realise this, one has only to recall with what precaution and indulgence, everyone concerned, treated the name of a Doctor Sternberg, the Jewish lover of the accused, in the Hedwig Müller criminal proceeding, which was heard before a jury in the Berlin Courts of Justice in the course of October 1913: counsel for the defence, witnesses, reporters and even the Judge — all united their efforts in this direction. Experienced newspaper-readers know, that for several decades, whenever the names, in a questionable case, are suppressed in any of our papers, Jews are invariably concerned as evil-doers.

XVII

THE JEWS AND THE WORLD-WAR

The wars of the Aryan nations have always served to enrich and strengthen Judah. Reference to this fact has been made many times in the course of this book. By usurious behaviour in connection with army-contracts, by financial manoeuvres with various securities, and by raising and depressing the rate of exchange, the Jews have always known how to make profit out of the agony and need of the various nations. The Jewish families, which have become rich, and have been ennobled, are almost always indebted, for their ascension, to war-time profiteering, and in this respect the "Semi-Gotha" contains some interesting disclosures.[77]

The World-War of 1914—1918 also, showed us Hebrewdom in a state of feverish activity. This time, again, they were the most important army-contractors, the most daring manipulators of prices, the most cunning clandestine dealers, formed the most powerful business rings, and absorbed incredible profits. By their behaviour they contributed, to a large extent, to the defeat of the Central Powers; one may even go so far as to say: they have emerged as the real victors from this monstrous war of the nations.

Directly after the outbreak of war, the Hebrews, Rathenau and Ballin, took over the organisation of the economic side of the war — ostensibly in the interests of the nation, but in reality to secure the lion's share of the army-contracts for their racial comrades, and to create almost a Jewish monopoly of the entire trade carried on, not only in Germany itself, but with neutral foreign countries as well.

---

[77] Semi-Gotha. Register of ennobled Jewish families, Munich. Kyffhäuser Press 1912.

An industrialist, who visited the Prussian War Ministry in September 1914 in order to tender, pictured to us his amazement when he found installed in this high office, not, as he had expected, officers and military officials, but preponderantly Jews. Herr Walther Rathenau sat in a large room, at an enormous secretarial writing-table, "dispensed" and gave away the army-contracts. Around him were seated, almost without exception, Jewish clerks and Jewish business-people. — Herr Ballin, Director of the "Harpag", seeing his shipping enterprise temporarily paralysed by the war, offered himself to the Imperial Government as a voluntary organiser and business expert, migrated with his entire staff of officials and clerks to Berlin, and organised the "Zentral-Einkaufs-Gesellschaft" (Z.E.G.) [Central-Purchase-Company], and other Jewish undertakings. The feeble government under Emperor William II, which had always formerly favoured Jews in all important positions, allowed this to happen, owing to its embarrassment and perplexity; and if, in the course of the war, any fact rose conspicuously to the surface, which, until then, had only been perceptible to those who see deeply, and which even then appeared incredible to German visionaries, it was the fact that since the beginning of William II's reign, the Jews had been the real rulers of the German Empire. For the last fifteen years, those in immediate personal contact with the Kaiser were Hebrew financiers, Hebrew manufacturers, and Hebrew merchants like Emil and Walter Rathenau, Ballin, Schwabach, James Simon, Friedlander-Fuld, Goldberger, Guttmann, Hulschinsky, Katzenstein etc.[78]

The old legend that the Kaiser was under the influence of the high nobility and of the Junkers, living east of the Elbe, was only a Jewish ruse to deceive the nation as to the real state of affairs, and to lower the Kaiser himself in the estimation of his people. It is quite true that the Kaiser, for the last decades, has gone mainly to the Jews for advice, who have flattered his weaknesses, and have contributed much to the follies, which led finally to the World-War, and to the collapse of Germany. — The German Nobility were as good as banished from the Berlin Court.

---

[78] Compare Rud. Martin: "Deutsche Machthaber" (*German Potentates*).

Hymns of praise have been sung to one of the Rathenaus in the press, conducted by his racial brethren, on account of his supposed services in connection with the organisation of the wartime economy, without which it is pretended that the war could never have been carried on. He arranged that he should be designated, behind the front, as "Chief of the Economic General Staff", to whom the German victories were really to be attributed. As a matter of fact, Rathenau created by means of his "War Companies", which exceeded 300, an absurdly complicated apparatus, which disordered and made more difficult the entire economic life throughout the country, and transferred, by a kind of jugglery, all the power and the advantages into the hands of the Jews. I do not hesitate to maintain, and can furnish convincing proof moreover, that Rathenau's "War Companies" contributed, in a large measure, to the defeat of Germany. They did not facilitate the German economic life but, on the contrary, disturbed and interrupted it — for reasons, which are not to be discussed in this work. This particular subject, as well as the general attitude of the Jews, throughout the war, calls for special treatment in a book, devoted to that subject alone, and it is to be hoped that an opportunity to accomplish this will soon present itself.

Here mention is only made of some grave facts, for which valid documentary evidence is forthcoming: the activity of the Z. E. G. as can be proved, has, in many cases, rendered the importing of the necessaries of life from abroad more difficult than it was before; and in other cases — a particularly glaring instance is that of the "War-Grain-Department" (K. G.) —goods have been sent backwards and forwards, from one end of the Empire to the other, time after time, in such an absolutely crazy manner that they have reached the hands of the consumers in a perished condition. Simultaneously the railways were burdened, in an unheard-of manner, beyond their capacity, and the cost of the commodities unnecessarily increased by heavy freight charges. What extraordinarily uneconomical business was perpetrated by the buyers of the Z. E. G. in Holland, Denmark and other countries, can be easily ascertained by referring to the numerous and instructive instances given in the *"Hammer"* publications from 1915—1918.[79] The annual volumes, 1915—1919, of the trade paper "Deutscher Müller" (*German Miller*) in Leipzig, contain numerous examples of the favouritism shown to the great mills, owned by Jews, and of the crazy transport, backwards and forwards, of grain and flour by the K. G.

It would be a great mistake to see in all this merely blunders in organisation and disposition; closer observation discloses that malevolence prevailed.

The attitude of the Hebrews is only comprehensible by attributing it to their deep aversion for all that is German, for the German form of government, and for militarism. Victory was begrudged to the German Empire. It is beyond all doubt that the Jews hate the Germans more than they hate any other nation — simply because German idealism is the natural antithesis to the Jewish Tschandala — disposition. It is quite obvious also, that the majority of Jews sympathised with our enemies, and were on their side, and especially on the side of England. Influential Jewish newspapers, such as the *"Frankfurter Zeitung"*, *"Berliner Tageblatt"*, the Vienna *"Neue Freie Presse"*, and many others also, knew well the whole time how to glorify the Western Power at the expense of the German people, whom they characterised as a horde of reactionaries, and of whom they could never say anything bad enough. It is this kind of newspaper, which, for decades, has carried on a steady campaign with the definite object of rendering everything connected with Germany, despicable in the eyes of foreign countries, by circulating as widely as possible, occasional scandalous incidents, such as the Eulenberg law-suit, various military excesses etc, and, by suggesting that the German Nation was addicted to a revolting vice, has procured for it the equally revolting term of abuse "Boche" — a word, the meaning of which cannot be

---

[79] These were collected and published by the *"Hammer"* under the title: "Complaints against the Z. E. G." Further, compare "The Z. E. G. and the Jewish Business-Monopoly", *Hammer* No. 377 from March 1st 1918.

reproduced in German book-language, for it denotes someone who is addicted to indulgence in unnatural lust (The desire for boys).[80]

The crime, which the Hebrews have committed against the German people by their unheard-of war usury, by their invention of the clandestine and secretly linked-up method of trading, known as "Schieber- und Kettenhandel" (linked-up smuggling), by raising the prices of all the necessaries of life, and thereby enriching themselves to an immeasurable extent, can hardly be estimated. All these matters call for a searching investigation at some other time and place.

Here it is only necessary to call attention to the fact that alone in the case of army supplies, a disproportionate increase in prices at once set in, because — in consequence of Jewish influence — direct delivery from the producers was evaded, and the orders were assigned to Jewish commission-merchants, agents and middle-men. It created almost the impression that the people of Judah had made it a condition with the German Government, from the very beginning of the war, that they should receive the lion's share of the army-contracts. For the cases are too numerous where German contractors, manufacturers, merchants, trade associations, guilds, etc have been "turned down", whilst, later on, Jewish middlemen have secured the contracts at considerably higher prices. In this way, the delivery of important supplies was frequently entrusted to dealers, who were without experience in that particular kind of business, and who had no technical knowledge of the goods required; it sufficed that they were Jews.

The Hebrews were seldom to be found in the trenches, but were more at home in the depots, in the offices, in the garrisons and — in the war-trading-companies. In consequence of the numerous complaints, which were made about this — even in the Reichstag — statistics were taken, notably in December 1915, which, however, have never been published — probably because they would disgrace even Judah.

---

[80] It Is quite possible that the expression is derived from the Hebrew word "Bocher" (boy).

The revolution, the object of which was certainly not to assist the honest working-class to obtain its fair share of political influence, but rather to enable the Jews to do away with the hated Monarchy and the military organisation, was principally the work of Jews. The Masonic Lodge at Milan (Latin Freemasonry is completely under Semitic direction) announced in a circular, dated July 30th 1914, that the object of the Lodges was, to introduce an age "free from thrones and altars". That is to say: the overthrow of all princes and the removal of all non-Jewish religions. Jewdom has been working at this task — openly and in secret — for decades. And they have very nearly succeeded in their purpose.

The ill-advised working-class, instigated by the Jews, has allowed itself to be made a tool of, in order to promote interests which are entirely Jewish. The destruction of all national feeling amongst the working-people, and the actual turning-to-contempt of everything German, are the work of a subtle Jewish press campaign. Throughout all the years of war, confidence in an ultimate German victory was steadily sapped by the influence, which the Jewish press exerted upon the public frame of mind, and the attempt was made to lay the entire blame for the war on German shoulders. And the collapse of our front was the result of sheer treachery. A person, who enjoyed the fullest confidence of the "*Hammer*", reported that a Jewish soldier had declared in July 1918: "Germany will not be victorious, for we (Jews) will make the revolution before the end of the war comes." The independent Social Democrat, Vater, admitted at Magdeburg that, since January 1918, his party had carried on propaganda at the front, inciting to desertion and mutiny. — Thus, the German people are indebted for the collapse and the annihilating peace conditions to those malicious forces, which, even in inmost Germany, played into the hands of her enemies outside — favoured by the blindness and trustfulness of the German people themselves. It is as if the old prophecy in the cloister Lehnin fulfilled itself:

"*Israel infandum scelus audet, morte piandum.*"
(Israel dares unspeakable crime deserving death).

CONCLUDING WORDS

Whoever weighs up all the facts, which have been imparted in the course of this work, will understand how frivolous and superficial those phrases are, which, clothed in the semblance of humaneness and tolerance, speak of an adaptation and blending of the Jews with the Aryan nations of culture. Only fathomless unacquaintance with real life, such as that of Friedrich Nietzsche and other stay-at-homes, can excuse such phantasy. The entire humanitarian assimilative idea shatters miserably at the first contact with the awful seriousness of racial heredity. The notion that all contrasts could be balanced, as it were, by men living in closer contact with one another, and by so-called civilisation, rests on a doctrinaire interpretation, which is contradicted, at every moment and at every turn, by the hard facts of actual life. Jewdom is something, which moves and acts beyond the sphere of the natural laws of life, something hostile to life, something unnatural, something demoniacal. And that doctrine also, which is equipped with a veneer of natural science, that, in the battle of life, what is better and stronger, conquers, is out of place here. A selective combat of this kind is only efficacious and warranted, when beings of kindred stock, provided with the same natural weapons, strive with one another for the mastery. No one will claim that an unrestricted sphere of action should be granted to the bacilli, which cause disease, that one should not oppose devastating pestilences with precautionary measures; no one will contend that the Cholera bacillus is a better and a stronger being than a human being, because the former is able to destroy the latter. This doctrine of a free field for all forces, requires the restraint of reason, for that singular destiny persists, which ordains that diseases work by infection, but that health does not. A single rotten apple in a basket will easily communicate its corruption to a hundred sound ones, but even a thousand sound apples cannot heal a rotten one. Here it is a case, not of selective combat and superiority, but of shielding what is healthy against infective illness, of warding off national poison. Intelligence commands that all corrupting and infecting forces must be kept at a distance from healthy life, and must be suppressed by all possible means. To avoid what is poisonous is the first precautionary law of life. "Find out what is good for your body, and do not give it what is bad for it."

Jewdom, however, is a symptom of disease within humanity, a fact, which even the Hebrew Heinrich Heine admits, for he calls it, "the everlasting plague, which has been brought away from the slime of the Nile." The Hebrew is the "under-man", who has passed into a condition of spiritual and moral rottenness, who carries disintegration and corruption with him wherever he is permitted to come. He is himself very well aware of this peculiar property, as the following outburst of the Hebrew, Dr. Münzer, shows. He has written a novel — "*The road to Zion*" — which has been suppressed on account of its filthily naturalistic contents. In the course of this book, he makes the hero of his story speak as follows: —

"Not only have we Jews degenerated in this manner, and are at the end of a civilisation which is used up and sucked dry; we have ruined the blood of all races in Europe — perhaps we infected them in the first instance. Generally speaking, everything is under Jewish influence at the present day. Our ideas animate everything; our spirit dominates the world. We are the masters; for what is power at the present day, is the direct offspring of our genius. However much we are hated, however much we are hunted down and persecuted, our enemies can only triumph over our weak bodies. We are no longer to be expelled. We have eaten into the nations, have tainted and dishonoured the races, have broken their power, and, with our mortiferous culture, have brought staleness and decay into everything."

Münzer tries also, in the usual way, to represent the war of annihilation, which the Jews wage against humanity, as a justified act of revenge, because of the pretext that the Jew has been unjustly despised and persecuted. He portrays the Jew as being insulted and spurned with the foot: he continues to portray him as ducking, dodging and twisting; and then adds in the same strain: —

"But, at the back of all glows triumph at the surreptitious victory. The world had been Judaized, and had decomposed into the Jewish mode of thinking and into Jewish vice. That was revenge!"

"The surreptitious victory!" The word describes the situation — involuntarily. Only by surreptitious falsehood and deceit has the Hebrew attained to his power. But surreptitious victory is no victory — just as little as the success of a thief is a proof of his power and superiority. Whoever, as guest in house, abuses the trust placed in him, and robs his host, has not thereby gained a victory, but has, on the contrary, committed an act of villainy. The Jewish "victory" is a parallel case. Now, it seems to us, that the triumph is somewhat precipitate. It is certainly true that the dull masses in civilised countries have been infected, both with the Jewish mode of thinking and with the poisonous blood bacillus of the Hebrew, and, before all, that certain higher classes of our society, who, devoid of instinct, have coquetted and fraternised to such an extent with the destroyer of nations, that they have fallen victims to the corruption, and are beyond rescue; but a sound core still lives in our nation, which, up till now, the foreign poison has been unable to get hold of. And, even if a tremendous collapse is impending over the imbecile masses, who have been Judaised both in body and soul — over those masses who crowd together in the great cities — our nationality will grow young again, and renew itself out of the unspoilt reserves, who live on the land.

It is to be hoped that the standard will be adopted, which the excellent Lagarde speaks about in his *"German Writings"*: "Every Jew who is burdensome to us, is a serious reproach to the genuineness and veracity of our life. — Germany must be German, and be full of Germans, full of itself like an egg… then there will be no room for Palestine."

It is perfectly true: the nations of antiquity have collapsed under racial degeneration and Judaisation, without any correct forebodement of what was gradually happening to them. We, however, have learned from history, and have discovered the source of racial destruction. Now, for the first time, the Jew is being unmasked and recognised for exactly what he is, and now, for the first time, the secret of Jewdom is being pitilessly unveiled. For many decades, intelligent men have been on the look-out, carefully observing every movement of this enemy. They have seen completely through him, have calculated in advance what his next moves will be, and have begun, as quietly and unobtrusively as possible, to protect the most important positions against destruction; no one now has the power to arrest collapse of our miry surface-culture, collapse of that structure of fraud, erected by Jewish speculation, collapse even of the Judaized system of government;[81] but one may well hope that the unspoilt elements will escape in an ark, as it were, from the deluge, and will land, after it has subsided, on a purified soil, to build up a new and better life — in a German world, free from Jews.

* * * * *

Leipzig, August 1922.

The contents of the present book have not been altered since the second edition in 1913. In the meantime the movement, directed against Jewdom has developed to an undreamt-of extent, and important political and economic events have taken place, which would possibly make it advisable that an amplification of the statements, made in this book, should be published. At present, this has not been done — chiefly on account of the unusual expense. The text of the book is cast in plates; alterations in the same would necessitate a complete resetting of the type. This would be bound to increase the price of the book considerably.

But there is, however, no urgent need for such a supplement. Whatever has been set down here, in the separate chapters, as characteristic of the Jew, still retains its validity. It has not been refuted by more recent events, but, on the contrary, has been confirmed in all that is essential. Moreover a new and extensive literature has come into being, which supplements in welcome fashion what is given here. (A list of such works is appended).

---

[81] These words were written in the year 1913, and have since proved themselves true.

The most remarkable literary event in this particular domain is the appearance of a book, written by the American, Henry Ford, the great and widely-known motor-car manufacturer and winner of the Nobel prize. The title of this work is: "The international Jew — The World's foremost Problem." Millions of copies of this book are dispersed throughout English-speaking countries, and there is also a strong demand for the German edition. The discriminating and careful manner, in which the author introduces the American public to this question, which is entirely novel to it, is masterly and works irresistibly. In particular, the accounts in the second volume present an engrossing picture of the machinations of Jewish High Finance during the World War, which latter stands revealed as the indubitable work of the Jewish "Golden International."

The discovery of the so-called *"Protocols of Zion,"* which in truth represent the programme of political action of the secret confederations of the Jews, is of further great importance. The Jewish plans, which are revealed therein, display such demoniacal malice that the uninitiated reader might well believe them to be a fabrication. Jewdom is straining every nerve to refute the genuineness of these "protocols"; what, however, speaks most strongly for their authenticity, is the circumstance, that not only during the war, but that even now, Jewdom acts, in unmistakable fashion, in full accordance with the programme laid down. (The essential points in these "Protocols" are also repeated in Ford's book.)

At the present moment, Jewdom is endeavouring, by means of the Government organs at its disposal, to stifle the ever-swelling anti-Jewish movement:[82] it hopes, principally by means of an artificial and disproportionate increase of prices on the paper-market, to render impossible any further publication of those books, periodicals and newspapers, which are hostile to the Jews (the paper trade lies under the dictatorship of Hartmann, a Hungarian Hebrew, who lives in Germany); all this, however, cannot prevent the spark of perception, which has fallen into the national soul, from

---

[82] Numerous patriotic and German-national associations have been dissolved and forbidden.

continuing to glimmer, and from bursting, one day, into a clear flame. Already, far down into the working-class, insight is dawning that the pernicious effects of the degenerate capitalist-system can be referred mainly to Jewish machinations, and that it is precisely from that quarter that the greatest danger threatens the freedom of the nations. The awful events in Russia have made it clear to every one what Jewish tyranny means.

The movement against the predomination of Jewdom is no longer confined to Germany: it has taken root in all civilised lands. Anti-Jewish periodicals and books are being published in England, France and the United States, and also in Poland, Hungary and Sweden, and a "White International", a league of all honourable nations to break a way for the departure of Jewdom, is now in the process of formation.

Peace and quietness will not return to humanity until the enemy of humanity has been completely unmasked, and has been warned to keep within his own boundaries. We are, however, on the right road to accomplish this.

* * * * *

OTHER TITLES

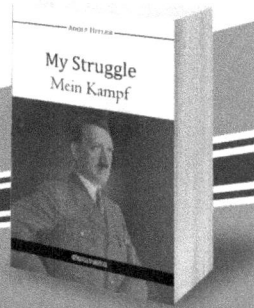

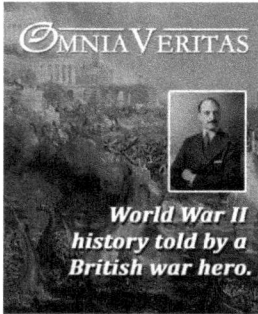

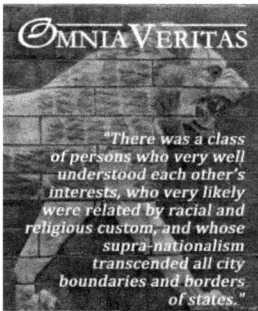

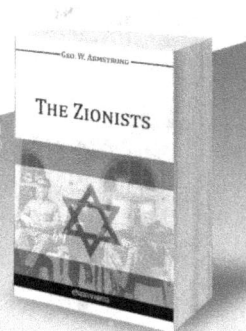

www.ingramcontent.com/pod-product-compliance
Lightning Source LLC
Chambersburg PA
CBHW061717270326
41928CB00011B/2019